HERE TO COMPLETE DR. KING'S DREAM

The Triumphs and Failures of a Community College

Lillian Cohen Kovar

University Press of America, Inc.
Lanham • New York • London

Copyright © 1996 by
University Press of America,® Inc.
4720 Boston Way
Lanham, Maryland 20706

3 Henrietta Street
London, WC2E 8LU England

Library of Congress Cataloging-in-Publication Data

Kovar, Lillian Cohen.
Here to complete Dr. King's dream : the triumphs and failures of a
community college / Lillian Cohen Kovar.
p.   cm.
Includes bibliographical references and index.
1. Bronx Community College--History. 2. Minorities--Education
(Higher)--New York (State)--New York--History 3. Bronx
Community College--Students--Economic conditions--History. 4.
Bronx Community College--Students--Social conditions I. Title.
LD6501.B758K69   1996   378.'.052'09747275 --dc20   96-20388
CIP

ISBN 0-7618-0402-1 (cloth: alk. ppr.)

*Dedicated to the students of
Bronx Community College and
to their teachers who try mightily
to make a difference*

Contents

Acknowledgments

I wish to thank Arthur Galub, a political scientist, George Lankevich, an historian, Carl Daley, a sociologist, and James DeMetro, a professor of English, for their careful reading and criticism of the manuscript as it evolved. All are on the faculty of Bronx Community College and so augmented my own view from the inside. My husband, Leo Kovar, a psychiatrist, read the manuscript with equal care, contributing an important perspective from the outside.

Chapter 1

Introduction

It was during the nineteenth century that Americans affirmed their enduring faith in formal education, universally accessible, as a means of acquiring usable skills and extending social and economic opportunities. There was less accord on the value of the intellectual quest. Such a venture was regarded as appropriate only for the aristocracies or leisured classes.[1]

Nevertheless, when free public higher education was introduced in the middle of the nineteenth century, children of the emerging urban middle class of America's greatest commercial city were ready to take full advantage of a broad and rich educational program. The first free municipal college in the United States, The Free Academy, to be known within a few years as the City College of New York, included in its early courses Mathematics, History, Languages and Literature, Drawing, Natural and Experimental Philosophy, Chemistry and Physics, Civil Engineering, Moral and Intellectual Philosophy, and Law and Political Economy.[2] Its first students were middle-class, native-born Protestants, the sons of merchants, ministers, lawyers, doctors, carpenters, and clerks.[3] They were joined in the last decades of the nineteenth century by Irish Catholics and Jews of German descent. By the early twentieth century scions of the working class appeared, predominant among them the sons of Jews who had fled the pogroms of Eastern Europe. After World War II Irish and Italian Catholics began attending the municipal colleges in increasing numbers.[4]

Admission to city colleges in New York throughout most of their history was based on academic merit. Though the colleges continued to grow in number and size, the growth could not keep up with the ever increasing demand for free higher education. Consequently, admission standards were raised to limit eligibility. High school graduation became a requirement early in the twentieth century, shortly after New York City's first public high school was established. In the years after World War II, the requirements to enter any of the city colleges included a high school academic diploma and a high school average exceeding a specified cutoff point for that college. Community colleges, opened in the 1950s and the 1960s, required of matriculants in transfer programs an academic high school diploma and, by the early 1960s, a high school average in the upper seventies. The more recently arrived blacks and Hispanics, migrants or children of migrants from the American South and the Caribbean, often lacking the academic high school background or the required high school average, found themselves excluded from the senior colleges and even from the newly-established community colleges.[5]

It was not surprising, then, that during the racial confrontations of the 1960s the demand for equity penetrated the city colleges, which had come under the jurisdiction of The City University of New York when it was created in 1961. Black, Puerto Rican, and white student demonstrators forced the closing of the oldest campus of the University, whereupon the meritocratic policy of the city colleges collapsed. Responding quickly to the demands of its latest constituency, the University instituted a policy of open admissions in 1970, five years earlier than anticipated, guaranteeing admission and free tuition at one of its two- or four-year colleges to every city high school graduate, though not necessarily in the college of choice. Eligibility for the four-year colleges required an 80 high school average or rank in the top half of the high school graduating class. The use of either high school average or rank was introduced to expand the pool of minority students entering four-year colleges.[6]

With the doors of the University's tuition-free undergraduate colleges fully open, blacks and Puerto Ricans joined white ethnics in the rush to matriculate.[7] Students of all ages and degrees of preparedness entered the college portals, searching for the education that would allow them to fulfill their version of the American dream. At Bronx Community College, the college of study, which admitted its first class of 120 students in February 1959, the full- and part-time student population expanded to 15,000 by 1972, 80 percent higher than its last pre-open admissions enrollment of 1969. Forty-three percent were attending full-time, a considerably greater proportion than at community colleges generally. Black and Hispanic representation increased from 42 percent of total enrollment in 1969 to 60 percent in 1972 and 90 percent by 1987.

Free tuition lasted only six years after the inception of open admissions. During the city's fiscal crisis in 1976 the Board of Higher Education, pressured by the city and state, mandated tuition in the city colleges -- nominal compared with private colleges but substantial for the new students. It also imposed more stringent standards of progress and retention. The student population of Bronx Community College fell precipitously to 8,800 by 1977 and hovered around 6,000 through most of the 1980s, though its percentage of full-time enrollees continued to exceed the national average for community colleges.[8] Contributing to the drop in enrollment, in addition to the introduction of tuition, were the decline in the borough's high school graduates and the departure from campus of Vietnam veterans. The latter, whose serious approach to academic life was gratifying to teachers, represented 42 percent of male enrollment in 1975 but only 22 percent two years later. Faculty retrenchment followed the contraction of students, and faculty population fell precipitously after its earlier rise.

Bronx Community College has been described as an island of hope in the midst of the desolation of the South Bronx, peopled predominantly by blacks and Hispanics. It stands high on a hill overlooking the Harlem River, its imposing neoclassical buildings designed by Stanford White juxtaposed with modern structures encircling a large expanse of lawn. In a ten-minute, steeply uphill trek from subway to campus, students and staff pass burned-out, abandoned apartment houses as well as stores and storefront offices in various stages of deterioration. The expansive campus seems a refuge left over from a more sedate and prosperous past.

Students at Bronx Community College differ substantially from traditional students and from those of the white-ethnic working class whom Cross, London, and others identify with the two-year public college.[9] During the 1980s they represent a seeming multitude of cultures comprising African-American, Puerto Rican, Dominican, Cuban, Colombian, Haitian, Jamaican, Antiguan, Barbadian, Nigerian, Guyanese, Filipino, Chinese, Vietnamese, Irish, Italian, Jewish, and a host of others, a panorama of the developing world in microcosm. They include the sons of a Jamaican fisherman and of an African chief, the daughter of a Haitian lieutenant slain during a political coup and the wife of an African-American slain during a family brawl.

The student body encompasses, too, a broad range of ages, from the late teens to the fifties and beyond. One-third of an entering class are recent high school graduates, another third are graduates who have been out of school a number of years, and the rest are equivalency-degree recipients. Only in economic class and minority status are the students relatively homogeneous.

Two-thirds of the students are women. A greater proportion of the women in the 1980s than in the 1970s are single mothers, many of them struggling to stay off welfare or remove themselves from the welfare rolls. Conspicuous is the disproportionately small number of African-American males, who seem to have lost faith in higher education as a stepping stone to a career and a good life. The failure of this predominantly black and Hispanic college to attract a greater number of African-American men is a recurring frustration to faculty and administration.

Students here are almost invariably poor, but they believe that they can rise in class and status if they work hard enough and long enough at their studies. Open admissions to college provides the opportunity, and it behooves them to take advantage. The questions to be answered in the pages that follow: Do they take advantage? And what does the college offer them to take advantage of?

They enter the college at a time of internal upheaval. A new president arrives on the campus in 1978, shortly after the city's fiscal crisis and the introduction of tuition. The college has ceased to be an expanding institution, it too faces a financial crisis, and it is redefining its mission. No longer primarily the liberal arts and sciences institution that it had been during the 1960s and early 1970s, preparing students to enter the junior year of a four-year college, it is fast becoming principally a college of terminal vocational studies. The new president envisions the college primarily as an institution for vocational education, designed to prepare students for jobs and satisfy the job needs of the community.

The change in priorities from the academic to the vocational is not unique to Bronx Community College. As early as the 1920s and 1930s, prominent junior college officials recommended that the two-year college abdicate its lowly status at the bottom of the hierarchy of higher education, looking "upward to the university," in favor of a position at the top of the vocational hierarchy, higher than the trade schools and "looking outward upon the community."[10] Presidents of most leading research universities welcomed the proposed vocational emphasis. They saw the expansion of the junior college and its concentration on terminal vocational curricula as a way of democratizing higher education while keeping masses of underprepared students away from their doors. Other proponents joined the bandwagon, and, by the 1970s, the two-year public college, with its emphasis on the vocational, gained recognition and financial support from state and federal governments, prominent foundations, and corporate leaders. It discarded the title of "junior" college in favor of "community" college and, blurring the distinction between terminal and transfer education, renamed its "terminal vocational" program "career education."

One important factor impeded the effort to vocationalize the community colleges through the decades: students opted for the transfer track as their pathway to mobility.[11] Professionals in the African-American community also resisted vocationalization, fearing its deleterious impact on educational opportunity for minorities.[12]

Not until the 1970s do students, responding to weakened economic conditions and mournful tales told by the media about the job plight of college graduates, begin to turn away from the transfer curricula and into vocational programs, whereupon community colleges across the nation rapidly expand their terminal vocational offerings. The "Great Transformation" of the community college from primarily an academic to a terminal vocational institution continues through the 1980s. The new president of Bronx Community College sees the turn from the academic to the terminal vocational as imperative for the survival of the college at a time of declining numbers and student preparedness.

The ascendancy of vocational curricula in community colleges occurs at a time when a call for academic excellence is surfacing, counterpoising in the 1980s the call for equity of the 1960s. Educators are increasingly concerned that curricula in American schools have gone awry and that students are falling academically behind their peers of other industrialized nations. The "leveling-down of literacy" in open-access colleges and, more specifically, in community colleges, is noted at least since the 1970s, when meritocratic higher education gives way to "mass" education, and terminal vocational curricula replace liberal arts and science transfer programs as the first choice of students.[13]

The community college is a crucial participant in the struggle to achieve equity without forfeiting some measure of academic excellence. A late-comer to the college scene, it has become the fastest growing sector in American higher education, receiving forty-four percent of all first-time freshmen in 1970, fifty-four percent, in 1980, and fifty percent in 1990.[14] Students are lured to the community college by the ease of entry, the low tuition, the short-term commitment, proximity to urban centers, and anticipation of a smooth transition to higher education.[15] They feel that they are being given an opportunity to earn the credentials for mobility. Their assumption of the triple burdens of family, job, and school with so little of the preparation for college that middle-class students take for granted from the primary grades arouses in teachers awe and trepidation.

Massive remedial programs in reading, writing, and mathematics are introduced at the college to prepare new students for college-level work. There is a presentiment early in open admissions among some of the faculty that excessive remediation will overwhelm the community college and destroy its academic character. A faculty delegation proposes to the Board of Higher Education that schools for remediation be set up elsewhere. Such a proposal is regarded as politically not feasible; the community college "has to shoulder the burden." With funding to public colleges reduced, the massive remedial program eclipses college-level offerings in basic areas, and the foreboding of the faculty becomes a reality.

Concurrent with or after completing remedials, students have the option of selecting a program on the terminal vocational track, leading to an associate degree and a job, or one on the transfer track, emphasizing the liberal arts and sciences and preparing students for transfer to a senior college. The course requirements and the standards on the two tracks are not equivalent -- "they differ across the board," attests a mathematics professor. By the 1980s, two-thirds of the students, with the advice or at least the consent of their faculty advisers, settle for the terminal track as more practical since it is intended to insure them jobs in the near-term.

The practicality of the terminal vocational track is problematic. Some coveted vocational programs do "insure a career within the students' grasp," though academic requirements in these programs are relatively stringent and acceptances far short of student demand. Other terminal vocational programs lead to dead-end jobs that are not what students anticipate when they come to college.

Community college administrators begin to express alarm, distressed not so much by the expansion of remediation and of terminal vocational curricula which they promoted for decades, but by the declining rates of retention and graduation. Although students at the college, recognizing by the 1980s that a two-year associate degree may be of limited value in the marketplace, speak increasingly of their desire to pursue a baccalaureate, only a small proportion graduate. Some of the dropouts do transfer elsewhere. Withdrawing and returning even after a considerable number of years is not uncommon among community college students.

Early withdrawal from college is rooted in poverty and family responsibilities as well as in failure to pass courses where greater rigor is demanded than students are accustomed to, prepared for, or perhaps willing to strive for. Students failing in their area of concentration may withdraw from college or, less drastically, find another major where teachers are more likely to deflate requirements and inflate grades.

While only a small minority of matriculants graduate from Bronx Community College, most graduates attempt to transfer to a senior college. Graduates from terminal vocational programs discover, often belatedly, that the senior college is unwilling to accept a considerable number of their vocational credits. Moreover, they enter the four-year college at a marked academic disadvantage.

Students here exhibit tremendous variation in academic development and in motivation for learning. Conspicuous academically is the large number who, having lived their lives predominantly at the oral level, in the realm of talk, are uncomfortable immersing themselves in reading and writing. And conspicuous motivationally are the seekers after knowledge, considerably smaller in number, who derive gratification from their study and strive to become academically all that they are capable of. I use these two orientations as points of reference in assessing students in the classroom.

Teachers at the college are distressed by students' deficiencies in reading, writing, and mathematics and their failure to work hard at learning. Tough-minded teachers respond by demanding of their students some semblance of academic excellence, refusing to compromise in course substance or grading. The more tender-hearted moderate expectations so that few students withdraw or fail their courses. Teachers poised between the two poles modify their tough-mindedness with some measure of tender-heartedness.

Some teachers are challenged working with the poorly-prepared oral-level students who would not have survived initially in a four-year college but whose persistence may lead to their eventual transfer in pursuit of a baccalaureate. Other teachers look to the knowledge-seekers to add intellectual excitement to the classroom dialogue. But many teachers feel little challenge and remain dispirited and disillusioned.

In the chapters that follow I trace students' trajectories, based on 284 in-depth student interviews and student writings over a fifteen-year period from the mid-1970s to the end of the 1980s. Integrated into the student narratives are extensive quotations from interviews with sixty of their teachers as well as reflections on my own experiences as a teacher at the college during this period.

Part One, "Constraints and Aspirations," is devoted to an examination of the fabric of students' lives -- where they come from, socially and culturally, what they aspire to, and the nature of their encumbrances.

Part Two examines "The Classroom Encounter," impeded by circumstances within and outside the classroom, generating triumphs and failures -- perhaps more of the latter than the former as the high hopes of the early 1970s among faculty give way to considerable disillusion by the end of the 1980s.

Students speak with candor and passion about the impediments of class, gender, age, race, and ethnicity, the difficulties with language and learning, and the pleasures and displeasures at the college. Through the students' words we begin to perceive their world. Through the words of their teachers we become increasingly aware of the ordeals of the classroom and college that impede teachers' missions and students' goals.

Student interviewees are self-selected. At the end of each semester I ask for volunteers. I feel that students who know and trust me are most likely to provide authentic statements. Most come to sociology to fulfill their social science requirement, a few, to discover what sociology is about. This self-selected sample of men and women, diverse in age, ethnic group, and academic accomplishment, is overweighted with the more serious student and with those who expect to derive some gratification from the interview -- either the intellectual gratification of participating in and observing an interview, or the psychological gratification of being able to talk freely to a friendly professional who will listen to their stories without condescension. Some memorable interviews come from students in departments far removed from the liberal arts: pre-engineering, nursing, secretarial, electrical technology, accounting, and pre-pharmacy. Each interview takes from one to four hours in one or two sessions.

Initially I began student interviews with specific open-ended questions. I soon discover that if I allow the students to talk freely for as long as they wish in response to my questions, they will tell me a great deal about what I should know but do not think to ask. The respondents are assured of anonymity. As more and more students are interviewed, themes emerge, some that I have considered earlier, others serendipitously. It does not occur to me, for example, that a recurring concern among many women students revolves around the frustration and envy that their mates experience at being left behind when they, the women, enter the classroom.

The sixty faculty members interviewed after the conclusion of student interviews comprise one-quarter of the full-time faculty and come from every department in the college. Included are some teachers who now serve as administrators. The teachers' free-floating responses to my prepared questions lead to new areas of questioning. As interviews with faculty proceed, new themes emerge and earlier ones are revised. My interview schedules are included in the appendix.

I came to the interviews with faculty as a partial outsider who had taught at large public universities and small private colleges before arriving at Bronx Community College. Having participated in governance only in my own department, my personal relationships outside the department and my knowledge of the inner workings of the college were limited. I was moved, sometimes shaken, by the willingness of almost all faculty I approached to talk freely in all areas that were broached and by the intensity of their feelings. It was as though they had been waiting for someone to whom they could tell their tales. One consequence of the extended interviews with faculty is a tempering of my own optimism about the students and the institution.

The span of time -- a decade and a half -- serves as a significant variable in the study, enabling me to contrast each of the two decades with regard to curricula, students, and faculty, and their impact on each other. Remedial and terminal vocational programs are in the ascendancy during the period. Increasingly, students are nonwhite, predominantly black and Hispanic, and increasingly they are foreign-born. The median age rises sharply under open admissions.

Student and faculty interviews are enriched with findings from the classroom. Other sources relevant to the study include student essays, school newspapers, the president's and deans' memos to faculty, external and internal evaluation reports on the college, school catalogues, and class schedules.

Let the students and their teachers speak. You will hear in their voices not a confusion of tongues but instead, a profusion of sober reflections.

Notes

1. Richard Hofstadter, *Anti-Intellectualism in American Life* (New York: Random House/Vintage, 1962), 309.

2. S. Willis Rudy, *The College of the City of New York: A History 1847-1947* (New York: The City College Press, 1949; Arno Press, 1977), 33.

3. Ibid., 68-69.

4. David E. Lavin, Richard D. Alba, Richard A. Silberstein, *Right versus Privilege: The Open-Admissions Experiment at the City University of New York* (New York: The Free Press, 1981), 3, 4; Harold S. Wechsler, *The Qualified Student: A History of Selective College Admissions in America* (New York: John Wiley, 1977), 264-265; James Traub, *City on a Hill: Testing the American Dream at City College* (Reading, MA: Addison-Wesley Publishing Co., 1994), 28-30.

5. Lavin, Alba, Silberstein, *Right versus Privilege*, 3-5, 22; Harold Wechsler, *Qualified Student*, 262-265.

6. Lavin, Alba, Silberstein, *Right versus Privilege,* 19.

7. Students admitted to the City University under open admissions who would not have been accepted under previous academic standards include whites as well as nonwhites. From 1970 to 1975, Jewish and Catholic students entering under open-admissions criteria generally outnumbered open-admissions blacks and Hispanics. Lavin, Alba, and Silberstein, *Right versus Privilege,* 67-69.

8. Beginning in 1988, the downward trend in enrollment at Bronx Community College is reversed. Total matriculants in 1988 number 6,070, in Spring 1994, almost 8,500.

9. K. Patricia Cross, *Beyond the Open Door* (San Francisco: Jossey-Bass, 1971); Howard B. London, *The Culture of a Community College* (New York: Praeger, 1978).

10. Walter Crosby Eells, "A Suggested Basis for a New Standard," *Junior College Journal* 3.1 (1932):1-2. Quoted in Steven Brint and Jerome Karabel, *The Diverted Dream: Community Colleges and the Promise of Educational Opportunity in America, 1900-1985* (New York:Oxford University Press, 1989), 42. Brint and Karabel describe the positioning of the administrators in fascinating detail.

11. Brint and Karabel, *The Diverted Dream,* 99-101.

12. Ibid., 100.

13. Richard C. Richardson, Jr., Elizabeth C. Fisk, and Morris A. Okun document "the leveling down of literacy" at the open-access college they studied. *Literacy in the Open-Access College* (San Francisco: Jossey-Bass, 1983).

14. Table 168 on first-time freshmen enrollment in college by sex, attendance status, and type and control of institution, fall 1955 to fall 1990. *Digest of Education Statistics,* U. S. Department of Education, National Center for Education Statistics, 1992.

15. Cross defines "new students" as those scoring in the lowest third among national samples of young people on traditional tests of academic ability. Most of the new students she describes were the children of white blue-collar workers. K. Patricia Cross, *Beyond the Open Door* (San Francisco: Jossey-Bass, 1971), 13, 15.

Lavin, Alba, Silberstein refer to the beneficiaries of open admissions as those students who would not have been admitted to a particular level by the criteria prevailing before open admissions. *Right versus Privilege*, 88.

My sample includes students who enter Bronx Community College after open admissions, whether or not they might have been accepted under previous academic criteria.

Part One
Constraints and Aspirations

Chapter 2

A Sampling of New Students

The students at Bronx Community College in the 1970s and 1980s are for the most part young adults of the inner city. Born here, they comprise its survivors -- often the parents, the siblings, or the children of others who have been crushed by the discord of urban life. Or else they are its in-migrants, who left the countries or the states of their birth, hoping to achieve here the mobility they crave. Native or in-migrant, predominantly black and Hispanic, they live in the ghettos of the South Bronx or Harlem and experience first-hand the desolation of their community.

As survivors, they face the risks and hard work entailed in striving to make the future better than the past for themselves and their children. Overwhelmingly they are poor. They are more likely to be women than men and are generally older than traditional college students. All come to take advantage of the open door.

We look in this chapter at a sampling of new students in terms of their class, gender, race, ethnicity, and age. Noted first is the pervasiveness of poverty and its impact upon students, especially upon African-American men. Next, we describe the experiences of women students, some attempting to cope with mates threatened by their matriculation, others bearing the burdens of parenthood alone. Finally, we examine the vagaries of older students, male and female, who return to school after long absences, seeking a second chance.

Impact of Poverty,
Especially on African-American Men

At any hour of the day men of all ages congregate on the streets and the stoops of the inner city. They have nowhere to go, nothing special to do. The scarcity of jobs available to them that pay a living wage has reached "catastrophic proportions" and portends a "tangle of pathology." [1]

The situation was not always so dire. From World War II through the early 1960s factories and wholesale and retail establishments provided jobs with steadily rising real wages. Unionized jobs in mass production industry brought good pay without requiring a great deal of formal education or special skill. Employment in the clerical sector was expanding, and in the late 1960s black women's earnings and employment possibilities in clerical work began to approach that of white women, though white women worked largely in private firms, black women, in government. [2] Professional opportunities, especially in the public sector, were increasing for minorities ready educationally to take advantage. Though drug dealing was common in the ghettos of Harlem and the South Bronx, guns had not yet become pervasive. [3] Even in what appears in retrospect to be the best of times, though, the black unemployment rate was high in the inner cities and was augmented by massive black migration from the rural South.

By the late sixties an economic restructuring is taking place, and the long post-World War II period of worker prosperity nears its end. Factories producing material goods are moving to suburban areas or abroad, and the city remains primarily a center of administration, finance, communication, and the arts. Most affected by the transformation of the economic structure of the inner city from manufacturing goods to dispensing services are unskilled or semi-skilled male laborers whose skills are not adaptable to the white-collar service world and who now have to compete for available jobs with immigrants and women entering the labor force in massive numbers. Especially vulnerable are poorly educated, unskilled black men. Even in the relatively prosperous year 1965 only 74 percent of black men were working. By 1983 the percentage of black men employed declines to 56 percent and remains disastrously low through the rest of the decade. [4]

A transformation also occurs in the class structure of the inner city. Its communities in earlier decades encompassed all economic classes. The exodus of the professional middle class to integrated areas within the city or to the suburbs, followed by the departure of many members of the working class, leaves behind a high concentration of "the truly disadvantaged."[5] The impact of class segregation occurring within the inner city should be a real concern at the college, situated in the midst of the desolation of the South Bronx, one of its teachers reminds us.

> I think there is some sort of common factor here at the college but it is probably more a common factor of class than anything else. It's one of the things we do not speak of at this institution, and I think it's a very real issue. With the advent of integration, you had the classes more physically removed from each other than they had been historically and I think that that in some ways works to the detriment of the community.
>
> There was a time when you had people separated only by blocks. It meant that you frequented the same church and that you saw each other in your daily pursuits of going to business or whatever, and it meant, even if you didn't want your children to marry the people on the other block, you were very much aware of that other block and its rules and regulations. It's a fascinating issue that has not been addressed, I think, in the broad base. This college has that issue and will not deal with it.

The departure of the middle- and working-class from the ghettos of the inner city removes its "social buffer," with serious repercussions for the underclass that remains, cautions William Julius Wilson. Their departure eliminates the support they provided for its schools, churches, recreational facilities, and other institutions and removes too the role models of educated blacks with steady work and family stability.[6] Inner-city black youth, segregated within the invisible but intractable ghetto walls and daunted by academic underachievement and the scarcity of jobs, see no future attending the community college. Black professionals are no longer living nearby, providing visible proof that education and hard work can lead to economic well-being. The underground drug economy is more visible, more profitable, and for many the easiest course to follow.

Though to the outsider, Harlem, the South Bronx, and Bedford Stuyvesant conjure up visions of drugs, violence, and despair, some students here have recollections of pleasurable excitement and tranquillity growing up in their inner city community. A Puerto Rican young man reminisces about earlier gratifications.

> My father prospered and moved out of Harlem. I couldn't cope with the idea of leaving my old neighborhood, so I moved back. To me, Harlem was a place of excitement. I felt it was too precious a place to leave behind. Though I was working, I was still attending school.

And a young African-American woman describes the resilience of
residents in her "run down" building in the urban ghetto:

> I was raised the early years of my life by my mother and father in a
> one-room kitchenette apartment located on 125th Street in what is
> known as Harlem. I remember the five-flight brownstone building and
> how well it was kept up. I also remember the friendliness of the people
> who lived in this house and how all were willing to help each other
> out. My parents, who always wanted the best for me, kept our one-
> room house clean and free from the roaches that were a problem in so
> many other apartments in that area. The neighborhood was considered
> pretty safe at that time and everyone on the block knew just about
> everyone else that lived there. I was only allowed to play in front of
> the house, where my mother would be able to watch me, because
> around the corner from us was where a lot of men hung out.

The camaraderie may have been limited to kin and city block.

The impact of poverty pervades the college. Most students receive
financial aid, covering tuition and books as well as partial living
expenses, and in addition work at part- or full-time jobs, not in order to
support a car or the girlfriend it might lure, one motivation among the
white working-class male students in Howard London's *The Culture of
a Community College*,[7] but, rather, to insure their own or their families'
survival. Those without young children to care for regard themselves as
fortunate if they have a midnight-to-morning shift, enabling them to
study on the job without incessant interruption in preparation for an
eight or nine o'clock class.

Even with financial aid, "tuition is keeping away a lot of students,"
a teacher protests. "It's now $1750 a year. Students are inundated with
loans. Many are on public assistance." "The college had no tuition
until 1976," another instructor interjects. "We had 15,000 students at
the time. It dropped to 7,000 over a couple of years. Tuition is going
up. A lot of students will be dropping out, you'll see. There are
students now who don't come to class They say, 'I didn't have enough
money for carfare.'" Eligibility for a New York State tuition assistance
grant requires full-time attendance. In order to qualify, many students
enroll in more courses than they can manage.

Some students postpone buying textbooks until book stipends are
available. "You have to wait about a month for the grant from the
federal government," a student complains, and this delay is confirmed
by others. Students are caught in an administrative bind. By college
fiat, book money is not dispersed until registration is completed. When
the registration period is extended, some students have had to wait
until the fifth week of a fourteen-week semester to buy their textbooks.

Jeopardizing a student's progress may be aging parents who require economic support or, at the least, escorting to doctors or to court. A young Chinese student supports his widowed mother, who speaks no English and never worked outside her home. "She could have done piece-work in a factory, way below the minimum wage," he recounts. "My father was a cook. He died when I was ten. The first semester here was dismal. I had to go without lunch, just enough for coffee. There were times I had no money for carfare." Chinatown in lower Manhattan is many miles from Bronx Community College.

By the end of the 1980s an unrecorded number of homeless students attend the college. "They have an address, a spurious address, but have no home. And they're here studying. It's incredible," declares a teacher of Engineering Technology. "School keeps me alive," confesses one of my students who now lives with her four children in a shelter for the homeless.

Students live with a feeling that disaster is imminent. Crime in the streets, precipitated by the prevalence of illegal drugs and guns, increases significantly within the inner city during the 1970s and 1980s. Mothers of young children often arrive in class late or leave early to call home and find out if their children made it through the streets rife with the sound of gunshots. A distraught single mother, distressed by her low grade in a sociology examination, confesses that she is also distressed by the carryings-on of one of her two drug-pusher sons who has just returned to live with her after being shot and hospitalized. He has already served jail terms. As soon as he recovers from his wound he expects to continue plying his trade. Nothing else pays so well, he feels, certainly not school work. "It's devastating to me," she demurs. "I always held my head high." The pressure she tries to exert on her sons carries no weight against the lucrative lure of peers and money. "'You're too old-fashioned,' my sons tell me. I didn't bring them up that way."

The crises students experience defy the imagination of middle-class professionals or students attending a private college. A young man who appears healthy a week earlier is now shaking all over as a consequence of an injury to his spine from an attack by a patient at the hospital where he works as a psychiatric attendant. Another young man is negotiating with city officials over his heatless apartment building. A young woman, living with her children in an abandoned building, does not heed the order to vacate, although there is no electricity and other apartments are being vandalized and set on fire. She is still there when the building burns to the ground with her possessions, though she and her children escape. Memories of a child's death haunt some students: a baby daughter, dead in her mother's arms in a hospital clinic as the mother impatiently awaits her turn to see the doctor in attendance; an adolescent daughter, killed while baby-sitting at the home of an irate husband. Though recurring crises are not confined to the poor and poverty alone does not bring disaster, they are likely to leave their powerful imprints.

Teachers accept the reality of students' disaster-prone existence and feel endless sympathy, but they are often nonplussed. Should they accept the veracity of every statement of a heinous murder or emergency hospitalization or death in the family? When are such misfortunes introduced as an excuse for the failure to do homework? Is the student baldly stating a sorry fact of student life or preying on the teacher's sympathies? An occasional teacher demands evidence of the occurrence. Most do not.

Confined largely to segregated settings even more than recent immigrants who have greater freedom to move elsewhere, inner city African Americans are increasingly isolated from mainstream culture,[8] and their social isolation spawns fear. "The same reason they don't talk in class," asserts one African American who attended an elite New York City private school during her early years. "They're afraid. They don't talk to strangers. I know a lot of Blacks and Hispanics who are afraid to go into a store like Saks and Bloomingdale's, restaurants, museums, they feel it's not for them. 'I'm scared to go in there,' they say." "They may have good reason to fear," notes another African-American student. "*They* ask for your identification. *They* watch you."

Fear and frustration may lead to aggression, largely against neighbors close at hand, who share the same devalued black skin. The black power movement attempted to efface low black self-esteem through a new image of the black skin as beautiful -- a "minor revolution" that bypassed large numbers of ghetto residents, declares an astute older African-American student who works at Harlem Hospital.

> Most blacks don't stick together, unlike the Puerto Ricans. They're afraid their brothers are going to rip them off, going to get more than what they're getting.
>
> Why do black people have such loathing, such low self-esteem? I am speaking of the group I know and the people I've dealt with in Harlem. A black person very easily turns on another black person: 'Nigger, you're always going to be a nigger, you ain't white.' The Panthers turned against the white man, but we have so many blacks destroying blacks. At Harlem Hospital the blacks would bend over to help a white person more than their own. The majority of the patients are black and the nurses are black -- blacks taking care of blacks. It's just not good care.
>
> You've had sort of a minor revolution with Carmichael and Rap Brown. They started something. It was like a re-brainwashing. The

only good thing that came out of it. They gave something to the younger people., but not to the thirty-and-over people. The muggings in Harlem. People on the block don't have a dime. Why would anybody mug them? Beat them?

We call each other 'nigger' to this day, in fun, but there's nothing funny about it.

In the classroom, the fear and frustration that arise from tortuously slow progress reading or writing may be concealed through "fooling around," displaying bravado, and even engaging in a brawl. An English professor describes the goings-on of some young men in his remedial writing class.

The black guys in my class don't generally do as well as the Hispanic guys. The black guys often bring the streets in with them. They don't do as well and that's one of the tragedies in this city. The women in the class work harder and they resent some of these wise guys in the class who are fooling around, who are kids, and they, the women, are not kids any more. Many of the women had kids when they were fourteen, fifteen, sixteen years old. They're mature people now. Maybe it's just much more difficult to be a black guy on the streets of New York nowadays. They have a tougher time, with the whole macho thing. The women have a different view of life than these guys. They worry about their daughters as victims of the boys. And they worry about their own sons getting shot or doing drugs with their buddies. That may also be why it's so tough for these kids to come back to school. Their friends may make fun of them. But they listen, they're willing to learn, they want to succeed.

The professor indicates his own frustration.

I'm getting a little burned out by the wise guys and the people who are too difficult to reach, even though I try hard. This semester I have trained a couple of guys not to walk in with their head sets on, five to ten minutes late, and carry on. One of my colleagues in the math department today had two guys who were almost having a fight in his class. I heard the noise and went out, and he said, 'Can you believe it. I'm not getting enough any more to work with that.' But otherwise, with almost any other student, I can feel inspired.

"There is potential for violence," a sociology professor concurs, and crowded classrooms help to incite this potential. "The classes are much more restless over the last couple of years, the classes are much more crowded, and they include some young people who are more violently inclined, so there are more arguments and some scuffling in the halls. Not too often, little confrontations. My style is more informal, which allows some of the stuff to surface, but the tension I feel is definitely stronger. I attribute it to a new type of student, especially the young, plus much more crowded classrooms. We take the brunt of all the financial problems. Fifty in a class in a crummy building just gets ridiculous."

An administrator sees deviant classroom behavior as part of a culture that pervades the college. "It's a culture that is reflected in their dress, their speech, their academic orientation. It's not a rebel culture. It's a life style with norms that have been part of their high school, part of their community, and they demand a kind of conformity. Some of their language I don't want to repeat. Cursing means nothing to them. I don't use that type of language. In conversations, while I'm walking across campus I hear someone is 'cool,' they're not 'with it,' or 'yo man.' 'She diss me,' or 'he diss me.' Disrespectful, insulted some one. It's in language, in dress, even in work habits. They're not tuned in to standards. It's like, if we want to do it, it's all right. People ought to conform to them rather than they conform to institutional standards. They throw garbage or paper or cans on the sidewalk. There isn't any sense of propriety, of being responsible for something greater than themselves. If it's all right with me, it's all right. There's not that respect for authority or for the environment. There's not the respect for others. Students from some of the Latin American countries, some of the British countries, have a very different attitude. They're very grateful, unlike some American students whose sense of gratitude is not there, the sense of respect is not there. Very different altogether."

This administrator, often confronted by students who create problems in and out of the classroom, is likely to stress the underside of student culture. He appears to be expounding on Cornel West's portrayal of the young black male style as "a form of self-identification and resistance in a hostile culture; it is also an instance of machismo identity ready for violent encounters."[9] Such encounters do not customarily erupt in the classroom.

Women predominate at the college. Conspicuous among the student population during the 1970s is the woman whose mate is threatened by her return to school, and conspicuous in the 1980s is the women without a mate who is burdened with the tasks of children, school, and possibly part-time or full-time work. The gender disparity is blatant in sociology and psychology classes, less so in mathematics and the sciences.

The Woman with a Mate
Threatened by her Matriculation

With admission declared open and free in 1970 to any college within the City University, many married women take advantage. The Hispanic and white-ethnic women students of the 1970s grew up in households where married women's labor was expected to be confined to the home, formal education deemed not sufficiently important to interfere with early marriage and homemaking.

A woman of Italian descent, almost fifty, recalls the parental push. "My mother was proud of my good school reports, but I always felt she thought it was incidental to what was important for a woman. She would often tell me that I should try to be like my older sister who knew how to cook and sew."

Two Jewish students voice the same parental theme: marriage and family are the woman's sphere. Says one: "Get married, have children, and live happily ever after: that's what I was taught. I believed that. My mother was sure that without a man you can't be happy." And the other: "There was not much vibration from my parents about education. My parents never derided me or encouraged me to do better. Maybe they expressed pleasure when I did well, I don't know. They would have been perfectly happy to have me marry rich. But since I am married and my husband is incapable of supporting me, there is pressure from them for me to have a career."

Two Puerto Rican young women were also seen as prospective wives and homemakers, presumably replacing obeisance to father with subservience to husband. One notes the difference in early gender role assignments: "Girls were to do well in school, be pretty and respectable, but girls will marry and be helpful to their husbands. My brothers, on the other hand, were expected to excel in school and were encouraged in sports. They were expected to be successful and a great help to my parents later on." The other speaks of her father's ambivalence toward her academic aspirations: "I was always told, 'Finish high school, go to college.' But when the time got closer, my father was negative. He said it was a waste of time and money, I would drop out and get married. He still feels that way. I'm the only niece who isn't married. My father and my relatives are proud that I'm still in school but they can't understand why I'm not married. I can't see myself getting married now. There's so much to do." (She is twenty-one.)

African-American women lack the early history of patriarchy prevalent in Hispanic and white-ethnic cultures. Black families from their earliest days in this country were usually two-parented, and women combined work outside with work at home, where they had relations of relative equality with their mates. Marriage they see as fraught with economic uncertainty. "Marriage as a goal in life was not one promoted by our parents," recounts a forty-year-old black nurse who never married. "Instead, they were more interested in preparing us for lives which would be emotionally and financially secure."

Difficult for the woman student of all ethnic groups to deal with is the man who becomes anxious and hostile at the prospect of being left behind when she enters college. She is growing beyond him, he fears, and may wrest control from him in the home or leave him in favor of another mate. The threat is recurring and real. Such a fear is expressed more frequently during the 1970s, when a greater proportion of women students are married, but continues through the 1980s.

The mate's expression of resentment at his woman's return to school may rise to a pitch of fury. One husband tolerates no discussion about school. Another derogates the education his wife seeks and flaunts his "common sense" as superior to her "book learning." He labels his wife stupid, hoping, perhaps, that his condemnation will prove prophetic.

The woman is resolute in her determination to remain at school. An Irish-born wife, who dutifully adhered to her husband's dictates when her three children were young, now grows increasingly restless. "I've done volunteer work in the school as a reading aide. I've bowled with the ladies. I need more. I didn't leave my children when they were younger, but they don't need me now. I'm married twenty years, and I've been home for twenty years." Daring to return to school, another Irish-born woman expresses some pride in her independent stance. "Irish culture is structured in such a way that a woman is a homemaker, a slave, there to take care of their every need. The majority of Irish women are interested in home and family. I'm somewhat of a rebel in my group."

An Irish-American student does little to alleviate her husband's apprehension that she may be sexually attracted to a black male student. Her husband has good reason to fear, she conjectures, apparently alluding to the myth of the black man's desire to violate the white woman sexually, and her fascination with that depiction.[10]

> My husband was very upset about my going to school. I guess he was jealous, afraid somebody would sweep me off my feet. He said, 'The children need you!' The white men I know are insecure, they are straitlaced. I'm talking about sex. They know that the black men are not insecure or inhibited. They believe in variety and try to get as much as they can. My husband asks, 'Are you ever attracted to black men?' I say, 'No.' Of course I am. I've been going to integrated parties. We live in an integrated neighborhood.

The myth of sexual prowess surrounding the black man is deplored by a young black woman student. "The black man plays that role because he's given that role. It's a self-fulfilling prophecy," she protests.

The black man in turn may suspect that the white man at school is cavorting with *his* woman, suspicions with historical precedent dating back to slavery, when a goodly number of offspring were products of such unions. He accuses his mate of taking his manhood, she protests, and wants her at home, on a pedestal, or else available as a scapegoat, presumably to absorb his rage.

> The blowup happened when I went to school three years ago and he decided I was taking his manhood, so he went home to his mother. He started school first, but he would have preferred me to stay home, on a pedestal. . .
> The black man feels the white people will take away his manhood and the black woman will do the same. He uses the black woman as a scapegoat.

The African-American man's preoccupation with his manhood may be a residue from slavery, when the white plantation owner treated him as "a boy" and had first claim on his woman; and a residue "after freedom" when he had to endure the degradation of Jim Crow, the recurring fear of being lynched, and the plodding along as indebted sharecropper or at other lowly work that provided little return and no dignity to him as a man. The black power movement, emerging in the late 1960s, for the first time fosters racial pride in blackness, though with machismo overtones. Black men might affirm their manhood most simply through asserting supremacy over their women.[11] Black women "who take initiative and work to become leaders in their own right" they see as "a threat to their attainment of manhood,"[12] and they express preference for women of color who are submissive and feminine, as they perceive white women to be.[13] Black women look askance, even irate, at the black man's demand for their subservience but, regarding race rather than gender as the primary source of their own affliction, they find it easier to denounce white women than black men.[14] "Racism creates an inevitable bond between African American men and women that many white feminists overlook," notes Johnnetta Cole.[15] Black men have the same divergent pulls.[16]

The woman, whatever her ethnicity, recognizes her mate's apprehension over her educational strides.[17] Books on the table" serve as a symbol of her as student, and her mate often turns livid when the books appear. "Not enough time with me," he protests.

She is likely to adjust her study schedule to avoid his displeasure. "I study Tuesday, Thursday, and Friday from one to five. I can't study otherwise because if my husband sees me with the books, he gets mad. Not on weekends or nights. When a teacher says she's going to give a test on Monday, I get anxious." But she cannot always determine her study schedule precisely. "It bothers me because I know what his attitude will be when he sees me with books"

She may respond to his fury by abandoning her books. "My husband says, when I open the book, 'You're opening your book! Nobody works so hard as you,'" a woman of sixty-five relates. "I like to read and take my own notes -- if my husband's not bothering me. When he comes home and sees the book on the table, he'll think I've been studying for hours. I'll usually close the book unless it's a test."

Or she may respond by abandoning her major. "I started out in nursing but I wasn't able to go through with it. My man was saying I was spending more time with the books, I didn't have enough time for him."

The woman with rising professional aspirations, though, may scorn her mate's interference with her ascent. "My husband is a male chauvinist pig," declares an African-American woman in her thirties. "He enjoys the fact that his wife is in college but he also resents it. They don't want you to get too far, it seems. He shouldn't try to stop me from climbing. I tell him, one of these days I might be a congresswoman. He says, 'I won't have no Shirley Chisholm.' I think today career is taking priority over marriage. If you see your marriage sinking, you have to better yourself. Even though I'm dependent on my husband economically, I have an independent attitude. I believe I can make it without him. I can't have him mould me into what he wants in a wife and have my identity taken away. I was naive, raised in an old-fashioned home. They conformed. But times have changed, and I must change with the times." Shirley Chisholm, a black member of the House of Representatives from Brooklyn and the first black woman elected to the U.S.Congress, has the temerity to announce her candidacy for President of the United States in 1972. She is not supported in her bid for the presidency by black male leaders.[18]

Even an understanding and seemingly self-sufficient husband expresses misgivings about his wife's schooling. "If school makes me happy, it makes no difference to him," relates another African-American woman in her fifties. "He went only to the third or fourth grade down South. He drives a cab. He'll say, 'I'll wash the dishes for you.' But he also joshes, "You in the books again, you going nuts." She indicates her own push toward college. "You get a little taste and are curious."

The rare blue-collar husband, black or white, responds to his wife's educational or career aspirations with unmitigated pleasure. A butcher who attended college for a year "even reads the sociology book" and a skilled construction worker, possessing "an inordinate amount of common sense as well as building and mechanical skill," critically reviews his wife's homework.

The husband who unequivocally encourages his wife's schooling is likely to be relatively young and to attend college himself, usually within the City University system. He may see his wife's education and career as an economic asset and insurance for the future. He may like having a student-wife. Busy with her own study, she ensures him the free time he needs; she appreciates the discipline required for study; and she talks with him at his academic level.

A wife is less likely than a husband to feel aggrieved over her spouse's return to school. A registered nurse wants her husband to continue his formal education full-time. And a wife with little education, a simple, beneficent woman, provides support and encouragement for whatever her husband wants. "My wife is a Jehovah Witness," confesses a Puerto Rican man in his thirties. "They promise you everything in heaven, nothing here. She's satisfied with that. It's lucky for me she understands the situation. A more worldly woman would not be as understanding."

But, working at a lowly job to keep her husband in college, a woman begins to show impatience. A forbearing wife, who works as a domestic, loses some of her forbearance after the arrival of their second child. And a wife who drops out of college after three years, frustrated that she must take many remedial courses without advancing appreciably toward a degree, regrets leaving college but now wants her husband to drop out in order that she might quit her job and assume a traditional housewifely role, "settling down and raising two kids."

When the man attends college and leaves a spouse behind his difficulty generally is solely economic. The woman's difficulties invariably transcend the economic. Leaving behind a distraught man who feels personally threatened and must be reckoned with compounds her difficulties but may no longer serve as a deterrent to attending school. Nor do young children inevitably impede young single mothers.

The Woman Bearing the Burden of Parenthood Alone

As the population of available young black men in the inner city declines through early death, imprisonment, or the move South or West in pursuit of a job,[19] the prospects of a young black woman getting and keeping a husband often appear slim.

The increasing rate of joblessness among black men "merits serious consideration as a major underlying factor in the rise of black single mothers and female-headed households," writes William Julius Wilson.[20] Young men, unable to prove their manhood through bringing home wages sufficient to support a family, may do so through displaying sexual prowess and fathering a child.[21] They appear to have no difficulty finding willing teenage partners.[22]

The college has been deluged with single mothers. Forty-four percent of the students in 1987 say they have dependent children but only fifteen percent are married and living with spouse (with or without children).[23] One-third of Bronx Community College students, with a significantly larger proportion of women, may be single parents. While many students of the 1970s mourn their rush into early marriage and family, students of the 1980s are more likely to indicate ambivalence about their rush into family but outside marriage.

Families headed by women are disproportionately living in poverty. However, the image of the beleaguered unmarried mother who thrives on welfare as an entitlement is a far cry from the single-parent student at Bronx Community College, single-minded in her determination to pursue an education and career and extricate herself and her children from dependency on Aid for Dependent Children.

Impressive among the women at the college who became mothers in their teens is the number who grieve over the premature foreclosure of their academic lives. Acquiring a college education they see as a glorious achievement and an inspiration to their children. A twenty-seven-year-old single parent of two boys, a native Antiguan, tells of her early academic accomplishments despite impoverished beginnings.

> I was the youngest of ten children and was only two years old when our mother died. My eldest sister, who was put in the position of nurturer, was only fourteen years old. I was born in Antigua, West Indies. This country is a third world country and was very impoverished during that period. Work was scarce. My father left for the U. S. to find work to help us.
>
> Most people, except for the privileged few, could not get an education beyond high school. I was fortunate to have passed a government examination and was allowed to attend the high school that was once exclusively for the paying few. Unfortunately, my education was cut short in the tenth grade when I became a pregnant

teen. So my education stood still until my enrollment at Bronx Community College. My desire to succeed stems from having my education taken away from me because of a mistake I made at fourteen, and I also believe in setting an example for my children.

A native Puerto Rican, a single parent of three, now in her thirties, recounts the tribulations that came with early motherhood, her childhood "stolen," her education, "halted."

> At fourteen I was seduced by an eighteen-year old boy, got pregnant, and had his son. Being a young mother, I did not know what was expected of me. After all, I was only a baby myself and having to be a wife to a boy was a frightening experience.
>
> By the time I was seventeen years old I already had three children. My relationship with their father was over. I had to bring up my children by myself. As my children and I grew up together, we were each others' nurturing partners. My childhood was stolen from me and my education halted. I scraped by on the welfare rolls, struggling to survive. My children became my entire life, and I pushed them to get an education and to work their way out of the culture of poverty, as my father had tried with me.
>
> I met a young man, and his encouragement, love, and support gave me the courage to go back to school. I have found out how important it is to have an education. Without it, no one can survive. I only hope that my children will see this and do the same, go back to school and try to finish. I know I will be a psychologist some day even if it takes me ten years.

And a young Antiguan student embraces the goals of her single mother whose yearnings for further education were aborted by early pregnancy.

> Although my mother left school at fifteen (when she became pregnant), she kept on reading. She read everything she could get her hands on. No college graduate could write, read, and comprehend more than my mother. It was because her education was cut short, and Antigua did not provide the facilities to further her education, she wanted me to become what she had envisioned for herself.

Single mothers do not necessarily regret becoming mothers in their teens, especially if an adult is readily available to turn to for help. One pleasurable reminiscence comes from a young woman born in Spanish Harlem.

The family I was born into was not a traditional nor a nuclear-structured one. It was a single-parent environment and a strong one, I might add. I was born into a matrilineal home where my mother and grandmother were providers of both financial and emotional support. There were no male figures around at all.

My mother migrated from Puerto Rico to the United States when she was ten and acquired most of America's cultural standards, so by the time my sisters and I were born, there were no traces of the Spanish culture she came from. I sometimes feel grateful that my mother did not instill the Spanish culture in us because when I was born, the culture was still a very strict one. We lived above the poverty line but didn't quite make it to the middle class.

At fifteen I became a teen-age mother. I have a vivid recollection of when I told my mother and how she accepted me with open arms and expressed to me how she would back me up on whatever decision I made in reference to my having the child or terminating the pregnancy. She never made me feel obligated to marry the father just because it was the right thing to do according to societal norms. I decided to have the baby. She's eleven years old now. She's the love of my life and I have never regretted having her. Her biological father never participated in her life and I kind of gathered he wouldn't, so immediately after giving birth to her I found employment and took care of responsibilities. I did realize I was missing out on a lot of things that teen-agers usually do. I didn't regret my new status in life, as mom and I did a good job of it, if I may say so myself.

No matter what, my mother raised us to respect and love our fathers, regardless of what happened.

Helped financially by Aid For Dependent Children, single mothers often move out from the parental household to one of their own. Members of the extended family or social network may be available for baby-sitting services or even a place to sleep, but cannot always be depended upon. The kin and network support for single black mothers that Carol Stack describes in *All Our Kin* is not always found here, "not in New York," I am told.[24] Yet the move from home is usually not far, just sufficiently distant to permit some independence while providing the possibility of assistance. "When I was twenty-two, I decided to move out on my own," one single mother recalls."I moved in the same building as my mother. She takes care of my daughter while I work and go to school." Some single mothers gravitate toward men to relieve them of part of the burden, while others express reluctance at this juncture to depend upon men for financial help or psychic satisfaction.

Grandmothers give support and solace for single parents in innumerable ways, often as baby sitters. A single mother expresses her gratitude. "When I was twenty, my grandmother came to live with my mom and I was able to attend night classes after work to acquire my high school equivalency diploma. I was eternally grateful for her staying with us because it was she who took care of my daughter."

And grandmothers instill an ethic of personal responsibility, recounts an African- American young man who is a single father for his young son.

> Both of my parents suffered from a drug problem and had little concept of what it meant to be responsible and committed. My mother is dead now, she died of lung cancer. My father is still alive, but to me he's been dead from the first day I realized he wanted nothing to do with me. My grandmother migrated to the North in the 1950s. She was a dear woman who taught me to be peaceful, wise, and grateful for whatever situation I found myself in. She was not highly educated academically but was a wizard at common sense thinking and teaching. She was hard on me in a good way. She is deceased now, but her presence is felt every day consciously and unconsciously.

If no adult is around to help, being an impoverished single parent can be excruciatingly difficult, and the students describe the difficulties they face in devastating detail: their daily trek from home to day-care center to school and/or work, back to day-care center to home, then feeding young children, supervising the homework of somewhat older children, and preparing the young for bed. Study at home is cut short by simple weariness or incessant interruption.

Being the child of a young, single, harassed mother who works outside the home while attending school is difficult, too, they acknowledge. "My child gets lonely, has a puppy, he likes to talk a lot, and sometimes I don't feel like listening." "He wants me to read a story and I'm exhausted. I spend too little time with him, having to support the apartment, my child, me. His teacher says I should spend more time reading to him -- reading, reading. I tell her I also have homework."

Students who themselves were bereft of fathers recall the distress experienced at their absence: "I was always yearning to see my father, but he only used to go to my house twice a month in order to avoid problems with my mother." "I felt cheated not being brought up by both parents." "I hated my father for not being around when I needed him and my mother for letting him go."

Mothers, and occasionally a father, bring children to class when surrogates are not available. Young children are ubiquitous on the campus and teachers must occasionally remind themselves that this was not always so on college campuses and is still not so at other colleges. Children become a classroom reality that most teachers and students learn to live with and soon take for granted. Only one student, a woman with young children who herself resists bringing them to class, ever expresses annoyance at the presence of other students' children in the classroom.[25]

The single mother's routine between mothering, schooling, and working can turn chaotic when an emergency arises. A young woman explains her low grade in a sociology quiz after having maintained a B average. She and her two children are supported by the Department of Welfare that usually sends a rent check to her landlord. But the Department was four months late, she was evicted and now lives in a dormitory, separated from her children. She is frequently absent from class seeking legal aid, attending court sessions, or waiting her turn at the Welfare office. She eventually drops the course.

Whether the single mother, deprived of the help of mother or grandmother and abandoned by the father of her children, is likely to forgive him is moot. Single parenthood may often contribute to long-lasting estrangement between women and men.[26]

The Older Student Seeking a Second Chance

"All generations of college students have in common their youth and their developmental status," wrote Nevitt Sanford in 1967. "Most undergraduates are still free of the responsibilities and commitments that people assume as they enter adulthood."[27] One of the great transformations that occurred in higher education since the early 1970s has been the return to school of people of all ages and levels of responsibility. Not since the time of the medieval scholar and the humanist have students of so wide a range of ages been so free to intermingle in the classroom.[28]

Students at Bronx Community College span generations ranging in age from the late teens to the fifties and beyond. A sharp rise in student age comes with open admissions. Students older than twenty-six comprise 3 1/2 percent of the entering class in 1970 and 24 percent in 1978 and reach 50 percent by the late 1980s. The proportion of older students here is large even compared with other community colleges.

Students in the 1970s recall with irritation their own rush into early marriage and family. A woman in her thirties, married at nineteen, bemoans being her "mother's little girl," then in short order becoming a wife and mother herself. "I did not have enough time to enjoy my youth," she reflects. "I resent the fact that I can't do most of the things that I want to do. I have to think about the welfare of my family, then myself." And a divorced man in his thirties, also married at nineteen, reiterates: "The family comes first, but where do I come in? I'm coming in now. I'm just starting to see me as an individual."

Accepting their role of homemaker, women postponed becoming "somebody" or "something." "It's important to be something before you're a mother," a student in her late twenties plaintively asserts. "If I had it to do all over again, I would just now be having children. My education would have been completed, and I would have gotten involved in a field first. That's the way my mom wanted it, but you can't tell hot-headed teenagers anything."

Women generally acknowledge, at least retrospectively, that there was much that was pleasurable in the early marriage and family experience that they would not have wanted to forego. Nevertheless, "There is an insecurity at being out of the mainstream of life for twenty years," reflects a women of thirty-seven. The "mainstream of life" is for her outside the home.

Students more than a decade beyond customary college age fear that they cannot now acquire the knowledge or make up the experience they missed. At the least, employers will assume a knowledge and experience gap. "I might have gone into psychology, but my age may be a problem. That's why I'm staying where I am, a Mental Hygiene Therapy Aide," says a forty-eight year old black man resignedly. And a forty year-old white women voices her desperation: "I know that I could get a job as a hairdresser, better than any professional career." (After graduation she does find a satisfying job as a counselor in a woman's prison.)

Family and job usually take precedence over schoolwork, leaving insufficient time for study and interfering with concentration on textbook or lecture. "A younger person without worries, obligations, or stress is able to grasp more quickly," a woman grieves, she would do better "without kids," and a man recalls the time he was part of a state and city layoff from his job as corrections officer: "It was the best year here, I got A's and B's. Then when I was recalled, it was difficult."

Older students lament that they have forgotten much that they learned in school in earlier years, "a lot of things" they used to know "faded away." The fear of being the oldest student, "with rusty brains," makes them nervous. They feel "old and tired, unable to compete with the young and the restless."

Dubious about their own academic achievement, they anticipate serving as mentors and models to their children. They want a college education "for their kids, to push their kids to go on." If they never get that degree, they "know their children will." At the least, they can follow in their children's footsteps, determined that the education gap between generations not be stretched beyond repair.

Whatever their lamentations over protracted role responsibilities and learning difficulties, the older students are grateful for the "second chance" at college and career. An African-American woman whose husband died violently after a tempestuous marriage expresses her gratitude: "I've been there. I don't think I could say again, 'Yeh, this is my man.' I'm fascinated that with my background I can do it. I dropped out of grammar school and I made it! I study at work (on the night shift) and in the morning before class. I have no days off from study."

The superior students at Bronx Community College are likely to be older than average. I discover one such student while reading essay examinations for the first test of the semester in a sociology class. Most papers are poor to fair but one is outstanding in conceptualization and clarity. I note from his student identification number that he matriculated seventeen years earlier. What happened to him in the intervening years, I want to know. He re-enlisted in the Armed Forces, married, helped to rear six children, and now works full-time as a computer technician while carrying sixteen credits, with a cumulative grade-point average of 3.9. His wife is also a student at Bronx Community College. He will soon graduate and transfer to a four-year city college. He is an African-American man of forty.

Teachers concur that age is an important parameter in learning:

> Younger students are not as interested, they come to class late, want to leave early, and tend to have more absences, whereas the older students are more serious. . .
> The older students are more aware of the valuable nature of time. They work harder, they won't put up with nonsense from the younger ones. . .
> They are more perceptive when they read, they bring more life experience to the reading, and it does make a difference.

Some older students compare their seriousness with the levity of the young:

> It's hard being out of school for so long and the giggling and whispering and note-passing and gum-popping of the eighteen, nineteen, and twenty-year-olds is distracting. . .

They're still partying. Life hasn't taken on its full significance. To
them, life is a game. I've been there. . .
I know the meaning of education high-school dropouts don't know.
You work a while at the lowest-paid jobs. You realize education is
a way to a better life.

Youth, though, has some advantages in the mathematics class:
"Younger students come to math courses fresher from math in high
school. Older students are probably more serious about studying. The
combination balances out." And youth is advantageous in a foreign
language class. "The students of forty or fifty might be more motivated
but more scared."

Relationships on campus between old and young are generally
amicable. The young are likely to express admiration for the older
student. "Older people are coming to get personal knowledge, they're
not always doing it for a career. I love to see them here. I think I'm the
richer for it" is a common assessment among the young. Though older
students occasionally express annoyance at the unmitigated levity
among some of the young, they also respond warmly to their presence.
"Much younger students make it easy for me. They talk with me, even
the male side," ventures a woman in her sixties. "I'm just a student and
that's it."

College, then, is no moratorium for these new students, representing
some years away from the job market weighing alternative careers, as it
has been for the traditional student. Almost all are poor, most are black
and Hispanic, more are women than men, and many are older than the
traditional college student.They enter college determined to reap the
advantages of open admissions and subsidized tuition despite
encumbrances from family and job that usually have prior claim on
their time and attention.

Notes

1. William Julius Wilson, *The Truly Disadvantaged: The Inner City,
the Underclass, and Public Policy* (Chicago: The University of Chicago
Press, 1987), 20-29.

2. Jacqueline Jones, *Labor of Love, Labor of Sorrow: Black Women,
Work, and the Family from Slavery to the Present* (NewYork:Basic Books,
1985), 302-304.

An African-American student at Bronx Community College in the 1970s who attended high school before World War II recalls that not until the war did a high school education begin to offer a black woman any emotional or financial security. "I quit Julia Richman high school six months before graduation," she reminisces. "I took the commercial course, it was all they had, and where could a colored girl get a job in the commercial field? That was 1939. They tried to get us into dressmaking or beauty culture. It made me angry. What were we going to school for? I couldn't see a job. My mother cried. The job market came with World War II."
(Even in 1950, though, only 5 percent of black working women had clerical or sales jobs. Jones, *Labor of Love, Labor of Sorrow* , 235).

The last time I saw this student she had just received her baccalaureate from a city college and was seeking a letter of recommendation from me for job applications. She appeared poised and self-assured.

3. Kenneth B. Clark, *Dark Ghetto: Dilemmas of Social Power* (New York: Harper & Row, 1965), 90.

4. Judith Cummings, "Breakup of Black Family Imperils Gains of Decades," *New York Times,* 20 November 1983 : 1, 56.

The "unemployed" include men looking for work as well as those who never worked or have given up seeking work.

5. William Julius Wilson, *The Truly Disadvantaged,* 7.

6. Ibid., 56-57, 49.

7. Howard B. London, *The Culture of a Community College* (New York: Praeger, 1978), 11.

8. Andrew Hacker, *Two Nations: Black and White, Separate, Hostile, Unequal* (New York: Ballantine Books, 1992), 146; Wilson, *The Truly Disadvantaged,* 61.

9. Cornel West, *Race Matters* (Boston: Beacon Press, 1993), 89.

10. The rapist myth did not exist during slavery or the Civil War but was circulated after Reconstruction to justify the savage lynchings of black men, complementing the continued rape of black women, both weapons of domination. Angela Y. Davis, *Women, Race, & Class* (New York: Random House, 1981. First Vintage Books Edition, 1983) , 184-185.

The white community circulated the myths of the black male rapist and the sexually loose black woman about the newly freed blacks in order to prevent interracial marriage and to assert the ideal of white supremacy. Bell hooks, *Ain't I A Woman: Black Women and Feminism* (Boston: South End Press, 1981), 60-61; *YEARNING: race, gender, and cultural politics* (Boston: South End Press, 1990), 58, 71.

11. Giddings, *When and Where I Enter: The Impact of Black Women on Race and Sex in America* (New York: William Morrow, 1984), 314-317; hooks, *YEARNING: race, gender, and cultural politics,*47. Hooks speculates that "Careful interrogation of the way in which sexist notions of masculinity legitimize the use of violence to maintain control, male

domination of women, children, and even other men, will reveal the connection between such thinking and black-on-black homicide, domestic violence, and rap . . ," 77.

12. Angela Davis is referring to some black male activists in the l960s. *Angela Davis: An Autobiography* (New York: Random House, 1974), 161.

13. Giddings, *When and Where I Enter: The Impact of Black Women on Race and Sex in America,* 318-320.

14. .Jacqueline Jones, *Labor of Love, Labor of Sorrow: Black Women, Work, and the Family ,* 315-316.

15. Johnnetta B. Cole, *Conversations: Straight Talk with America's Sister President* (New York: Doubleday, 1993), 94.

Bell hooks speaks of racism and sexism as "interlocking systems of domination which uphold and sustain one another. Cannot black women remain seriously concerned about the brutal effect of racist domination on black men and also denounce black male sexism?" she asks. *YEARNING,* 59, 62.

16. Jones, *Labor of Love, Labor of Sorrow,* 312.

17. Michele Wallace, *Black Macho and the Myth of the Super-Woman* (New York: The Dial Press, 1978), 173.

18. Ibid., 28-30. A black comedian television star "joked" that he would prefer Raquel Welsh, a white sex symbol, to Shirley Chisholm any day. Black men savored and repeated his "joke."

19. Jones, *Labor of Love, Labor of Sorrow,* 326.

20. Wilson, *The Truly Disadvantaged, .*83.

There has been an unprecedented increase in the *proportion* of births out of wedlock among young black and white women, the rates for blacks considerably higher than for whites, though the fertility rate of young unmarried women has changed only moderately since the late 1950s. Women are more likely than in earlier decades to remain single or marry at a later age and married women are having fewer children.

21. Jones, *Labor of Love, Labor of Sorrow,* 326

22. Elijah Anderson, *StreetWise: Race, Class, and Change in an Urban Community* (Chicago: The University of Chicago Press, 1990), 112, 113, 126, 134. Hacker, *Two Nations: Black and White,* 69-77.

23. According to social survey findings, many men neglect to report children who do not live with them. They are reluctant to acknowledge children they neither see nor support. Frank F. Furstenberg, Jr., "Good Dads-Bad Dads: Two Faces of Fatherhood," in *The Changing American Family and Public Policy ,* ed. Andrew J. Cherlin (Washington, D.C.: The Urban Institute Press, 1988), 201-202.

24. Carole B. Stack, *All Our Kin* (New York: Harper and Row, l974).

25. The generally cheerful acceptance of children in the classroom at Bronx Community College contrasts with the aversion to their presence

among white students in Weis' study, who felt that their education suffered as a consequence of black children appearing in class. Lois Weis, *Between Two Worlds: Black Students in an Urban Community College* (Boston: Routledge and Kegan Paul, 1985), 112.

26. Jones, *Labor of Love, Labor of Sorrow,* 326. Jones refers to the possible estrangement between black men and women.

27. Nevitt Sanford, *Where Colleges Fail* (San Francisco: Jossey-Bass, 1967), 30-31.

28. Philippe Aries, *Centuries of Childhood: A Social History of Family Life,* trans. Robert Baldick (New York: Alfred A. Knopf, 1962).

Chapter 3

Discrimination and Segregation
In School and Out

Bronx Community College opened its doors in 1957. During its first decade, matriculants were predominantly white. With the advent of open admissions in 1970 there was an exodus of whites and an influx of blacks and Hispanics. The ethnic pool expanded through the 1970s and 1980s to include an increasing number of foreign students: from Ghana to Guyana, from Vietnam to Pakistan, and from every Caribbean island.

Students of color describe their experiences as nonwhites in a country dominated by whites. Color in the Caribbean islands is seen as closely associated with class, while in the States the ramifications of color are regarded as more personally vilifying. Students who grew up in the United States allude to their racist encounters here, newcomers to their racial shock.

Discriminatory History:
Race Here, Class There

The belief that the color white alone is beautiful is disconcerting to black students. "Women represent what beauty is in this society and too much emphasis is placed on white beauty," protests an African-

American woman. "I think we've been conditioned for a long time. Just recently we've been considering that black is beautiful."

"Next Life, I'll Be White," headlines an editorial in *The New York Times* written by a black man.[1] The black man remains obsessed with whiteness all his life, writes Kenneth Clark in 1965.[2] The color black may have become increasingly beautiful since the 1960s, but the world is still divided between the dark and the fair and it is good to be fair, even among blacks themselves. An Antiguan student notes this fact resignedly: "In Antigua, most people are black. There is no discrimination there. Yet the fairer blacks discriminate against the black blacks. They pick the fairer girls to be on the floats."

Growing up in a black ghetto and attending a neighborhood school, black students felt shielded from racism in their early years.[3] "I saw discrimination and didn't see it," a student who grew up in Atlanta reflects. "I never really thought about it. There was never any visible racial tension in Atlanta when I grew up. With teachers themselves there was a color consciousness. All teachers were black. And there was strata consciousness. You were a teacher's kid or a post-office kid, higher than the ordinary worker. There was a preference for the lighter skin student. We were victims of prejudice ourselves."

Nevertheless, nonwhite students develop an acute sensitivity to race and speak freely of their racist encounters: on the street, at work, and in the Armed Forces.

Dark-skinned male students remain ever fearful of being picked up and detained by the police for an innocuous offense not of their own doing: arrested for a traffic violation and remanded to jail overnight or suffering through a succession of encounters with the law, feeling fortunate if each charge is eventually dropped.

Discrimination at work is commonly alluded to. To be young, black, and female without work experience "is enough to make one paranoid about a working atmosphere," a young African-American woman laments. Nor is it better to be young, black, and male, contends a young African-American man whose jobs, he feels, never demanded what he was capable of giving. "I feel people have a tendency to want to take care of their own first," he concludes.

The stereotype of the black as lazy and shiftless appears inescapable. "I applied for a job at Macy's," a young woman recounts. "The interviewer asked how I spent my time and told me, 'If it wasn't for Christmas holidays, I wouldn't hire you because you don't seem to want to work.' I took it all in because I really needed the job." The degrading label is imposed upon Puerto Ricans too. "If a Puerto Rican man makes it, he's a nigger or Spick who made it," complains a Puerto Rican student. "'You're a Puerto Rican? I never knew that,' people say. They don't expect me to be industrious or attractive. If you're a good student or a good worker, you hear, 'You're not like the average Puerto Rican.'"

One of the most poignant among the discriminatory army tales comes from a young Chinese-American student who does not recognize himself as the enemy until he arrives in Vietnam. "Since I'm an only son and my father, who was a vet from World War II, died, I wasn't supposed to be drafted. I feel I was mentally raped and it can never be erased. I was glad to see what it was like in Vietnam instead of through the media but I regret being there. I was under the impression we were fighting the bad guys and I was considered the bad guy by my comrades. I was picked on and officers would beat me up for no reason. I could have stripped them of their rank but I didn't. I had a constant feeling of being watched all the time I was in the Service. I had some really good friends there, too."

A nonwhite soldier either learns to endure discrimination or he leaves the Service, concludes a young African American who resigned from his lowly position in the Navy after five years of duty. "All the blacks have the same low jobs. It was hard to deal with."

The anticipation of racism is so strongly embedded in black students' consciousness that in the late 1980s some assume that it lies latent even if never exposed. Racism today can be very subtle, speculates a young African-American woman. "One can almost get the feeling that it is unfashionable to be boldly racist anymore. Today people try to cover up their real feelings. I can honestly say that if I were being discriminated against, I would never know it."

Foreign students, new to American culture, speak of their distraught reaction to discriminatory treatment in this country. A young Nigerian, the grandson of a Yoruban king, finds "extremely unbelievable" the double jeopardy he experiences here as a native black-African. "To be black is a jeopardy in this society, and I realize that to be a native black African is a double jeopardy. People are prejudiced towards Africans because they see Tarzan and the Ape and they think we jump from tree to tree. To be an African is to realistically experience discrimination and prejudice to the fullest degree possible."

A young Indian woman of Asian descent who arrived recently from Guyana, where her great-grandparents from the Punjab settled as laborers several generations ago, resigns herself to the fact that "There will always be some barriers in my way. There will always be discrimination and prejudices wherever I go."

Students from Caribbean countries discern discrimination in their native country, but discrimination there, seeming to arise from class differences, does not evoke the same personal humiliation. Students are caught off guard by the epithets hurled at them in this country: "black bitch," "nigger," "damn black." "In Dominica, which is ninety-nine percent black, race had no negative meaning to us," one young woman attests. " But I experienced a very nasty racial incident here. I was at a certain bus stop at 10:30 P.M., awaiting my bus. A white man about fifty who was obviously drunk approached me and called me 'black bitch.' He then continued with the nastiest insults I had ever heard, ending with, 'Nigger, go where you came from, we do not need you all here.' There were other white people at the bus stop who had the look of disgust but didn't say or do anything to help."

The class discrimination that prevails in their own native country, not so pointedly vilifying and devastating, can more easily be endured. "We have problems in the Dominican Republic but not like the United State," maintains a Dominican student."There it's social and economic discrimination, rich and poor, it's not color. I saw the problem here -- 'You damn black' or 'blacks are not as smart' -- and I panicked. In the Dominican Republic, if you say something against the president, you can go to jail. You can't talk freely. Otherwise, you can do there what I am doing here."

Class discrimination in their homeland is closely allied with color discrimination. "In the city, most of the black people are poor and most poor people are black," a Dominican interjects. "In Puerto Rico too," a Puerto Rican corroborates. "There's a color line among Latins, very obvious racial discrimination in Puerto Rico. It's done especially through jobs and housing. The unemployment rate in Puerto Rico is 12 percent to 15 percent, but among blacks it is over 50 percent."[4] The color line intrudes in personal relations as well as jobs, asserts another Puerto Rican. "When you want to get married, if the man is darker, there is objection from her family who would like her to get somebody better than you, and 'better' means 'lighter.'" [5]

The high correlation between class and color is noted in Jamaica too by Nettleford. "In the minds of many Jamaicans, it is still a poor black, a middle-class and privileged brown man, and a rich or wealthy white man."[6] And a Barbadian student finds color a crucial stratifying variable in Barbados. "There's a different kind of discrimination there," he points out. "Here it's more open. There, on the surface it looks like no discrimination. You work together, you are invited into the homes. But there is never dating or marrying among Barbadians. There's great disparity in income on the same job. The lighter you are in color, the greater the possibility of getting a good job. In 1964, when I graduated from high school, there were no black bank tellers and no black salesmen in the stores. There was not much somebody of my economic class could do there except a clerical job in government. I worked there for five years, then got a student visa. The only outlet, get a degree here, then go back. I might even enter politics, who knows. Economic control still rests with the white minority, though political control is now with blacks."

Caribbean students refer to discrimination in class rather than race in their native countries, yet class and color appear intertwined.[7] Racial discrimination in the States, though, is experienced as more personal, agonizing, and humiliating, an aversion both new and distasteful.

Three Distinctive Ethnic Enclaves on Campus

White Americans are increasingly becoming nonethnic in character and culture as their ancestral country becomes more distant and they intermingle and intermarry, notes Andrew Hacker. They are now more likely to differentiate themselves by economic class than by ethnicity.[8]

Ethnicity at Bronx Community College is a strong divisive variable. Group life revolves primarily around three distinctive ethnic enclaves: African-Americans, blacks from former British colonies in the Caribbean, and Hispanics, black and white.[9] Students with British credentials speak pridefully of themselves as British-educated and refer to African Americans and Hispanics in stereotypical, derogatory fashion. They are not alone. Each ethnic group expresses misgivings about others, even Vietnamese against Cambodians. In the cafeteria one large section of Vietnamese don't speak to Cambodians, a teacher observes, "so you realize how many sub-subcultures there are."

Language differences, prefiguring other cultural differences divide Hispanic students from African-Americans. "The hostility between Hispanics and blacks is great when the Hispanics don't know English very well," an African-American student proposes. "There's not the same humor. You don't feel the same things funny." Hostility may persist even when the Hispanics do know English well.

A common language unites Hispanics from varied homelands. Puerto Ricans, Dominicans, Cubans, Colombians, and Hondurans "hang out with other Hispanics a lot. We are often close friends, though some are more white than me, some darker." Despite the common language, though, Hispanics create cleavages among themselves. Puerto Ricans predominate among Hispanics during the 1970s and 1980s, but, by the late 1980s begin to be eclipsed in number by the Dominicans. Hispanics from countries other than Puerto Rico dislike being identified with Puerto Ricans, whom they see as divested of their nationhood by the Yankees. "Here in New York, the Spanish-speaking people -- Puerto Ricans, Mexicans, Cubans, Dominicans -- we're grouped together," one Puerto Rican young man observes, "but the others don't like to be called Puerto Rican. People from South and

Central America have respect for their own country. They call Puerto Ricans 'Yankees.' They see a cop out by the Puerto Ricans. 'Operation Bootstrap' was not a Puerto Rican goal but a U.S. goal. All we got was a minimum wage on factory work and chimneys pouring out dust and dirt."[10] Yet Dominicans and other Hispanics try on occasion to pass as Puerto Ricans because of the "full rights" Puerto Ricans possess as American citizens.[11]

Themselves derogated by other Hispanics, Puerto Ricans turn against African Americans, whom they stereotype as being tough, assertive, and self-pitying. "A black person moving next door in Puerto Rico wouldn't bother us, but here the black men and women are trying to be tough," declares a native Puerto Rican, white in color. "We owned a house (here) and a black lady moved to the next house. My husband sold the house. The way they talk and walk, they try to be better." "Look at us, and not always at the American blacks," demands another young Puerto Rican woman. "There were black slaves, Indian slaves, white slaves, Jewish slaves, and they all suffered, not only the blacks. A lot of people want others to feel sorry for them."

African Americans reciprocate, venting their grievances against Puerto Ricans, who enjoy what they, the African Americans, fought for: welfare, jobs, public housing. "The Puerto Ricans come here and get on welfare. They don't have to pay taxes then. I don't have strong prejudices. It's harder for blacks to get welfare," an African-American student complains, and a young Puerto Rican confirms that he has heard such grievances before, though they are somewhat muted at Bronx Community College. "With students it is different. We're almost equal. We have the same problems: reading and writing."

The amalgam of disparaging voices is embellished by British West Indians -- Jamaicans, Barbadians, Antiguans -- who seek to emphasize their British credentials as they preserve their social distance from both African Americans and Hispanics, whom they see as lower on the ladder of respectability. They allude to their own superiority in manners: "West Indians are well-mannered. They grew up with the British system. They stand when the teacher comes in. They talk politely." American blacks they characterize as "much too loud." "You can get your point across without yelling or screaming. Why do they have their mouths open so wide? The Hispanics? Forget about them. They are aggressive to a point where they are ill-mannered."

Manners were the only resource left the Antiguans in confronting the British, notes the Antiguan writer, Jamaica Kincaid.[12]

The British West Indians speak with pride of their middle-class community, situated in the North East Bronx, far from the devastation of the South Bronx, where the college is located. "The whole North East Bronx -- doctors, lawyers, teachers, nurses -- is predominantly

West Indian. I have my own house there. We don't sit on steps in the streets. My son's friends are not a lot of black children. He is intimidated by them."

They decry what they see as the spiritual empoverishment among African Americans, mired in drugs and overcome by violence, failing to utilize their own resources to make for themselves a better world. "Black Americans are being left behind because they are still reliving their ocean voyage to this continent as slaves. They are still crying about their second-class life style. They commit racial suicide with crack and kill each other. They listen to Martin Luther King, Jr., "I Have a Dream," and forget to dream, too. Instead they think society owes them their dream. They must realize for them to survive they have to develop a future-oriented style of thinking. They need to go out and look for that dream and make it reality." [13]

They regard many of their American-born counterparts as unworthy of the financial aid they receive from the government. Such aid, they maintain, encourages deception and indolence. "A lot here who are getting financial aid don't appreciate their education as much. They say, 'That's all I'm here for, to get that money.' A lot of them do work and also collect financial aid. There should be more screening. They don't clarify that they're living at home or have a job. They lie." "I'm very critical of the American system. I, a Jamaican, have to work weekends to pay my tuition. Financial aid encourages people to be lazy."

They are appalled by what they regard as black racism exhibited by African Americans against them as black in-migrants. A Caribbean student recalls with dread his first job in this country collating papers at a Wall Street firm. "It was terrible. For the first time in my life I experienced racism. The irony: it was not white racism but black racism. The black Americans cursed and abused me and the other West Indians so badly I just could not take it. I quit. I was miserable, depressed, and angry."

And they are scornful of African-Americans' seeming hostility toward whites, as evidenced by their not wishing to share a table with white students in the classroom. "There is one incident that took place in my biology class that I found very disturbing," recalls a black Jamaican. "I shared a table with some fellow students who happened to be white and, to my surprise, some of the black students in the class began calling me 'a white lover.' I was furious and shocked because in my country people were not conscious of the color of their skin. I felt very hurt and ashamed for those people who cannot see past their skin color. In Jamaica I was not exposed to prejudice and racism because almost everyone was of black descent, so people saw themselves as a person instead of a black person." This black Jamaican does not mention that American whites often share the same myopic vision.

"We're all in the same boat" is outweighed, then, by, "Look at our differences." Status linked to ethnicity and life style is introduced as an important differentiating variable in this population of black and Hispanic students.

Segregation Between Cafeterias by Life Style; Segregation Within a Cafeteria by Race and Ethnicity

Inside the classroom "everybody seems to get along with everybody," though lapses occur. Casual friendships arise among students who find themselves sitting next to each other or attending the same classes. There is an awareness of racial and ethnic differences, but little discernible discrimination. "They have their own groups, but in classes or walking on campus, it's not an issue." "If I feel someone is giving me a cold shoulder because I'm white, I try to show them usually I'm not prejudiced, and it works out fine. It rarely happens."

Outside the classroom and in more informal surroundings -- in the cafeteria or on the lawn -- life with peers becomes a microcosm of the life in the wider multiethnic community. Students splinter into subgroups segregated primarily by ethnicity and race but also by academic or extracurricular involvement.

In the 1970s, during the early years of the study, two student cafeterias are maintained on campus, each attracting its own clientele. The groups are differentiated on the basis of life styles: one, at Silver Hall, inclined toward the academic, the other, at Gould Cafeteria, disposed to anti-intellectual and social pursuits. "Those in Silver Hall are trying to learn, they are quiet and clean. Those in Gould cafeteria are spending their time partying, with loud music, disarray, disorder. There are no differences in social variables. It's the students themselves. I like to eat at Silver Hall. Maybe because I'm older," one student recounts, and another confirms: "There's a segregation, and those who feel they're a higher intellectual level are at Silver Hall. It's not on a racial or ethnic or class level. I know both crowds and I relate to both but I stick with friends in the classroom and then I go to Silver Hall."

Students critical of the clientele at Gould cafeteria refer to it as a hangout for those smoking pot, snorting coke, playing cards, and cutting classes. The noise level and levity are disconcerting to a student new to the college, who sees the students hanging out at the cafeteria as the same ones who talk revolution but never turn papers in in class. "If you're interested in learning, don't want noise, don't want to dance, but want to exchange ideas, there's no place to go." He has not yet discovered Silver Hall.

By the late seventies, only Gould Cafeteria remains as a student dining hall. Guards are stationed in and around the cafeteria, and non-students are forced to leave. There is no further talk of the drug scene on campus, although there are scattered indications that no place is off limits for drugs.

Within the remaining dining hall, as in the world outside, segregation by race and ethnicity persists. "In the cafeteria, blacks sit on one side, Latin-speaking on one side, Caucasians sit in the middle. They look at me constantly," observes a student who bridges the gap. "'Why do you talk to everybody,' they want to know. I think it's out of fear, fear of getting involved with something they're not familiar with."

One's own ethnic group and its culture breed relaxation and ease in talk, an extension of the "we-feeling" of the primary group. "Humans will always look for their own kind because of convenience in communication. The talk, the gestures." "I guess you know where you stand, you know you belong and there won't be too many problems." Moreover, there is the basis for networking. "Segregation here is a matter of security. Security with your own. I need a job, they help me. The students are interested in meeting other people, but there's the security."

Students at Bronx Community College seem fatalistic about the perpetuation of racial segregation, which in their view has never been obliterated. "In the army, there was definite segregation. In prison where I work, there's even more: all blacks, all whites, all Puerto Ricans." And "In all colleges, blacks stay with blacks, whites with their group, Puerto Ricans with theirs," is the consensus. "Overall, the same thing here, too." The segregation "is depressing to me," ventures an older African-American woman. "I felt with the younger students it would change and I don't see the change." The college is no ivory tower but mirrors the attitudes and relations that the students have encountered elsewhere.

The White Student as Outsider

White students at Bronx Community College, likely to be of Irish, Italian, or Jewish ancestry, comprised 45 percent of the student population in 1970, the first year of open admissions, but only 5 percent by the late 1980s. The precipitous decline in white students results from the reduction of the white population in the borough as well as the apprehension among whites regarding their minority status in a minority college, an apprehension that appears short-lived when they participate actively in extracurricular activities. "Everybody knows me," boasts a young white man known for his skill at basketball. And a young white woman who is editor of a poetry magazine, active in dance, and on the Parents' Board of the Nursery School, declares: "When I first came, I felt uneasy, but I got used to it. Everyone was friendly."

White students who have no extracurricular involvement express an uncertainty endemic to outsiders. "There are so many blacks and Puerto Ricans, I feel I'm the minority," a young woman reflects. "Most of my friends are Spanish-speaking. I feel I really don't belong. Why am I here? It's a problem. Being Jewish, you can't meet that many people. I'm finding that people are just like me down inside. They've got the same feelings."

The black woman's seeming self-confidence and assertiveness is threatening to some white woman. A student of Irish descent who spent twenty years mothering and housewifing before entering Bronx Community College in the 1970s expresses her ambivalence toward the black woman, admiring and castigating her. "I personally think that black women I have met here are enormously more confident in themselves and more aggressive than I am, and I attribute that to differences in upbringing. I was very protected. Any woman who has worked is more self-confident. A very overbearing, self-possessed woman throws me. I feel as though I am reporting to the principal." "The stereotypical image of the black woman as strong and powerful so dominates the consciousness of most Americans," bell hooks writes, "that even if a black woman is clearly conforming to sexist notions of femininity and passivity she may be characterized as tough, domineering, and strong." [14]

Admiration for the resourceful, self-reliant black woman is expressed by another white woman student, also of Irish descent, who has mingled in upper-class circles: "It's been an enlightening experience here at college, especially the black women. I really have to admire them. They work all night and come to an eight o'clock class in the morning. They don't seem to resent that their husbands took off (as hers did)."

Uneasiness over being Jewish may be greater than being white in this predominantly black and Hispanic college. "The people I hang out with are white but I don't feel very uncomfortable," a Jewish nursing student confesses. "I'm more uncomfortable about my religion. I have more paranoia as a Jew than as a white here. Jews have a poor reputation with blacks. It can come up. I'm not unhappy." She "doesn't feel very uncomfortable" and is "not unhappy." Through the use of the double negatives, she seems to be setting limits to her protestation of comfort and happiness. Whether this mode of expression is a personal proclivity or a response to the situation is difficult to assess. She has heard "white girls bitching it's below their level. It's fulfilling what I came for, " she declares.[15]

A black woman, in turn, is resentful of the white woman, seeing her as a competitor for black men. Bathroom conversation and graffiti on the bathroom wall bespeak black-white rancor. "If there is a black crowd in the bathroom and whites come in, conversation stops," a student observes. "Maybe they couldn't say it face-to-face. Somebody writes, 'Black guys like white women and not black woman because they smell,' and somebody else responds, 'What! Black is beautiful. I wouldn't think of fucking a white bitch.'"

The relations among students are succinctly described by one of the relatively few white Anglo-Saxon Protestant young men at the college: "There is no real black-white conflict, but they don't get along as well as possible. There is a basic fear on both sides."

Transcending Racial or Ethnic Boundaries?

Students at Bronx Community College blur ethnic and racial boundaries when they study together "and give each other moral support." Participants in sports and clubs that meet weekly on campus also create their own multiethnic bonds.

Notable in the 1970s is the camaraderie that persists among Vietnam veterans. Looking forward to graduation, one veteran speaks of his sense of responsibility for those he left behind. "The guys I run around with are all nationalities, mostly vets. It means something to me to get that piece of paper (the diploma). I'm living the dreams of those guys who never came home from 'Nam.' Sometimes I feel they're watching me. "

Students at the college generally spend a limited number of hours on campus and live their lives elsewhere. "I don't look to campus for my social life" is a frequent comment. "I'm too busy, I don't notice what goes on here." "I get very little sense of there being a community of college students," a teacher speculates. "There are just a few leaders who call themselves a community and speak for the community. Because of the passivity of the general student body, they're able to get much more notoriety than they probably deserve."

Peer interaction on campus, then, is largely an extension of life outside. There appears a surface cohesion within the ethnic subcultures but equally clear is a latent antagonism between them. Racial and ethnic boundaries are transcended only in the classroom and in specialized voluntary group activity. Outside the classroom, students erect invisible walls and suffer the segregation that they themselves impose.

A more benign relationship may have begun to emerge on campus in the late 1980s, a new and seemingly pervasive interest in and tolerance of others resulting from the increase in third world representation from distant countries. "The ethnic make-up at Bronx Community College of people that span the globe has been very enriching," affirms one African-American student. "It has opened my mind and heart, so that I will not be ignorant or insensitive toward the plight of the newer Americans." "At first, they seemed a little stand-offish, but now, as I see and get to know them, they are friendly and always eager to talk about their cultures and homelands," confirms a second student. Such effusive remarks are new, due perhaps to the students' desire to be identified with newcomers who share with them a non-European heritage.[16]

Notes

1. Laurence Thomas, "Next Life, I'll Be White," *New York Times*, 13 August 1990: A 15.

2. Kenneth B. Clark, *Dark Ghetto: Dilemmas of Social Power* (New York: Harper & Row, 1965; Middletown, CN: Wesleyan University Press, 1989), 65.

3. Alphonso Pinkney observes that in some respects middle-class blacks were more likely to encounter racism than poor blacks who lived in the slums and were not surrounded by whites. *The Myth of Black Progress* (New York and London: Cambridge University Press,1984),109.   Kenneth Clark speaks of the psychological safety in the ghetto where one does not risk rebuff from strangers. *Dark Ghetto,* 19.

4. According to the anthropologist, Elena Padilla, "Racial attitudes in Puerto Rico involve ambivalences that rotate around the cultural ideal that there is no racial prejudice. . .while social class is strongly associated with race." *Up from Puerto Rico* (New York: Columbia University Press, 1958), 75.

5. "One phenomenon that puzzles the observer in Puerto Rico is that one person will identify an individual as white or trigueno (ranging between white and colored), while a second person will identify the same

individual as colored," records Joseph P. Fitzpatrick, *Puerto Rican Americans: The Meaning of Migration to the Mainland* (Englewood Cliffs, New Jersey: Prentice-Hall, 1971), 105.

Ancestry and not pigmentation determines the assignment of color in Puerto Rico, declares one white-skinned Puerto Rican student at Bronx Community College who sees herself as black. "Being white has nothing to do with skin color. I'm Puerto Rican. I could look at my family. You'd see my father is black and my grandfather is definitely black. So it's there. My mother's family is light."

"Having immediate Negro ancestry does not necessarily peg an individual as Negro (unlike the United States)," Padilla writes, "for race is more a matter of 'appearing to be' than of ancestry." At the point of marriage, though, ancestry is a concern in socially mobile groups. Padilla, *Up from Puerto Rico*, 72-73.

6. Rex M. Nettleford, *Mirror, Mirror: Identity, Race and Protest in Jamaica* (London: William Collins and Sangster, 1970), 24-25.

Discrimination by color occurs in primary as well as secondary relations in Jamaica. Fair women are likely to be hired in shops, offices, and banks, and successful black men look for women of a "higher" color in marriage. Fernando Henriques, *Family and Colour in Jamaica,* 2nd. ed. (London: MacGibbon and Kee, 1968), 61-63.

7. Though some of the most deplorable features of slavery were worse in the West Indies than in the United States, West Indians had more experience taking care of themselves. They were assigned land to raise their own food and could sell surplus in the market. Thomas Sowell, *Ethnic America: A History* (New York: Basic Books, 1981), 218.

In the eighteenth century, slaves in the American South were often treated with brutality, even dismembered, writes Willie Lee Rose. Under new nineteenth century slave codes, the slave owner was responsible for providing his slaves with decent care and more humane treatment, though he could still buy or sell them at will. They were no longer regarded as barbarians but as children who would never grow up. Their movement was restricted, especially their association with free blacks, and their education eliminated. Though a Christian master had to provide religious instruction for his slaves, he was not likely to accept the Protestant dictum that to save their souls they had to read and interpret the Bible for themselves. Willie Lee Rose, *Slavery and Freedom,* ed. William W. Freehung (New York: Oxford University Press, 1982), 22-28.

8. Andrew Hacker, *Two Nations: Black and White, Separate, Hostile, Unequal* (New York: Ballantine Books, 1992), 175-176.

9. Hacker speaks of Hispanics' nonracial character, as indicated by a recent Census report in which one-half of the residents of California who describe themselves as Latin or Hispanic say they have no race at all, they are neither black nor white, but Hispanic. Ibid., 6.

10. "Operation Bootstrap" was a program of industrial development begun in Puerto Rico in 1948 and criticized for introducing values discordant with traditional values of family loyalty and personal relationships. Fitzpatrick, *Puerto Rican Americans,* 48.

11. The statement by a Puerto Rican real estate agent in New York City appears in Thomas Kessner and Betty B. Caroli, *Today's Immigrants, Their Stories: A New Look at the Newest Americans* (New York: Oxford University Press, 1981), 120.

12. In *A Small Place* (New York: Farrar, Straus, Giroux, 1988) Kincaid reminisces about the "bad-minded" English who used to rule over Antigua, her birthplace. "Nobody who did not look exactly like them would ever be English, so you can imagine the destruction of people and land that came from that." (24) The headmistress of a girls' school on the island, hired through the English colonial office, "told these girls over and over to stop behaving as if they were monkeys just out of trees. No one ever dreamed that the word for any of this was racism."(29) "We felt superior," she writes, "for we were so much better behaved and we were full of grace. . . (Of course, I now see that good behaviour is the proper posture of the weak, of children.)" (30). "But what I see is the millions of people, of whom I am just one, made orphans: no motherland, no fatherland, no gods, . . and worst and most painful of all, no tongue. . . . Nothing can erase my rage -- for this wrong can never be made right. . ." (31, 32.)

   Antiguans perceived the British as ill-mannered, not as racists, says Kincaid. (34)

13. From a student essay.

14. bell hooks, *Ain't I a Woman: Black Women and Feminism* (Boston: South End Press, 1981), 83.

15. Hostile feelings toward blacks were expressed by lower-middle class Jews living in close proximity, whose children attended the same schools, and who, as shopkeepers and teachers of the ghetto, felt themselves vulnerable to black rage. Murray Friedman, "The Jews," in *Through Different Eyes: Black and White Perspectives on American Race Relations*, eds. Peter I Rose, Stanley Rothman, and William J. Wilson, (New York: Oxford University Press, 1973), 148-165.

   Cornel West outlines "three basic pillars" on which black anti-semitism rests: (1) Black-Jewish interaction in business and education "cast Jews as the public face of oppression for the black community." (2) Regarding Jews as "natural" allies because of their history, some blacks hold them to a higher moral standard and feel "betrayed." (3) Underdog resentment and envy probably exists toward another underdog who "made it" in American society. *Race Matters* (Boston: Beacon Press, 1993), 76-77.

   Elijah Anderson writes of black hostility directed toward Asian business in the inner city, in contrast to the lack of hostility aroused by Jews who had run similar business establishments. Asians are seen as new competitors, taking over businesses that might have been taken over by blacks. Elijah Anderson, *StreetWise* (Chicago: University of Chicago Press, 1990), 61-62.

16. Black Americans, Cornel West observes, increasingly identify with other oppressed peoples throughout the world, a practice arising more from sharing political and social experience than from a common skin color. *Race Matters*, 53.

Chapter 4

Student Aspirations Run the Gamut

Little that occurred in the early lives of most students at Bronx Community College would predict their attending college. Their parents' knowledge of higher education was scanty and high school teachers and counselors saw them as unfit candidates.

Nevertheless, having matriculated with the help of open admissions and financial aid, they believe they can rise in class and status through their own efforts. Their reservations about society's benevolence remain, but for now they berate themselves if they lack the drive to succeed against surmountable odds.

Their professed motives for attending college run the gamut from finding a satisfying and well-paying job to serving their community and enriching themselves academically, aesthetically, and socially. The disparity is often great between their goals and the means they utilize to achieve these goals.

No Early Push toward College

To go or not to go to college cannot be a paramount concern when the exigencies of daily survival all but foreclose its implementation. A Puerto Rican young man recounts:

> My mother always said, 'Go to school, get a good education, get a good job.' But she didn't know how to explain the whole thing to me or how to motivate me to try to achieve a high education. My father died when

I was ten, and my mother had seven other babies. I was the oldest and I learned to deal with life. Lots of responsibilities -- work and school, guide sisters and brothers, cook, wash clothes, scrub floors, so my mother wouldn't have so much to do.

The parents of most Bronx Community College students of the 1970s and 1980s dreamt the universal American dream: that their children would advance beyond them in education and occupation. Deficient in formal education themselves, they wanted "more" for their children. Their sights, though, were not set on college, but on a trade for a son and a high school diploma for a daughter.

A son recounts that his Barbadian father, a jack of all trades, went to Cuba to cut cane, where "he saw a man reading a book. He saw the more education you got, the less manual work you did. He would tell us about his experiences, encouraging us to be different from what he was. He was sure all eight of us would get an education. We all went to high school."

Another student, of intellectual bent, describes the push toward a trade from his Irish-Catholic family. "I was never advised to go to college. I was advised to go to sheet metal at $8.40 an hour. My brother and his wife are anti-education."

A trade where the son shows talent might be encouraged. An astute young African American who aspires to journalism or the law recalls that his father thought he was an excellent cook and should become a chef. "I didn't laugh, but I had no such intention," he declares.

A government job seemed to parents to offer prestige and security. "My mother always stressed civil service work, though not anything special," recalls an African-American student born in New York City. "My father was a cop." The son becomes a police sergeant.

Parents who encouraged formal education beyond high school could give no guidelines, only, "Be something;" "Make something of yourself;" "It doesn't matter what you take, just go." When parents were more specific in their push -- "Be a teacher or a doctor" -- they could not propose how a child might get from here to there. "I guess the whole family had dreams of me being a doctor at one time," a twenty-eight year old African-American student recalls. But no one in the family could serve as model or mentor. Instead, the neighborhood cop was a real, live model. "He would drive around in a patrol car looking for us, knowing that we would be playing stick ball." The young boy becomes a cop, a Transit policeman.

A boy's early freedom to move about on his own without supervision impedes his remaining in school, a young Puerto Rican spokesman conjectures. He is victimized by the freedom accorded him which his sisters envied.

> When I grew up, parents would tell their daughters, 'When classes are over, I want you straight home.' The daughter stays home, eats, does her homework, and may later go to college. The son returns late from playing and may reluctantly do his homework. Many Puerto Rican males drop out. There seemed more to working than to school. I got lectured from my parents, 'Go to school.' But you can't compare an A with money to buy a record or go to a movie. My parents were working parents, and when they divorced, I dropped out of school.

Paradoxically, Hispanic parents who regard their son's education as more crucial to their own well-being in old age than their daughter's undermine their own interests by the freedom they give their sons.

Parents trying to push their children toward college gave directions that were vague, and high school teachers and advisers didn't try. They considered them "not college material," a pronouncement which became a "self-fulfilling prophecy." Students deplore the poor career counseling in their secondary schooling which did not include an academic curriculum as an option. One serious student recalls:

> When I was young, in a poor area of Brooklyn, teachers would look at you as though you were stupid. It was blatant. And the way they talked to your parents! You learn to accept it, but that's the worst part of it, you have the attitude that you can't do anything about it.

The push to college comes in more recent years from a friend, a relative, a co-worker, or an employer, whom the prospective student envies and seeks to emulate. A friend, different from others in the neighborhood, may provide the impetus. "I had to see someone I knew achieve from going to school," says a young African-American student. "I met an Italian kid. His parents were very poor. He had a paper route, was very disciplined, always had time for everything. He continued through college." Or an older sibling with academic credentials becomes the model. "All my mother's efforts were geared toward getting her an education."

College-educated co-workers, far removed from neighborhood peers, provide incentive for a tenth-grade dropout. "Getting a good education for the future didn't mean anything to me," she confesses. "My parents saw what was happening, but they didn't know how to deal with me. I was rebellious. I got an internship on the State Council of the Arts. Away from my friends, around highly educated professional people, it started to make sense to me. I came here to start all over. My whole first year was remedial. I expected lousy grades and was surprised. Now I want to go as high as I possibly can. A B.A. in International Affairs and an M.A. in Economics or Law School."

Parental aspirations for students attending the college in the l990s reveal a sea change. "You can't make it in this country without going to college," parents seem now to counsel, whether they themselves have attended college or are barely literate.

A Belief in Individual Mobility

Most black Americans blame the system for their failure to get ahead, says the anthropologist, John Ogbu.[1] Students at Bronx Community College, though, assert that they can rise through their own strivings. If they fail, they must blame themselves. They are imbued not with overpowering naivete but with a sense that they must be their own masters and rise above their blighted past and even their blighted present. "My young daughter (in college) and her friends would never say blackness is stopping them," asserts a black woman in her late thirties. "They think blackness should inspire you, and you're letting your people down if you haven't worked into your full potential." "I am reconciled to black-white discrimination," this student seems to be saying. "You have to be weak internally for the external factors to affect you."

A member of a black family of the underclass who is attempting to rise out of poverty and debauchery on his own scorns family members who show no similar inclination. His alcoholic father, in and out of jail, often sleeping in the hallway of his ghetto tenement, discharged his anger on the family. "The five of us half the time didn't go to school. He almost killed my mother, so she took off one day. She likes to play cards, numbers, gamble. One brother is locked up. They're typical blacks, messing around with other men, strung out on drugs. I try to stay away from them. Every time they call, it's a problem." He spent five years in the military and sought help through transcendental meditation. The sociology course too he sees as an instrument of self-help. "I don't feel the majority (of students) understand what the sociology course is all about," he asserts, "what they can do to apply what they learn, situations where they can use it. The burned down houses, the junkies -- why are so many black junkies hanging out? Half of the students are not concerned. Maybe they're afraid to ask questions. A lot feel inferior about themselves, stereotyped, even from high school." He finds no exemplar in his family and apparently few among his peers.

Students may castigate the teacher for any failure in the classroom. "He gives too much work. Doesn't he realize we have other classes?" "Half my class is failing. We can't all be that stupid." But ultimately they consider themselves personally accountable:

> Nothing is standing in my way but me. We don't know nothing about slavery days. Those were yesterday's problems. We're blaming ourselves now. If you have a high school diploma or an Equivalency, you can get accepted into New York City colleges. . .
>
> I think it's up to each individual to get all the education, rather than hanging on street corners and complaining about the system, the establishment. . .
>
> You hear people say, 'If you're the right color you can get everything,' but I never believed that. In every city you have important people -- writers, entertainers, politicians -- of every class imaginable. It's how hard you strive. Doors may be closed, but that can be overcome. . .
>
> If I don't succeed, it's not only due to my children or my poverty or race but to me, a lack of effort on my part. . .
>
> You should have responsibility for your own destiny. I don't think minorities are responsible enough. My psychology teacher assigned an article on bilingualism from *The Times* four weeks ago. The students hadn't read it. She said a question on it would appear in the exam. 'You didn't discuss that in class,' they protested.

Open admissions they see as providing a unique opportunity for blacks to rise as individuals and as a group. "It's time black people banded together and got their education first. If you don't have an education, there's really nothing you can do." "If every black man educated his black son, there would be no subordinate class."

Yet Reservations Persist about Society's Benevolence

Many high school graduates, white and black, turn away from college during the 1970s. They are responding to the seemingly insecure job market for college graduates and the increase in the loan proportion for financial aid but the reduction in grants. The turn-way in the 1980s is most visible among black men. The gap in the college enrollment rate between white and black male high school graduates, almost eliminated in the late 1970s, hovers at 7 to 9 percent through most of the 1980s and stretches to 15 percent in 1988.[2] For the first time ever, after 1975 the college enrollment rate for black men is lower than for black women. The decline in college attendance during the 1980s among black males coincides with the decline in government hiring, a foreboding of trouble for young black college men who depend for employment.on public and nonprofit agencies.

Rumors of disillusioning experiences in the corporate world circulate among black men, who must now compete not only against white men but also against women, "squeezed out" even under affirmative action. "Black Men Are Last," headlines Robert Goldfarb's editorial in *The New York Times* in 1980.[3] "As early as 1970," Harold Cruse affirms, "it was obvious that with the newly arrived gender issue in civil rights, the black male was in serious trouble." [4]

The demand by government and expanding service industries for highly skilled, well-educated workers will increase, and equal employment legislation and affirmative action will abet recruitment of black college graduates for professional and managerial jobs, predicts William Julius Wilson, writing in 1978.[5] Kenneth Clark, noting in 1978 the paucity of blacks in executive, managerial, and policy-making positions in government and private corporations, is less sanguine. The number, he says, "remains miniscule." Tokenism prevails rather than genuine compliance with affirmative action and equal employment opportunity requirements.[6]

Black male high school graduates who forego college turn to the labor force or the military or else to non-collegiate vocational/ technical schools that provide direct training for jobs and careers.[7] The military is attractive to those who lack viable job alternatives in civilian society.

Black women fare better than black men in getting professional, technical, and managerial positions, though not so well in the "higher" professions such as medicine, law, or engineering.[8] Unlike black men, they are not seen as competing for power with white men, and unlike white women, they are not perceived as possessing the "feminine" mind or feminine emotions. Nor do they express anxiety about being unmarried. Yet constraints attach to being a double minority in the workplace, at least in the private sector of the economy. Most black women find employment in the public sector in traditionally women's areas.[9]

Assessing the black man's precarious status in the white world, students regard the white man as the prime conspirator. "The White Anglo-Saxon has tried to keep the black man under his foot. Black men confront racism more often than black females," asserts one student, and another corroborates: "It's been hard for the black man to move, with white supremacy."

Anguished and articulate, a young African-American man cries out that white racism is insurmountable: "I feel black people are still in slavery. I feel manipulated. I feel depressed. The white man has money, control." His commitment to his own race is so great, he confesses, that it interferes with his thinking logically and objectively.

> I study here, but I'm not satisfied with myself. When I think, I put my feelings, my prejudices in it. I don't know how to take myself out of a situation and deal with that situation. We're talking about blacks. I like to defend blacks. They have a lot of faults, but even if they're wrong, I still would defend them. I get the feeling of anomie. I don't know what is right and what is wrong.

His frustration spills out and he doesn't know how to cope. He is an intense, serious student, highly motivated to absorb the lecture in its entirety as he sits directly in front of me every session. He lets me know that he studies in the library during the day and two hours at home each night. "I just have to do good, get good grades, make myself get good marks," he repeats insistently. He recalls with disdain his high school evaluation: "You are not college material." Yet, having spent five years in the Navy and several years at Bronx Community College, he does not feel he has reached his potential. "At this point it's up to me," he acknowledges. "But my consciousness is raised. It's more complicated now. I love and hate this society."

Perhaps even more fatalistic is a young Puerto Rican who fears he has been given a whiff of the good life at college, only to be cast off once again after he leaves school. His record is marred by a felony. "Is there a total turn-around with me?" he wants to know. "The guy who broke out of the ghetto and made it?   Now I know that's a farce. The financial aid is a token. Let the poor guy go to school. Tokenism burns me. There's enough to let you know what you're missing. I go up and down. I'm doing well, but what happens when this is through? I don't see the opportunities because of my record. My drug and jail record makes me, a Puerto Rican, untrustworthy in dealing with the white establishment."

Being forced to attend what he views as a second-rate college is abhorrent to a young Jewish student. Even if he transfers to a four-year city college, career options upon graduation he feels will be limited: "My priority is not school but finding a good job. I would like to be a lawyer some day, but they pick very few people from public colleges for law school. Compare Columbia University with a city college, with the same average -- who would get in? I would settle for owning a business or a chain. I know some people with Bachelors and Masters degrees driving cabs or unemployed. I have to be realistic. Maybe college would have meant something ten to fifteen years ago, but not now. Going to college is not a high priority now. If you can find something better, take it." He now works full-time driving a tow truck during the night and attends classes from eight in the morning. His grade point average is 3.7.

Recent immigrants from the third world are fearful that their status as immigrants may impede their progress.

> Do I believe in individual mobility (muses a young Filipino, born in a remote village four hundred miles from Manila). I have yet to search for an answer because my life-long experience taught me that there isn't such mobility. I started out as a country boy in a place where there is no electricity, and technology is practically at a standstill. After graduation from college, I had to move to the nation's capital, Manila, to look for a job and in this experience I learned that life was not as simple as I thought. In a society where the most important object is money, morals decay fast. I learned there is rampant corruption, and Filipinos see it as a normal way of life. The moral values that I learned in the grade school differ invariably in the real world.
>
> Now I'm in America and the technological difference from the Philippines is overwhelming. Yet it is society that makes a world civilized or uncivilized, not the technological advancement that it embraces. (He is now "shifting into nursing, a new career," where he hopes for acceptance.)

Though women students at Bronx Community College are less likely than men to speak of career misgivings -- "Unknowingly," one young woman concedes, "I have always stayed in my place" -- they do allude to discrimination in the workplace, even in occupations thought to be women's province.

A young black registered nurse voices her displeasure at the discrimination against women nurses from all sides and their feeble counterattack: "The majority of nurses are women, and we do not have the unity to fight together. Nurses are mistreated by everyone -- patients, relatives, doctor, supervisor, and the nurses themselves. Some people feel that we are supposed to behave like Miss Florence Nightingale, without thinking we are living in a different time and world. As for applying for a higher position, in administration, they prefer a male to a female nurse."

A young Puerto Rican woman speaks despairingly of the sexist attitude of professional men at work, who feel that married women should be confined to the home: "I worked five to six years in the State Health Department. When I told the men I was quitting to come to college, they were all surprised. 'You have a nice job here. You hardly do anything. Why do you want to go to college? Women belong in the house. Don't you plan to get married?' They weren't joking! A Latin man, I could see him saying that. But American men, even with their

Masters' degrees, also feel that way. They're more tolerant, putting up with it, but they don't really feel it."

Being a woman of color compounds fear of sexual assault on the job, especially if the job is that of barmaid. "My boss at the bar job took liberties," one young Puerto Rican women attests. "He wanted me to have his child. I'm sure a lot of white Americans go through this, but not as much as a minority person. I always have my boy friend come up to meet bosses. It never got to me before."

Though students express reservations about society's benevolence, they are likely to consider it imprudent to dredge out and commiserate over the past and blame their present troubles on discrimination. Students mention racial or sexual or other indignities -- they are a part of memory and current experience and cannot be erased -- and then try to move on and take the responsibility for their future into their own hands, not stymied by external constraints.

Aspirations: Pragmatic, Altruistic, Aesthetic, etc.

Students generally come to Bronx Community College to qualify for a good job and its emoluments, but they also profess additional motivation. Some desire to serve their community, offering a counterforce to our dominant individualistic ethic. Some want to expand their intellectual horizons as an end in itself; learning they regard as a deeply aesthetic experience. And some see attending college as enabling them to engage in talking relationships with thinking persons.

Notable about students' non-vocational aspirations is the fact that they exist. Exposed to tracking in city high schools, dropping out of high school and into "the real world," many of the students might easily have circumscribed their aspirations. Like Cross' new students in the bottom third of their high school class,[10] they could have limited their occupational choices to auto mechanics or typing. Instead, under open admissions and with free or subsidized tuition, though their goals do not usually soar, at the least they rise substantially.

Getting a good enough job

Students of the community college, having worked at lowly jobs, now clamor for ones that offer comfort and status.

> If you don't have a college education, you do all the menial tasks, you use the back entrance. Working made me want to go back to school. . .

I would otherwise have to stay in what I have done -- behind the
counter in a restaurant. We are living in a capitalist society, and a
person has to have a diploma if he wants to survive. . .
If I achieve it, my son will have it. After high school, materialistic
things were more important to me than education. As I got older, years
went by fast. I realized that if I wanted to rise, I better get an education
now.

Throughout much of the 1970s and 1980s, a considerable number of
Bronx Community College students turn to a branch of business -- data
processing, accounting, administration, marketing, secretarial studies.
Some already work in the business world; others flock to where they
think the jobs are. The nursing program, with its reputation for rigor
and the presumption of a permanent yet flexible career, also attracts
many students to the college.

Two disparate groups of students gravitate toward liberal arts:
potential transferees to a four-year college and flounderers. The latter
seek refuge in liberal arts when their goals are uncertain or when they
have been cooled out of the career program of their choice -- nursing,
perhaps, or engineering, or accounting. Students in liberal arts are
likely to choose what they regard as a "practical" major -- human
services or psychology rather than history or literature. Science majors
in turn select pre-engineering, pre-pharmacy, or the technologies rather
than biology, chemistry, or physics.

Serving their community

Black and Hispanic students throughout the City University of New
York, more often than whites, come to college with an altruistic goal.[11]
"I want to help people," they state, and they want especially to help the
young within their own neighborhood and ethnic group. There is ample
precedent for working where they know they are needed and wanted.
The black middle class, excluded early from serving the white
population, resorted to meeting the needs of the growing urbanized
black community where monetary rewards were moderate but their
professional or skilled work commanded greater respect and they had
less fear there of prejudice and discrimination.[12]

"Helping" professions -- nursing, psychology, social work, human
services, and teaching -- are popular career choices. They are the
nurturant professions, the traditional province of women more
frequently than men. And they are the professions that are likely to be
fully open to minorities.

Speaking with authority out of their own experience, students want as professionals to forewarn youngsters about the dangers of the streets. Drug and alcohol abuse loom large as a clear and present danger. "Drug use is still rampant, even with the stiffer terms," affirms a former drug addict, incarcerated during his adolescence. "The men who come back to the city from prison and don't know how to adjust turn again in desperation to drugs and repeat the vicious cycle." He wants now to work within the criminal justice system. And a veteran of the Vietnam war and of the streets, back from the Service, hears his friends mourn, "Our son is on drugs." "Many Puerto Ricans get educated, move to Riverdale or Scarsdale and want to forget where they came from," he discovers. Starting to work with the New York City Youth Board, he sees his own need to understand people in greater depth and comes to college.

Adolescent motherhood is cited as another danger in the community. A young student recalls that her classmates in junior high school, "already with bellies," cut other classes but attended gym class. "The gym teacher would talk to them, get them motivated to stay in school. She helped so many. Here, too, in college, I met some gym teachers who have really become idols." She would like as a gym teacher and unofficial counselor to alter the lives of young girls.

Students want to ensure that the child of poverty not be robbed of childhood, a replication of their own history. "I like dealing with kids," says a prospective teacher. "I didn't have an infancy or childhood. There was no welfare in Puerto Rico."

Some speak of transmitting their competencies to children. A bilingual aircraft mechanic hopes to teach "bilingual kids" in a trade school. And a young poet wants to kindle a love for poetry among those for whom poetry is an alien tongue. "A lot of people scoff at poetry, but I learned that poetry is more than an intellectual exercise. It's a spiritual thing. And it's not only for the higher strata. It can be related to life."

Students empathize with the immigrant youngsters living within two cultures who speak Spanish at home and learn English at school at the same time as they try to catch up with everything else in class and among peers. They know the difficulties of learning a second language and think they can teach it better than most professionals.

They would like to minister not only to their young but also to first-generation adults who transplant their alien culture onto North American soil and now resist becoming acculturated. "As a social worker, I can help the people, especially the Spanish," maintains a young Dominican. "They need someone with a Latin orientation. The anomie of these people. They read the same paper, eat the same food from their own country."

They look with objectivity and compassion at the men from a patriarchal tradition who suffer in New York City a deterioration of status within their families and discrimination and humiliation outside and react with general suspicion and mistrust. "My goal," says a Puerto Rican student, "is to learn about changes the Puerto Rican family is going through when they come to poverty areas of the United States. With my parents and my uncles and aunts, the father was the head and you respected him, you didn't talk back. Now I see a Puerto Rican young man screaming at his father and telling him what to do. Older men are going through a great change and don't know how to cope. Women take it in their stride, don't blow their top. But my father says, 'Don't trust what's out there.' He remembers his humiliation at having to go to a social worker and not understanding her and being unwilling to ask her to repeat what she said. He fears his children will be discriminated against."

African-American students, born in the rural South or the children of Southern-born migrants, wish to help poor blacks cope with the complexities of an urban environment. "I had a poor education but a lot of street experience," recounts a young black Vietnam veteran. "A lot of blacks are on a lower level, but if you break it down for them, what it's all about, then they could apply it. They don't have the know-how. Many of the older generation are poorly educated and hostile to their children, they abuse their children. 'Shut up,' they say in answer to questions. I sympathize with the children. If their minds are warped, they'll be scared. They're the next generation."

Prospective nurses recall their earlier desires to care for loved ones at home. A retired black police officer, brought up in a family of twelve, saw both parents die after long illnesses. "I know a lot about helping other people as a nurse. It's a change from beating people over the head with a night stick."

The law may be a "helping profession, greatly needed for those who are poor and deprived," but the money and the prestige from a career in law are not to be scoffed at. "I've been poor all my life, I'd like to see the other side, the prestige," muses an aspirant to the law. "In my whole family, the greatest education is an M.A., my uncle, my model, he worked his way up. I'd like to surpass that, set an example for my children and my nephews."

The desire to minister professionally to the poor among their own ethnic group thus pulls students to college and career. They see themselves as uniquely qualified for service jobs, their minority status an asset in empathizing with the victims of deprivation. There is the sense that they can go home again, this time as guide and mentor, to help or lead the way. "Stay close to your roots, teach what you know most intimately," is, then, a recurrent theme.

Learning as an aesthetic experience

The German sociologist, Max Weber, presents in historical context two educational goals: one, to produce the "cultivated man," the other, to train the "specialist."[13] An articulate minority of the students at Bronx Community College aspire to the former goal. They want all the trappings of an academic education: the language, the literature, the philosophy, and the psychology that make one a cultured gentleman or -woman, able to look at the world in broader perspective. If there are career rewards, so much the better. If not, the learning experience is nevertheless worthwhile and even glorious in itself. They reveal their yearnings in their own impassioned words.

> Education is a challenge, expanding my mind. . .
> It is not given to you. You have to bring it out. . .
> I love to come to school and read the books. This is an escape here. I want a career and just the idea of keeping my mind open, continuously learning. . .
> I find everything stimulating that has to do with education.

"Job-centered reasons (for coming to college) were primary among younger people, whereas the goals of older adults were much less pragmatic and utilitarian," wrote Cross and Jones in 1972.[14] This is generally true at Bronx Community College, though the seekers after knowledge who want "just to know" include students in their early and mid-twenties.

Knowledge-seekers express gratification at learning to view the familiar in a new context, reinterpreting their experience. "Sociology, psychology, and communication were eye-openers," reflects a former army police officer who left high school before graduation and now, at forty-three, hopes to study law. "So much material was enlightening. It linked my experience with someone who was formalizing it in the text. It fell into place very fast because of that. The adjustment to me here was beautiful."

Stopping to reflect before acting and in the process deterring otherwise impulsive behavior seems to some a by-product of their education. "I think it's natural for people of one group not to like another group," asserts a forty-year old. "The important thing, how do I handle it. When I was younger, if I experienced prejudice, I probably would have reacted physically." An intense twenty-five year old concurs: "I've learned to think logically and rationally, dealing with discrimination and prejudice -- to think logically under pressure."

Sitting in the college classroom is a new venture, an enriching experience, even if no professional job is forthcoming.

> If you sweep a floor, maybe you went to college for nothing. But it still is a new experience, something that you are benefiting from. . .
> I'd like to have an education even if I was a shoe-shiner. My thinking has been very narrow. I don't think and feel like I used to. . .
> I have children, they're being educated, why not me. . .
> I would continue even if I couldn't have the career I want for the satisfaction it brings. It really enriches my life.

The thrust toward learning found among students sampled here differs from that of the prototypical new student described by educational researchers. New students "tend not to value the academic model of higher education that is prized by faculty," concludes Patricia Cross, "preferring instead a vocational model that will teach them what they need to know to make a good living." They "possess a more pragmatic, less questioning, more authoritarian system of values than traditional students." [15] Neither willing nor able to work with ideas, they must work with things and with other people, and this cannot be taught them through such subjects as history, English, literature, or sociology. Consequently, "Group work, shop work, and experience in industry and the community may be the best techniques for teaching excellence in the people and things spheres." [16]

Historical and literary evidence has been cited to demonstrate that the lower classes have been slow to profess an interest in schooling. "The desire to carry adult education to the lower classes has been a constant theme in both history and fiction," but, "in the long run, the record of success of such ventures has been poor." Evening schools have been most successful in middle-class suburbs, and public library patrons are predominantly middle class. The lower classes, thus, do not seem to respond to what the middle classes prize. [17]

An alternative scenario might be posed. Ever since the spread of literacy during the sixteenth century, some of those no longer struggling for survival have wanted to make of themselves "cultured" persons, adept at reading and talking with others at all intellectual levels. With the financial and academic requirements eased, many denied an opportunity in the past are scrambling for it now.

A talking relationship

A college education is seen as having value beyond the practical, the altruistic, and the aesthetic. Discussing and exchanging ideas with spouse and children, with friends, or even with strangers, at all levels of sophistication, all the while thoughtful and relaxed: this, some students feel, is the by-product of a college education.

> When I started meeting intelligent people and couldn't converse with them freely or even understand their vocabulary, I got interested in college. . .
> How can I associate with people at a high social and intellectual level without knowing what's going on?. . .
> With exposure to more, your vocabulary and range are greater. If you don't come to college, you're so boring, not fun to be with. . .
> It's exciting dealing with people above my level. It makes me want to be just as good as they are. Mainly teachers. . .
> I have to go to college to learn how to express myself, how to listen to the teacher. I don't have to play, to fool around. A lot of friends say, 'I go only for the money they give.' Not me.

At the least, a student can talk with somebody other than children. "I've gotten so much out of this college experience," declares a Pakistani woman of forty. "Just the experience alone of meeting people. At times it was just me and the children. You need other people to talk to, to stimulate your mind."

A child may lead the academic quest, and a parent follow. "My older son was beginning to ask me questions about homework," confesses one mother for whom serious study is a new experience. "I started going to libraries, museums. The whole purpose, to grow up with them. My ten-year old is in fifth grade with a twelfth grade reading level. I'm so proud of him."

A student becomes increasingly sensitive to the perspectives of others and increasingly confident articulating her own. "Psych helped me understand my husband's attitude, but I also try to make him understand my point of view," declares a young woman of twenty-four who left school in the sixth grade. "I feel I have a right to express myself and make him understand. I'm more satisfied now."

The requirements in a mate begin to change. A student in his thirties is now looking for a mate to talk to, "a lady who is not only good-looking but one who is intelligent and affectionate." He never looked for the "intelligent type" before.

A goodly number of students thus find satisfaction in extending their talking relationships, a by-product of their college education.

"Born again:" a new identity

The dogged insistence, "I want to get somewhere and be somebody, not a nobody," seems pervasive. A formal education, students believe, is the path that leads to a career and makes one "somebody." They seem to accept the statement of Riesman and Jencks that "it has become increasingly hard in our society to maintain a sense of worth without a degree." [18]

A single mother is "tired of the humiliation" she goes through on welfare. She wants to be "somebody" for herself and her son.

A student in his forties, attending college for the first time, reminisces about his life-long objective, even as a boy in Puerto Rico, to become a professional.

> It was my common sense. Why be a nothing? I saw this boy had nice clothes, toys. His father was a construction foreman. My father died when I was two. I was smart in school. When my mother took me away from school at ten, the teacher was angry, and I was rebelling against the destiny of poor people.

A young man speaks of his transformation from drug addict to student.

> I was thinking of an associate of arts degree, some kind of degree that would show society I have some value. Being a successful college student is a whole new life style for me. Before I was silly, using drugs, using heroin. I was labeled a drug addict. I feel if I were lucky enough to hit the lottery, I would continue to a doctorate. I want contemplation, relaxation.

A young professional dancer who toured the States and Europe with Ballet Hispanica for six years now looks elsewhere to enlarge the scope of her world.

> I watched people in the dance company, thirty- to forty-year old dancers, fall apart when they realized they couldn't dance anymore. They audition and are still hoping. It was so sad. They have a career until thirty, then they teach. I want something to fall back on. I want to do other things, I don't know what, and I think dancing brought it about. I enjoyed it, but it's a very small world. I always wanted to do more than what I was doing. I wasn't satisfied with my performance. And it's not going to last forever. I want to use my head too.

"Learning that one has a brain" is a serendipitous revelation according to a divorced mother of thirty-nine.

> My mind opening up is the most wonderful thing that's happened to me. I was a terrible student. I flunked out of college, I went one year. My values were different then. My model was probably someone pretty, an actress kind of person. Coming here was instrumental in changing my values. Now it is Barbara Walters, women that have made it. Now I love getting good grades. Being here has changed my life absolutely. I like myself. I finally realized I do have a brain, I am smart. It's reaffirming.

Attending college helps thwart a sense of drifting and poses alternatives. One thirty-year old student roamed through Europe in his twenties. "Those years (the late 1960s) everybody was doing their own thing. Going to school was not hip," he recalls. He toured Spain and Holland, spent a year in Paris, then returned home, married, and started working as an interpreter for the Legal Aid Society. Wanting more, he came to college and maintains a grade point average of 4.0. Instructors in the humanities and the sciences vie to have him pursue a career within their areas of competence but, encumbered now with wife and child, he enters nursing. . . Another thirty-year old succumbed to temptations on campus during his first try at college. "My character and the character of the school didn't help me during the early years," he concedes. "Disco music was in the lunch room, pool tables were in the game room. They were too accessible. Now I'm in a different frame of mind." Finding themselves through their twenties "going nowhere," the two thirty-year-olds return to school.

Seeking stipend or averting boredom

Some students are drawn to school by the anticipated camaraderie or the government stipend. "I see so many faces that should be in the classroom but are outside or in the cafeteria," an older student observes. "The library is empty, but the cafeteria is always crowded. It's noisy and the record player is going. At Spelman College the supervision was tighter. If a teacher saw you outside, he wanted to know why you were there."

That some students attend college solely for financial aid is suspected when they do no home work and fail all the tests but continue attending class, then attempt to withdraw legitimately after all financial aid has been dispersed. Other students express resentment.

Money is not coming out of their own pocket. Therefore students don't do as much. I know my father is working hard to send me through. This way, I have to study. . .

There's no welfare in my country (El Salvador). Even little kids start working. When they give you something you don't work for, you don't appreciate it.

Students recommend tighter faculty supervision, higher academic standards, and greater wariness in giving financial aid. More rigorous standards for retention have been imposed since these remarks were made, and castigating comments about the lure of government stipends become somewhat less frequent.

Some students are running away from an empty life at home or responding to family pressure. "Learning now seems uninteresting to me, but my parents want me to come," acknowledges one young man. "My brother went and he bettered himself."

Most students though do not come to Bronx Community College to seek the stipend or avert boredom. Rather, having survived life in the raw, they appear to be setting new sights for themselves and their children.

The aspirations of many students here are reminiscent of those found by The Carnegie Commission on Higher Education in the early 1970s. "The prospect of a higher-paying job," its study found, "is by no means the only reason for attending college. It may not even be the most important reason in many cases. The cultural advantages, the opening of new avenues of intellectual interest and appreciation, and the enhanced social prestige associated with the college experience are likely to continue to stimulate rising enrollment rates even if the income differential associated with college graduation declines." [19]

The students' aspirations are also reminiscent of those found by Lavin and his associates in their study of two- and four-year college students at the City University of New York under open admissions in the early 1970s. Black and Hispanic students, they say, are more likely than are Jewish and Catholic students to view college as critical for their occupational future and broad cultural growth and to place greater emphasis on college as preparation for service to their community. [20]

Why, then, are students here? Students refer to jobs, community service, the trappings of an academic education, a talking relationship, a new identity. Teachers' perceptions are less lofty. They note that "Most are coming for a specific career. They want to be a nurse, an accountant." Often they appear to be coming "for lack of choice." And most frequently they "want to get out of the situation they're in."

"Mothers find themselves in a situation where they are single parents. Education is the only way they can get out of this morass and so the motivation might be stronger for them than for men."

A student, wounded in the drug trade, "was a drug dealer who one day got shot in the leg. He is now graduating with the fifth highest average. He said, 'I gave up $1000 a day to be on poverty row, but it's the best thing I've ever done in my life.'"

Dropouts from "wretched high schools, where in most cases no learning took place, couldn't get jobs or were in some sort of dead-end situation and needed to support families. It finally dawned on them, maybe education would be a help. Now they're coming back."

And "Some come because they cannot stay home doing nothing if they're not in school. Some do begin to like it and get into it. 'I can really make something out of my life,' they say."

The disparity is notable between the students' appraisal of what draws them to college and the faculty assessment. The faculty sense that students are "pushed" to college to get out of the dire or disheartening situation they're in. Students speak of being "pulled" in a supreme effort to remake themselves, most simply through work and its recompense but also through expanding their social, cultural, and intellectual worlds.

A Disjunction between Goals and Means

Education has traditionally been the most important criterion of status in the black community, more important than wealth or occupation because of the greater variation in education level.[21] African-Americans have extolled literacy and formal education, the prerogatives of the master class, since the days of slavery and Reconstruction.

Students at Bronx Community College affirm their belief in education as a path to the good life and admire seekers after knowledge in the classroom, but they themselves do not necessarily attempt to excel. Though black Americans have a great respect for education, notes Thomas Sowell, most are not greatly concerned with intellectual interests and intellectual values.[22]

Castelike or involuntary minorities are not likely to exert painstaking effort in the classroom since they know that their minority status blocks mobility, Ogbu speculates. He distinguishes between *immigrant* or *voluntary* minorities, who moved to this country in search of economic and political gain and regard schooling and hard work as the primary means of achieving their aim, and *involuntary* or *castelike* minorities, who came here through conquest, slavery, or colonization and may verbally endorse education as a means of achieving success, but, anticipating continuing institutionalized discrimination, do not make the necessary effort in the classroom. [23]

The foreign-born students at Bronx Community College would probably accept Ogbu's assessment of the difference between voluntary and involuntary minorities as they contrast their own effort with what they perceive to be the poor study habits among many African Americans at the college. "I came to the United States in hopes of furthering my education," is a familiar refrain among students of developing nations who look to the United States as the promised land of higher education.[24] Their desire for education appears sometimes to be imbued with a religious zeal. "My parents believed there were only two ways to ensure salvation from poverty," reports a young Jamaican woman. "One was to get the best education you could and to always, no matter what, trust in God and be a good Christian."[25]

American-born students, the descendants of involuntary or castelike minorities, protest that they, too, are capable of displaying persistence. They are willing to consider, albeit tentatively, the findings of William Julius Wilson that in the economic sphere, class has become more important than race in determining black mobility, and, through hard work, they believe they can rise in class. [26]

The practice among many African-American students (and other students, too) of extolling educational achievement while ignoring the hard work entailed may not differ substantially from the practice in earlier decades among Jewish immigrant students. There is a romanticized notion, observes Sherry Gorelick, that most Jewish children in the early decades of the century were passionate about learning. "What is forgotten is that, although more and more students were Jews, very few Jews were students. The entire graduating class of the City College of New York had only 209 students in 1913."[27] For Jews, as for other groups, educational achievement followed economic advance, rather than preceding it.[27] But. as James Traub reminds us, strong institutions did mould young Jewish students from an early age. "The family, and the larger community, imparted the values that made them self-disciplined and confident and ambitious. The schools, and the libraries, and the specifically Jewish culture of argument and debate, trained their minds and made intellectual work seem like the most natural thing in the world."[28] Many of the students entering Bronx Community College lack such early stimulation. Moreover, impoverished groups today are living in an age when formal education is more crucial than ever before in achieving some modicum of economic security.

Terminal or Transfer Curricula:
Which Promote their Goals?

A precedent for educating African-American students at the highest academic level was established in the mission schools after the Civil War by dedicated Northern white teachers who were sent to the South by the American Missionary Association. "Instead of carrying on a practical education, designed to meet the illiterate and unskilled on their own level, they boasted courses of study taken directly from the programs of New England colleges replete with Latin, Greek, and the higher mathematics," records the black educator, Horace Mann Bond. "Based on the academic successes of first, second, and even third generation descendants of the students of the early mission schools, available evidence suggests that these institutions provided for Southern Negroes some of the most effective educational institutions the world has ever known."[29] The elite liberal arts education of the mission schools offered the credentials for social mobility. Its students came from families who had already experienced some mobility.

Bond discovers four distinguishing characteristics of the black families who produced scholars over several generations: (1) Such families had three or more generations of literacy. (2) They had sufficient income so that their children might be educated in private schools. (3) They had access to superior schools — principally missionary schools. (4) And their children had extraordinary motivation and aspiration, spurred on by parents and teachers.[30] Only a very small proportion of African Americans could satisfy these social prerequisites for academic success. They were likely to be free persons of color, already free in the antebellum South, or else the children of white slave owners and black mothers. Most free persons of color were literate in 1850, and, however poor, had a head start in acculturation.[31]

Early in the twentieth century, two prominent black leaders, Booker T. Washington and William E. B. Du Bois, espoused opposing views on what should be the nature of the educational system for the children of former slaves.

Washington advocated a system of Negro common-schools, supplemented by industrial training, in order that the black rural masses might learn basic skills and discipline. Such subjects as science, history, and mathematics he did not deprecate but considered impractical.[32] The American Missionary Association had introduced in their school curricula trade education for black children, but Washington made of the trades not a "by-path" but "a veritable Way of Life."[33] Some historians of the period saw Washington's educational prescriptions, supported by the white South, as promoting "education for the new slavery."[34]

Du Bois espoused a college education with academic depth for students of talent and promise, "the Talented Tenth." He invited them to accompany him on the journey into the literature and philosophy that inspired him. In his essay, "Of The Training of Black Men," he writes:

> I sit with Shakespeare and he winces not. Across the color line I move arm in arm with Balzac and Dumas . . . I summon Aristotle and Aurelius and what soul I will, and they come all graciously with no scorn nor condescension. . . . Is this the life you grudge us, O knightly America? [35]

Community college leaders did not adhere to the precedent established by the black mission schools and Du Bois or by private junior colleges, established early in the twentieth century, that emphasized the liberal arts and sciences. Instead, they attempted to carve a niche in higher education that was primarily vocational and terminal. Critics saw the terminal vocational emphasis failing to prepare students for active participation as citizens in a democratic society, perpetuating instead educational and occupational inequality.[36] And most early community college students, associating liberal arts and sciences with upward mobility, could not be persuaded to accept the terminal vocational curricula. Only in the 1970s, with the economy in a recession, the media detailing the poor job prospects for college graduates, and some college administrators and teachers voicing their assent, do students begin to show a preference for the terminal vocational.[37]

Bronx Community College students, like community college students elsewhere, have turned to fields that looked "practical," notably, a branch of business or health care. Some students, though, find the seemingly "practical" choice insufferable. A young woman expresses the fear that, guided by practicality, she has chosen majors prematurely -- first, medical lab technician, which she found "hard and boring," then secretarial, which she "hated, except as a stepping stone." Her "true passion," she confesses, is acting. "I can make people pay attention to what I'm saying. People at the end of my performance (in the leading role at a school play) stood up. I got a standing ovation. But I wouldn't dare go into the field." If she were rich, she could "feel free to major in acting and not worry financially about getting a job." But," she reflects, "I don't live my life thinking of being rich." Then, in an ostensible non-sequitur, she queries, "Did you ever think what it would be like to be black?"

By the end of the 1980s, students begin to reevaluate the practicality of a terminal, two-year degree. Word has come back that entry level positions often become a dead-end for students who terminate their studies with a two-year associate credential; in the interests of "practicality," some want to aspire to a baccalaureate. Their curricula of choice remain largely career- or job-oriented, but increasingly they want their choice to lead to a bachelors degree and are eager to know the mechanics for bringing it about. Perhaps the obstacles to achieving the baccalaureate prove daunting, for most students who leave the community college prematurely forego, at least for the present, both graduation and transfer.

It becomes apparent that, despite the constraints of poverty and race and children come too early and wasted years in and out of school and dire warnings that they are "not college material," the students enter the college portals because they perceive education as a panacea, capable of transforming their lives, and they regard themselves as personally accountable for the outcome. If they work hard enough and long enough and receive the appropriate credentials, they feel that at least they will be eligible for better jobs than heretofore and at most they may satisfy their other aspirations -- altruistic, intellectual, aesthetic, and social.

Notes

1. John U. Ogbu, "Minority Status and Literacy in Comparative Perspective," *Daedalus*, *Literacy in America* 119:2 (Spring 1990): 141-168.

2. Table A-7 on High School Graduation Status, College Enrollment, and Attainment for Persons 14 to 24 years old by Sex, Race, and Hispanic Origin, 1967-1988. U.S. Bureau of the Census, *Current Population Reports*, Series P-20, No. 443.

Indicator 2:3 on Race Differences in participation in higher education, 1971-1988. U.S. Department of Education, National Center for Education Statistics. The Condition of Education, 1990, V. 2 Postsecondary Education, 20-21. Source: U.S. Bureau of the Census, *Current Population Reports,* Series P-20, "School Enrollments . . ..various years."

3. Robert Goldfarb, "Black Men Are Last," *New York Times*, 14 March 1980: A-27.

4. Harold Cruse, *Plural But Equal : A Critical Study of Blacks and Minorities and America's Plural Society* (New York: William Morrow, 1987), 366.

5. William Julius Wilson, *The Declining Significance of Race: Blacks and Changing American Institutions,* 2nd ed. (Chicago: The University of Chicago Press, 1980), 99. He identifies the middle-class black men as those employed in white-collar jobs and as craftsmen and foremen. (127)

In his 1987 publication, *The Truly Disadvantaged,* 109, Wilson cites a 57 percent increase from 1973 to 1982 in the number of blacks in professional, technical, managerial, and administrative positions, compared with the white increase of 36 percent. U.S. Dept. of Labor, *Handbook of Labor Statistics* (Washington, D.C.: G.P.O. December 1983).

If only managerial and professional positions are compared from 1983 to 1988 (excluding technical, sales, and administrative support occupations, which Wilson includes but Kenneth Clark omits), blacks increased 35 percent from 1983 to 1988, whites, 22 percent. The 1983 managerial and professional numbers represent only 14 percent of employed blacks but 24 percent of employed whites. Ibid., August 1989.

6. Kenneth Clark, "No, No. Race, Not Class, Is Still At the Wheel," *New York Times*, 22 March 1978: A-25.

7. Solomon Arbeiter, "Black Enrollments: The Case of the Missing Students," *Change* 19.3 (May/June 1987): 14-19; Elias Blake, Jr. "Equality for Blacks: Another Lost Decade or New Surge Forward?" *Change* (May/June 1987): 10-13.

8. Andrew Hacker, *Two Nations: Black and White. Separate, Hostile, Unequal* (New York: Ballantine Books, 1992), 115-116.

9. Cynthia Fuchs Epstein, "Positive Effects of the Multiple Negative: Explaining the Success of Black Professional Women," *American Journal of Sociology* 78 (1973): 913-918.

For some negative effects of the multiple negative, see Elizabeth Higginbotham, "Black Professional Women: Job Ceilings and Employment Sectors," *Women of Color in U.S. Society*, Maxine Baca Zinn and Bonnie Thornton Dill, eds., (Philadelphia: Temple University Press, 1993), 113-131.

10. K. Patricia Cross, *Beyond the Open Door* (San Francisco: Jossey-Bass, 1971).

11. Jack E. Rossman, Helen S. Astin, Alexander W. Astin, and Elaine H. El-Khawas, *Open Admissions at City University of New York: An Analysis of the First Year* (Englewood Cliffs: Prentice-Hall, 1975), 43, 44; David E. Lavin, Richard D. Alba, and Richard A. Silberstein, *Right Vs. Privilege: The Open-Admissions Experiment at the City University of New York* (New York: The Free Press, 1981), 108.

The need of the black community was regarded as "important" or "somewhat important" in career decisions for 96 percent of black students. Richard B. Freeman, in Margaret Gordon, ed., *Higher Education and the Labor Market* (New York: McGraw Hill, 1974), 105.

12. Johnnetta B. Cole, "The Black Bourgeoisie," .Peter I. Rose, Stanley Rothman, and William J. Wilson, eds., *Black and White Perspectives on American Race Relations* (New York: Oxford University Press, 1973), 36.

13. *From Max Weber: Essays in Sociology, eds. H.H. Gerth and C. Wright Mills* (New York: Oxford University Press, 1946), .242-243.

14. K. Patricia Cross and J. Quentin Jones, "Problems of Access," in *Explorations in Non-Traditional Study,* eds. Samuel B. Gould and K. Patricia Cross (San Francisco: Jossey-Bass, 1972), 51.

15. K. Patricia Cross, *Beyond the Open Door* (San Francisco: Jossey-Bass, 1971), 159.

16. Ibid., 167.

17. Cyril O. Houle, "Commentary: The Motives of New Adult Learners," *New Colleges for New Students*, eds. Laurence Hall and Associates(San Francisco: Jossey-Bass, 1974), 60-61.

18. David Riesman and Chrisotpher Jencks, "The Viability of the American College," *The American College: A Psychological and Social Interpretation of the Higher Learning* , ed., Nevitt Sanford, (New York: John Wiley and Sons, 1962), 76.

19. Carnegie Commission on Higher Education, *New Students and New Places: Policies for the Future Growth and Development of American Higher Education* (New York: McGraw-Hill, 1971), 53-54.

20. David E. Lavin, Richard B. Alba, and Richard A. Silberstein, *Right versus Privilege,* 107-109.

21. Murray Milner Jr., *The Illusion of Equality: The Effect of Education on Opportunity, Inequality, and Social Conflict* (San Francisco: Jossey- Bass, 1972), 84; N.G. Glenn, "Negro Prestige Criteria: A Case Study in the Bases of Prestige," *American Journal of Sociology* 68 (1963): 652-657.

All other factors remaining constant, a variable's importance as a criterion of prestige depends upon how unequally it is distributed and not necessarily how scarce it is. As income differentiation increased among blacks, income became more important as a prestige criterion. Glenn, 656-657.

22. Thomas Sowell, *Black Education: Myths and Tragedies* (New York: David McKay Company, 1972), 220.

23. John Ogbu, "Minority Status and Literacy in Comparative Perspective," *Daedalus, Literacy in America* (Spring 1990): 141-168.

24. Third world students were not necessarily exhilarated by their initial experiences in this country. "The transition from life in a slow, underdeveloped third world nation like Belize (West Indies) to that of the first world nation of United States was a hectic, at times, traumatic one for me," recalls one student. And another: "When I landed in 1986 (from Antigua) I did not feel any thrill or excitement. I got a shock when I entered my parents' home. I could not believe that I left a palace in Antigua and came to America to live in a dump."

25. Students speak of the dominant role that religion played in their early lives: being roused at five in the morning to have daily prayer; praying together before meals and before going to bed; being taken to church every Sunday until they were "old enough to understand its meaning, and its effect on life and the attitudes you have about right and wrong, good and evil." "Sunday was a day of serenity and was set aside for worship."

26 . William Julius Wilson, *The Declining Significance of Race.*

27. Sherry Gorelick, *City College and the Jewish Poor: Education in New York, 1880-1924.* (New Brunswick, New Jersey: Rutgers University Press, 1981), 121-125.

See also Colin Greer, "The Assimilation of the Immigrants: The Schools Didn't Do It, " Chapter 5, *The Great School Legend* (New York: Basic Books, 1972).

28. James Traub, *City On A Hill: Testing the American Dream at City College* (Reading, MA: Addison-Wesley Publishing Company, 1994), 42.

29. Horace Mann Bond, *Black American Scholars: A Study of Their Beginnings* (Detroit: Balamp Publishing, 1972), 23.

30. Ibid., 56-57. Thomas Sowell enumerates some distinguishing characteristics of academically excellent black high schools that in the mid-twentieth century produced a disproportionate number of distinguished alumni. (1) They were situated in four urban communities with a long and illustrious cultural tradition, though most of the students were probably not of the black elite or middle classes, nor were they necessarily academically excellent. (2) Students were not divided into ability groupings, but were excluded only if they could not accept the prevailing standards of order and respect. (3) Their principals were invariably persons of extraordinary character and ability. *Education: Assumptions versus History* (Stanford, Calif.: Hoover Institute Press, 1986), 7-38.

31. Thomas Sowell, *Ethnic America: A History* (New York: Basic Books, 1981), 195.

32. John Hope Franklin and Alfred A. Moss, Jr., *From Slavery to Freedom: A History of Negro Americans,* 6th ed. (New York: Alfred A. Knopf, 1988), 246. First published, 1947.

33. W. E.. B. Du Bois, *The Souls of Black Folk*, Introd.,Arnold Rampersad (New York: Alfred A. Knopf) 38-39. First published, 1903.

34. Franklin and Moss, *From Slavery to Freedom*, 247.

35. Du Bois, *The Souls of Black Folk,* 88-89.

36. Steven Brint and Jerome Karabel, *The Diverted Dream: Community Colleges and the Promise of Educational Opportunity in America, 1900-1985* (New York: Oxford University Press, 1989), especially 226-227.

37. Ibid. , 99-100.

Part Two
The Classroom Encounter

Chapter 5

Curricular Emphasis:
Remediation and Vocationalization

Salvaging through Remediation

Students arrive at the college with anxious anticipation, aware that they matriculated under relaxed admission standards. Tested in reading, writing, and mathematics, most are informed that they must take non-credit remedial courses in order to qualify for college-level study. During their first year, their program is likely to be rife with remedials.[1]

Faculty and students who view with alarm the expansion of remediation have dubbed Bronx Community College a "remedial" college. Over 90 percent of matriculants in 1987 are assigned at least one remedial course in reading, writing, or mathematics, a proportion greater than the average among community colleges within the City University and considerably greater than at Miami-Dade, regarded as a model among community colleges, where 60 percent of the students have entered with deficiencies in at least one of the basic skills areas.[2]

The most elementary course in remedial mathematics is arithmetic. "Its students may not even be conversant with whole numbers," concedes a mathematics professor. "If they have no idea that 5+7 =12, it is not easy to learn in six months." Elementary algebra at the ninth grade level and intermediate to advanced high school algebra follow the course in arithmetic. A fast remedial track is available for science students.

Even after immersing themselves in intensive remedial courses students are often unable to perform at the college level in mathematics, writing, or reading. "It takes so long because in all the lowest-level remedial courses, there is no bottom," a mathematics teacher cautions. "You get people who do not know whole number arithmetic or can't do fractions or are weak in percents. The same thing in English. You get students who are almost completely illiterate and students who are not so good in case agreement or something like that. By the time you get to the second remedial level, you have a bottom, a floor of sorts." "The students at the lower remedial reading level read below eighth grade standards and we don't know how low is low," a remedial reading teacher corroborates. "In the higher remedial reading sections, students read at the eighth-to-tenth-grade level."

Students starting out at the elementary remedial level are less likely to succeed at the upper remedial level than are students who begin at the upper level initially. The number of remediation courses a student requires in any single subject and the number of remediation subjects provide a forewarning of success or failure in college level work. Two students who started at the elementary writing level agonize over the difficulties they encounter moving to college-level work. One fails college-level English composition after receiving A's in two remedial writing courses. "The teacher is telling me I don't belong there (in the college-level course)," she notes plaintively. The other passes college composition but has misgivings. With a strict teacher, she might not have passed.

Whether students demand mere "brushing up" or more prolonged help, they generally appear satisfied with their remediation experience. A young Jamaican, having "gone two years without any math at all," is delighted with her two remedial mathematics courses, and a young man who left Haiti during his senior year in high school expresses gratification for his two remedial writing courses. "Now I understand everything," he exults. "How to proof read. Fragments. Run-on sentences." An African-American grandmother whose program has been saturated with remedials feels she "would never have gotten through without them." In math, she "was having anxiety attacks. 'Ms. D., are you sick,' the instructor wanted to know." She eventually graduates from Bronx Community College and transfers to a four-year city college.

Some students begrudge the extensive time required for remedials. "They stretched it out," one protests. "It could have been done in three months: chemistry, English, math. But it was helpful. Refreshes your mind." Some begrudge the "wasted money" on non-credit courses, prolonging their stay and forcing them to exceed the time limit for financial aid. "Lots of people come here thinking they'll spend two years here. It's not like that, with remedial courses we don't get credit for," an irate young woman complains. "And we can't get a loan on these credits. Free money for college lasts only four years. That's a slap for minorities. It cuts us out at the associate degree, we can't get a B.A. What the hell is that?" An extra year's subsidized tuition is added to cover remedials, and the irate young woman receives her community college degree. After completing one year at a senior college, she interrupts her studies to become an assistant administrator at one of the city agencies, a level up from her pre-college years as a waitress.

Other students are exasperated at their undeserved placement in a remedial course, based on one test given under adverse conditions. "Chemistry I needed," a student concedes, "but reading and writing remedials I passed with A's. I found them helpful, but don't think I needed them. I lost a lot of time." Instructors hear of a grievous error made in remedial placement -- about the student required to take remedial mathematics though he had passed calculus in high school. A letter of apology is sent him at the end of the remedial semester and, after taking a qualifying examination, he receives college credit for his high school calculus course. "The system is taking advantage," concurs a former tutor in the mathematics department. "Some are ready for calculus and they place them in Beginning Math. They did poorly in the evaluation test. Most students aren't into protesting. They wanted me to take the (evaluation) test. I said, 'No way.' I had already had a year of calculus. I came with my transcript."

Students do not usually regard remediation as humiliating unless it is protracted. Only once did I hear that "remedials are segregating. To assume they are needed is insulting." Prolonged remediation, though, is lamented as a forewarning of failure. "Bronx Community College tends to make students feel that they do not have a chance by keeping them in remedial classes for several semesters," complains one student bogged down in remedials. And another: "Sometimes I feel depressed, like I'm not making it. I think that's why a lot of people do drop out. If these are not college courses, why are they taught in college? Why not in high school?"

Whether remediation should be an integral part of the curricula at Bronx Community College was a matter of contention early in open admissions. By introducing remediation into the curricula, faculty opponents alleged, "you destroy the character of what a college should be." They suggested an alternative site for remediation studies. Its adherents feared, though, that separating remediation from the college would "siphon off students" and have negative political consequences. "The whole idea: you have them here physically, and once they're here, they can take certain courses that do not require remediation. Everyone was looking at it from that perspective."

After almost two decades of open admissions, sections in non-credit remediation dwarf college-level sections in mathematics and English, and the debate over remediation continues. Eighty-five percent of the mathematics sections and sixty percent of the English sections offered at the college in 1987 are devoted to remedials.

The impact on the college-level curriculum is deplored. "We have canceled upper-level courses, canceled drama, canceled Shakespeare because they have only nine students. That, I think, made our reputation suffer," declares one member of the faculty.

Others express skepticism as to whether students untutored in the rudiments of writing during their earlier years can catch up to grade level in one or two semesters of college remedials, however good the instruction. A history professor complains:

> Students come to class after taking the two non-credit remedial composition courses and the first college-level course and they still don't know what a paragraph is. So what has rubbed off? One of the problems is you learn many of these things the first ten years or so of public schooling, and it has to be drilled into you again and again and again. If you don't master it in those first ten years, I don't think our one or two semester remediation is going to change the picture much. Now you have all these psychological blocks. There are exceptions, but I'm thinking of 80 percent or even 90 percent of the students.

A critic of extensive remediation recommends that remediation be reduced to one or at most two semesters. "Any student, then, should be thrown into the kettle, sink or swim, and I think most of them would be able to swim." The students' inadequate preparation for college-level work demands extensive remediation, its proponents reply in defense. Students distance themselves from other institutions that might help them. "High schools do offer evening courses and people don't take advantage of them. Maybe it's psychological. They feel that they are now in college. We say, 'Well, you're not quite ready,' and they're willing to put up with that because now the foot is in the door."

Remedial faculty at the college have developed keen sensitivity to student needs and devoted much of their teaching lives to fine-tuning courses in order to serve those needs. They have edited a number of textbooks appropriate for remedial students. "We are moving toward remedials as our field, of necessity, and we have adjusted," notes the chairperson of the English Department.

The academic gains of those enrolled in remedial programs have, at best, often been modest, claims Ernest Boyer.[3] Educators, though, generally concur that remedial or compensatory programs enhance persistence and reduce dropouts.[4] While not successful in compensating for the ills of earlier education and bringing all students up to "college level," remediation does prevent open admissions from becoming a travesty for many underprepared students.

Away from Broad Exploration and into Early Specialization

Matriculating at Bronx Community College, students encounter two diverging tracks: one emphasizes vocational specialization terminating at the community college; the other enables greater exploration in the liberal arts and sciences and prepares students for transfer to a senior college.

Through most of the twentieth century the transfer track predominated at two-year colleges. Though community college leaders were successful in persuading federal officials, foundations, and business leaders that the two-year college should become a terminal vocational institution, its students, perceiving that the transfer track insured the upward mobility they sought, resisted terminal vocationalization until the 1970s. Almost two-thirds of the matriculants at Bronx Community College in 1971 enrolled in transfer curricula. By the end of the 1980s, the situation is reversed and two-thirds turn instead to the terminal vocational track.

Students often select their curricula with little comprehension of course requirements. "When they enter the college, suddenly we open up for them a world which I don't think they're expecting," observes a member of the faculty.

They go to admissions and are asked, 'What's your major?' It hits them unexpectedly and they say to themselves, 'Oh my God, what can I do?' If they say, 'I want to do computers,' somebody puts them in computer science. They have no idea what this curriculum consists of. Their decision on curriculum often varies from semester to semester, depending on what they know of the labor market. Many select pre-nursing and don't realize even the simple fact that they're going to have to take biology. They don't see that in a nursing curriculum their deficiencies are going to keep them here longer than almost any other curriculum. Somebody who may have to take three courses in English as a Second Language, two of them remedial, then three English composition courses, two of them remedial -- six semesters minimum, and some courses may have to be repeated -- will be here for years in pre-nursing and doesn't realize that completing the nursing program is almost an impossibility. Students are not forewarned. At one time we had counselors who presumably were trained to counsel these students. Now students see counselors for only six months and then faculty do the counseling. I've seen faculty who don't know what they're doing.

Students attracted to two-year terminal vocational programs by the prospect of jobs are encouraged in their choice by vocationally-oriented teachers who believe that nontraditional students should specialize early. Wanting a job in the short-run, they shun the transfer track, which might in the long run serve them well. Some run from one program to another, looking for one that is sure to provide job security, and in the process they amass excessive credits. Although sixty-six credits are required for graduation, "many students have already accumulated eighty credits, of which thirty or forty have nothing to do with their curriculum," observes a history professor.

Students discover that jobs are available for community college graduates in various allied health programs but learn, perhaps belatedly, that the number of applicants vastly exceeds acceptances.

"Jobs can be found in x-ray technology throughout the country, it's a tremendous field for our students," reports a physics professor. "The students don't see the need to go on for the bachelor's degree. But there is room for only about thirty-three students in the program and we're already filled in April for the September class. You cannot get into x-ray programs at some of the other community colleges for the next two or three years."

One thousand pre-nursing students clamor for acceptance in the nursing program, which has total space allotted for three hundred. Some spend years fulfilling pre-nursing requirements and waiting for acceptance. Others begin to look elsewhere.

Nuclear Medicine technology is another attractive health specialty requiring only a terminal degree, but its science requirements eliminate many aspirants.

Students fare no better in business curricula in the terminal vocational track where they compete with applicants holding higher degrees.

The Programming and Systems Curriculum requires forty-six specialization credits out of a total of sixty-eight credits for a terminal degree. "Trained programmers are in demand because of the ever-growing use of computers," the catalog notes.The Program Coordinator exercises great restraint in evaluating job opportunities for his students.

> A relatively small percent of our majors in Programming and Systems curricula graduate, and among those who do, a large percentage don't get jobs in this field. There is a prejudice against two-year graduates. Employers can choose from people at the masters' level for the same job. Some of our students will get jobs working on a personal computer, just doing data entry, unfortunately. Some will be lucky enough to get a job using data base or spread sheets, but it's all fractionated. We have not been able to upgrade what we teach to the extent needed on the outside.

In the transfer track a Programming and Systems option requires seventeen fewer specialization credits than its counterpart in the terminal track and is "designed to articulate" with senior colleges within the City University.[5]

Accounting students are unlikely to get a job in accounting with a terminal track degree, requiring thirty-eight specialization credits. (The transfer track requires twenty-six).[5] "The students have an opportunity to test out whether they're going to like and be successful in the business-type courses, so they take the accounting early," suggests the Dean of Academic Affairs. "Testing out" may be beneficial yet impractical for the student with limited time and money.

Overloading terminal vocational curricula with specialization requirements appears pervasive. "I don't know exactly why the process grew, so that every terminal track curriculum is totally loaded with specialization requirements," a mathematics professor notes disapprovingly. "Our community college students take too many specialized courses in the first two years. I think it's a fundamental mistake." If they decide at a later date to transfer to a senior college but have adhered to the regular terminal vocational curriculum, they will have completed watered-down courses in mathematics, the sciences, and art which are not acceptable for transfer credit at the senior colleges of the university. And their study in the liberal arts is likely to have been minimal. A sociology professor deplores the narrowness of their education.

> They do not know what alliteration is, they know nothing about the structure of poetry, they have never read a novel. I asked how many of them read a novel from cover to cover. 'I read a novella,' one said. I explained to them that when I was a student at this community college, I had to take two years of French and two years

of English. It's a big problem. Freshman and sophomore years should really be liberal arts years. Not to take the liberal arts subjects I think is unconscionable. The president thinks we're doing so wonderfully. He's Mr. Fantasy. He's in Never-Never Land. Nobody wants to bite the hand that feeds them. So we rip off the students in order to pay our mortgages.

Some students, after reviewing all options, may deem it in their best interests at this time to aspire only to an associate degree. They may look forward to jobs upon graduation in a terminal vocational curriculum - electrical technology, perhaps, or paralegal or secretarial studies. Taking the desired option while meeting transfer track requirements in the liberal arts and sciences would ensure their entrance to the senior college with the least loss of credit at transfer and thus facilitate their later pursuit of a higher degree.

"City College and City University have always prepared students for jobs," a history professor points out. "Students did not go just for the love of learning. The mission for many of our students has always been economic, but in the meantime, by giving them the enrichment and the exposure, they may then see other choices." The enrichment and the exposure for students on the terminal track, two-thirds of the total student population, are cut to the bare bone.

Squeezed between remedial and vocational specialization courses, the humanities shrink, their function reduced to serving other curricula. Few students look to them for areas of specialization.

Literature courses are among the first casualties. In 1973, shortly after the introduction of open admissions, one-third of the English department sections were devoted to a remedial non-credit Writing Laboratory, another third, to Written Composition for college credit, and the remaining third, to thirteen literature courses, including Prose Fiction, Drama, Poetry, Shakespeare, American Literature, The Bible, Journalism, The Black Writer in America, Black Poetry, and Hebrew and Yiddish Literature. Fourteen years later, in 1987, 60 percent of the English Department sections are allotted to the remedial, non-credit Writing laboratory, 25 percent to Written Composition for college credit, while the four or five literature courses that remain constitute only 15 percent of the English sections. A considerable number of the twenty-five professors in the English department now teach only remedials or English Composition. "We try to accommodate," acknowledges the chairperson of the English department. "Those teachers more interested in teaching literature, we let them do that." The number of literature courses, though, is limited and instructors who draw their gratification from examining with students the language and ideas embodied in great books are now required to consume countless teaching hours explaining run-on sentences, sentence fragments, basic grammatical errors, and the rest; their leisure hours are spent reading and correcting papers. Faculty in the two-year college may be more amenable to such a program than those in the four-year college, or more resigned, regarding it as their mission rather than their burden.[6]

History, another staple in the humanities, fares no better. The history offerings in 1973, twelve each semester, reflected the cultures on the campus and more. In addition to the History of Western Civilization and American History, offerings included History of the African American, Africa, Puerto Rico and the Caribbean, Latin America, The Third World and the West, the Far East, Modern Russia, the Jewish People, and the City in History. By 1987, offerings are reduced to three a semester. The two-semester course on History of Western Civilization is replaced by a one-semester History of the Modern World. "The one-semester course is more relevant and more manageable. Euphemisms for easier," the history department chairman states sardonically. Other 1987 offerings are limited to Values and Ethics in the American Experience and African American or Caribbean history.

The decline in the variety of offerings in English and history between 1973 and 1987 results from the smaller student population in 1987 as well as the substantial increase in remediation and vocational specialization, the latter a phenomenon occurring nationwide.[7]

Many teachers at the college are dispirited by the turn away from the liberal arts. A history professor observes with misgivings a sign appearing in the city subways that dubs Bronx Community College a "College for Careers."

> The tone we have set is that we are a college that is going to get people jobs, train them for the marketplace. I asked the president, couldn't we have said, 'A college for careers and personal development,' which would encompass the liberal arts, and his response was, 'Well, first we have to get them here.' I didn't know that the two were mutually exclusive. We can get them here for careers and also tell them that they can enrich their own lives.
>
> The president talks a lot about sociological achievement but not enough about broad educational objectives. Educational leadership should deal with more than just the sociological conditions that students face. We are trying not only to enable students to earn a living but to understand the universe, the physical, the social, the personal universe, and fit in happily.

The emphasis on jobs in the short-term "conveys a narrowness in occupational choice," a political scientist concurs.

> We train our students for concrete, narrow careers. There is no sense that the liberal arts degree is a useful goal and there are jobs out there for broadly-trained people. Middle-level jobs with advancement. Jobs that require the ability to meet people and solve problems.

Proponents of terminal vocational curricula counter that vocational specialization meets the needs and the desires of nontraditional students. Minority students attending Bronx Community College view with skepticism a liberal arts emphasis, asserts one of the deans.

> Most minorities in higher education are in community colleges. That affects our kinds of offerings. We try to feed them into the entry level jobs in industry. We don't say, 'You're going to be the manager or you're going to be on Wall Street.' Maybe in many ways we're at fault in that. But you cannot convince students that liberal arts is the track that will get them a better job. You cannot talk them into going into history when the other option is to be able to take Data 30. (Introduction to Systems). We tried. We must give them all the options that are available to them.

Students are more likely than are administrators to believe that the community college should place greater emphasis on preparing them for a four-year college, according to an internal study conducted in 1978.[8] Most students, though, are willing accomplices to being shepherded into the terminal vocational track. They seek advisement at matriculation with "such trepidation" that they deprecate their abilities and select a terminal vocational curriculum which they think they can master with the least difficulty. "They've done poorly before they came here and they have no gauge of their abilities," a mathematics professor observes. "It's very difficult to say to them, 'Don't sell yourself short. Try the more difficult path. If you can't do it, then fall back.' Part of the problem is a failure of good counseling. Counselors here set up individual appointments with every student, but only for six months and after that they're thrown out on their own." He discounts the value of any counseling done later by teachers.

Ironically, though less than 20 percent of Bronx Community College students graduate within four years of matriculation, graduates from a terminal as well as a transfer track continue their studies at a four-year college. Had all students who transfer to a senior college devoted their community-college years to improving their reading, writing, speaking, and mathematics skills and their knowledge of science, history, and literature, they would enter their junior year on a level playing field with students who start out as freshmen at the four-year college.

The attempt to reinvigorate the liberal arts as a major area of study at the college has long been stalemated. One of its proponents recalls the internecine struggle among faculty over the issue.

> Quite early, when they were first revising the liberal arts curriculum, I fought many a battle on the curriculum committee trying to protect the integrity of the liberal arts commitment. The wounds and the blood-letting were tremendous. We used to have a two-semester, six-credit introductory course in history. The course had a continuity. Now we lump everything into a one-semester course and rush it right through. Everybody, teachers and students, after a while goes crazy over it. We lost out, we reduced history from six credits to three credits; then other areas were similarly reduced. The humanities areas found themselves a division within the faculty. One person yelled at me at the curriculum committee, 'What is it that you want, Dr. C.?' 'What I want is to protect what I think is the best, sound academic plan.' Liberal arts areas were predominant at the time (in the 1970s). They were recommending all sorts of programs that were right off the wall, and departments would band together for their own reasons. Now we have all these programs. They keep us alive and going.

Prospective liberal arts students, forewarned by peers and parents or by high school teachers and counselors, have little incentive to want to attend Bronx CommunityCollege.[9] If they slipped by their gatekeepers, they themselves soon discover that the emphasis in the college is strongly terminal vocational.

A feasible alternative would be to design all curricula as transfer curricula. Students would have the option of choosing a major and taking introductory courses in the major of their choice but all curricula would include exploration in the humanities and the sciences equivalent to that of the first two years of a four-year college. Increasingly, students at the community college speak of aspiring to a baccalaureate. Their aspirations should be encouraged.

Notes

1.   In the senior colleges within the City University of New York, 53 percent of all the 1971 freshmen, and in the community colleges, over 80 percent needed at least some form of remedial work in language skills and math. David E. Lavin, Richard D. Alba, and Richard A. Silberstein, *Right versus Privilege: The Open-Admissions Experiment at the City University of New York* (New York: The Free Press, 1981), 234.

2.   John E. Roueche and George A. Baker III, *Access and Excellence: The Open-Door College* (Washington, D.C.: The Community College Press,1987), 29.

3.   Ernest L. Boyer, *College: The Undergraduate Experience in America* (New York: Random House, 1987) , 77.

4.   Students who passed at least some remedial courses were somewhat more likely than comparable non-remedial students to remain at school and to graduate or move on to a four-year college. Lavin, Alba, Silberstein, *Right versus Privilege,* 252, 256; Arthur M. Cohen and Florence B. Brawer, *The American Community College* (San Francisco: Jossey-Bass, 1982), 234.

5.   Bronx Community College Catalog, 1990-92, the programming and systems curriculum, .pages 77 and 59, accounting, pages 55 and 57.

6.   ". . By treating the problem of literacy in English and mathematics as a burden rather than a central mission, the urban educational model of the seventies missed its greatest, most profound opportunity," wrote Theodore L. Gross, *Academic Turmoil: The Reality and Promise of Open Education.* (New York: Anchor Press/Doubleday, 1980), 59.

7.   The 6,000 student population at Bronx Community College in 1987 numbered somewhat less than half that of 1973, though 63 percent attended full-time in 1987, 45 percent in 1973.

Arthur M. Cohen noted in 1979 that nearly half the mathematics and English taught in community colleges was at the remedial level. "What Next for the Community Colleges? An ERIC Review," *Community College Review ,* 17.2 (1979): 55.

8.   "Perceptions of the College Community Regarding What the Goals of the College Are and What the Goals of the College Should Be," Bronx Community College, Spring 1978, 19.

9.   See Chapter Nine, pages 163-165.

Chapter 6

Divergence among Students: Two Typologies

Growing Up In An Oral Culture

Students enter Bronx Community College poorly prepared for the encounter with teachers and textbooks. Many grew up within the confines of a predominantly oral culture, where newspapers were read and letters were written, but the mind-set of the culture was determined by orality.[1] Words were to be spoken, or read only minimally. In talk, the speaker gets immediate feedback not available in reading or writing, which are solitary activities.

Reading assignments are fraught with difficulty for students who spent their early years in an oral culture. They are more likely to respond positively to assigned homework if their texts use simple language, most like talk, and are replete with amusing and relevant pictures. "Otherwise students have a tendency to get overwhelmed by content and by the number of pages," conjectures a student well-qualified for college-level work.

Students who read little have scant aptitude for written examinations. Writing involves arranging ideas in a logical sequence around a theme or thesis. Talk has no such requirement. Written examinations are relatively new in human history, having come into general use in the West thousands of years after the invention of writing and only after print had its effect on consciousness.[2] Students indicate their difficulty taking written tests which demand more from them than circling the correct answer in a multiple choice test.

Words seem so much harder on paper. You can understand a person better than you can understand a piece of paper. I get afraid of taking tests. Like a voice saying, ' If you don't know that word, you're going to fail and repeat the course.' . . .
Students here know what you're talking about, but to put it down on paper, it's kind of hard. Like what happened in 1715 to such and such a person.

When I tell a student that she talks with clarity and self-assurance in my office but her tests are not always comprehensible, she queries: "My chopped-up test answers? A test situation is totally different from real life. I get tongue-twisted." It is her "tongue," which presumably she wants to use, that gets "twisted" in the written examination.

The spoken language of students growing up in an oral culture comes from the home and the streets, and not from the classroom. Though students talk spontaneously in an informal setting, they fear the jeers of peers and teacher when they talk in class. "There isn't enough good student participation in the classroom. Even though students don't understand, they won't speak up," an active participant complains. Another describes her unease. "Sometimes I get tongue-tied. I get nervous. I'm afraid I'm going to say the wrong thing." When alone with me during the hours of interview, they talk freely and informatively. Some reveal penetrating minds, well able to deal with the complexities of social situations, and an intellectual sophistication that they never display in the classroom.

Students who feel at home only in an oral culture speak of the arduous process involved in learning standard English.

(Says one young man who grew up in the segregated South):
I'm really beginning to understand the system of the English language through doing exercises. Just like a puzzle, you can begin to see the pattern. It comes naturally now. English is almost a second language.

(And another young man, who feels most comfortable with the language of the street):
I have difficulty only in the English course, with subjects and verbs. I go on my own to writing workshops. I learned what 'illiterate' means and I found out that if you talk slang, you write slang. It's all right to talk like that if you want to be on the corner. That's the hard part, making that transition. When you change the way you talk, you also change the way you think.

African-Americans may have greater ambivalence toward standard English than did the white ethnics of previous student generations.[3] Preserving in talk the language of the street bespeaks loyalty to one's people and rebellion against the conventions of white society. "I be writing 'standard' but I talk 'non-standard' to my friends or they look at me like I'm crazy," an African-American young woman declares, and an African-American young man ponders his ambivalence: "There's a lot of slang in the streets. It's a minimal language. When I went to speech class, I just learned 'this' instead of 'dis.' It's part of you. You really don't want to change. You rebel. If I want to, I can write in the correct words. I have a rebellious, negative attitude about this class thing, the way we interact. I relate to crazy talk. I feel comfortable with you, so that's why I make the mistakes. I think black people take on different personalities depending upon who they're with. You want people to accept you as you are. My family, my friends. A Southern way of being. It's a rebellious attitude. I know these things are hindering me."

The linguist, Basil Bernstein, distinguishes between the "restricted" speech code, largely oral in origin, of lower- or working-class English dialects in Britain, whose sentences are short and grammatically simple, and the "elaborated" code of the middle and upper-class dialects, formed with the aid of writing and print, where meanings are analytic and abstract. Middle-class children have a distinct linguistic advantage in school.[4] Walt Wolfram notes distinctions between Black American and standard American English like those between Basil Bernstein's "restricted" and "elaborated" codes.[5] The young and very bright African-American young man with the "rebellious, negative attitude" quoted above is saying, "a pox on your elaborated codes." Though he could easily attain proficiency in standard English, yet his family, his friends, his "Southern way of being" are tied up with vernacular black speech. He is expected to reject all of this if he wants to rise in the white world.[6]

Classroom dialogue between teacher and students is probably more important for those raised in the oral tradition than for students who feel at home reading and writing. Any teacher at Bronx Community College who does not accede to the requirement that there be dialogue may lose the attention of the class.

English as Their Second Language

Four out of ten students at Bronx Community College surveyed in 1987 speak Spanish or some other non-English language at home.[7]

Those arriving during their teen years or beyond who speak in their native tongue almost exclusively outside the classroom feel "nervous" when classes are conducted in English and are aggrieved by the innumerable hours required to comprehend English texts. Facility in the English language appears to depend largely on the age at arrival here, the continued exposure to English, the acceptance of this country as a homeland, and the freedom to err.

The mastering of English is a slow, tortuous process for those who mourn the move from their mother country and fail to become immersed in English-speaking situations. A Puerto Rican student in his forties who spent most of his life in a Spanish-speaking milieu and now labors diligently "to become a professional" expresses frustration at his difficulty reading and writing in English while continuing to think and talk more comfortably in Spanish. But a Colombian who came at eighteen and now at twenty-nine speaks flawless English asserts that it took no great effort. "In six months I was able to attend regular classes. I don't have a profound attachment to Colombia."

A foreign accent which is neither English nor Spanish remains an embarrassment to a Nigerian student who perceives himself an outsider at the college. "English is my second language," he indicates. "At home my native dialect is Yoruba. I learned English at the elementary level at school. I don't talk in class because of my accent. In one of my English classes the professor asked me to read the assignment. As I was about to read my first statement, I was taking the role of the other. I fear people will focus attention on me because of my accent." Other foreign students with accents unfamiliar to Americans do participate freely in class discussions.

Students who grew up in a predominantly oral culture and enter Bronx Community College with limited facility in reading and writing find their difficulties compounded when English is their second language.

There is no typical student at Bronx Community College. The variation in academic development and in motivation for learning exceeds that at most institutions of higher learning.

In academic development, I categorize students as either *Oral-Levels* or *Readers-Writers*. Oral-Level students, having lived their lives largely in the realm of talk, with insufficient inroads into classroom reading and writing during their pre-college years, have difficulty meeting college-level standards. Readers-Writers can, at admission or soon thereafter, read and write at an appropriate college level.[8]

In motivation for academic learning, I classify students as *Requirement-Meeters* or *Knowledge-Seekers*, two of the four orientations relating to student motives devised by Richardson, Fisk, and Okun in *Literacy in the Open-Access College*.[9] Requirement-

Meeters take courses in order to fulfill curriculum requirements, their primary motivation being acceptable grades. The Knowledge-Seekers' lust for learning is unequivocal. Their reading, writing, and classroom participation bespeak a critical bent that exceeds practical goals.

Though there are probably as many Oral-Level students at Bronx Community College as Readers-Writers, and significantly more Requirement-Meeters than Knowledge-Seekers, the types especially challenging for the instructor are the Oral-Levels, low in academic development, and the Knowledge-Seekers, high in motivation for learning. I shall concentrate on these two types.

Oral-Level Students

College is "unknown territory" to Oral-Level students who are likely to be the first in their family to enter college. "They must become oriented -- how to manage time, how to study," a Spanish professor proposes. Teachers determined to conduct classes at an appropriate academic level must perpetually remind themselves that these students are confronted daily by such basic difficulties as failing to comprehend the teacher's lecture, the substance of a reading assignment, or even the meaning of their own class notes.

Students intend to work hard at learning but other obligations constantly intrude. If a teacher simplifies the assignments, perhaps providing a list of questions whose answers are readily apparent from a cursory reading of the text, student performance may be satisfactory. They are gratified when the teacher writes extensively on the blackboard so that memorizing what has been written will ensure a good grade. "On the whole, they take their work seriously, they do want to learn, but often they don't understand how much work is involved," an instructor concludes. The Dean of Students details the procedures that school work should entail and that Oral-Level students are likely to find incomprehensible.

> It means struggling over something, putting it down, going back to it, looking at examples. It means taking out your dictionary, looking up words, going to other books. It means doing all those things. I don't believe it's a commonly distributed trait. I don't think the public school system generally trains students to do independent work and independent thinking. So much is, 'We give it out and you give it back to us.' It doesn't require the student to engage in the kind of process that goes into hard work.

Teachers complain that homework is too often postponed or neglected. "One-third of the class doesn't bother to complete the assignment." "Some start one hour before class to do the assignment, then copy from somebody else." Yet, "If I assign homework, they do it," one teacher affirms. "They have so many distractions: illness, family, jobs, social welfare, bureaucracies, appointments in the college, too."

The demands on students to work hard and the attendant sanctions if they do not are less stringent here than in other countries, foreign students attest. "There would be shame in my country if you didn't work hard. You're given no second chance," asserts a student who grew up in Jamaica. Teachers corroborate:

> We (in this country) don't have the kind of homework requirements that others have. Even when we give homework, we don't have the sanctions attached to it: 'If you don't do it, this is going to happen,' and it happens. It's a life-long process. . .
> We don't push students to study hard. This country has been so wealthy, it has so many advantages, there's no great pressure, whereas in other countries, people know if they don't work hard, they're not going to survive. . .
> Students from the Caribbean and from Ghana and Nigeria are very conscious of the amount of work they must put into a course. Local youth have to be taught that. . .
> You have a very small percentage of students in each class who do understand the work ethic involved.

The difficulty that Oral-Level students experience in attempting to master a subject is compounded by the discomfort they feel as intruders in the classroom. "Sometimes they show their nervousness by being very aggressive," observes an English professor. "They bluster, they hide it. It helps to understand that."

They may dispel their discomfort through loquacity -- annoying to the class and the teacher. "They don't try to be disruptive but they lack social savvy. Some talk while class is in session; they're quieted, and they talk some more."

Their discomfort may be dispelled through rushing to leave class. They put their coats on and assemble their books and papers while class is still in session. The teacher is reproachful.

Do students, then, work hard at learning? Compared to what many of them might otherwise be doing, they work hard, states the Dean of Academic Affairs in equivocal fashion."Overall, partly because it's the City of New York and partly, a general situation, our students could be any place that they wanted to be, they could be working, they could be hanging out, they could be selling drugs. But they choose to come here to get an education. That has to be recognized, that they are working hard to get an education, even if all you say is that they're foregoing a salary. There are a lot of distractions out there. I've had plenty of students whom I've recommended to go to a State University unit upstate in a dormitory environment because there are too many distractions down here." The Dean is defining hard work not in terms of what it entails but what it foregoes.

Many don't read,
teachers complain

How to get students to complete reading assignments becomes a constant teacher preoccupation. "If I say, 'Next time we want to look at this or that,' when they come back the next session, they really haven't done anything," laments a history instructor. "Or, if they have, they don't display it, because if I ask a question, I don't get the responses. They just don't read." "There are many days I go into class and I'm the only one who has done the reading," an English instructor concurs. "It's demoralizing. I don't want to come down to giving little quizzes. Sometimes you have to do that to make sure they read." And an accounting instructor notes resignedly, "They rely a lot on what is said and done in class. It puts a lot of extra pressure on the teacher, who then has to compensate in some ways for their not reading the textbook."

Oral-Level students "want instant learning," a Reader-Writer speculates. "Reading for them is a chore. They never enjoyed it. They can't read two or three books at the same time, even if the books are in different fields."

Not all Oral-Level students demand "instant learning." Some take little time off from study. "I had to read the chapter three times," one student recounts, complaining perhaps, but also expressing pride at her persistence. Another comes frequently to my office, plying me with questions which initially show minimal understanding. She too persists and, by the end of the semester performs satisfactorily in examinations and writes a commendable term paper, given her impoverished academic beginnings. The following semester she searches for me and glowingly lets me know that she has not sold her sociology text; she continues to reread it.

College textbooks are often written at a level beyond the comprehension of the Oral-Level student. "We put together a text geared to the seventh and eighth grade level," notes a remedial writing professor. "Many of our students are at that level of reading. The history teachers and the science teachers tell me they can't find books at an appropriate level."

Perplexed at the inability of his students to understand the text, a physics instructor wonders why other teachers have permitted this state of underpreparedness to persist. "I don't want to cast aspersions on my colleagues," he avows, "but I think there are other courses these students are getting through without having to work. I think students are being lulled into a false sense of security. Then when they get to the physics course, they realize there is something amiss, and that's part of the problem. I have students taking my physics courses who have been here three semesters and have passed English, but they still cannot read a paragraph in the physics book and understand what they read. And the physics textbooks are at the twelfth-year level."

The dilemma is perhaps unresolvable: how can Oral-Level students who have scarcely mastered reading at considerably lower levels comprehend history or science texts written at or near the college level.

They have difficulty writing

Only 35 percent of remedial writing students passed their remedial writing courses in Spring 1987. The difficulty inherent in raising the writing level of students sufficiently to meet appropriate college standards is viewed as a major problem facing the college.[10]

Asked to write a paragraph on an experience of culture shock at the college, an Oral-Level student includes the following statements:

> We all have a different culture. Culture is our value, and language. I come from the Dominican Republic. The culture of Dominican Republic is wonderful.

A Reader-Writer, responding to the same assignment, describes her experience at registration.

> Looking back upon my completions of Elementary, Intermediate, and High School (Parochial), I had felt familiar from most of the difficulties of academic life. Unfortunately, I was mistaken. Upon arrival to the college, for registration, I was shocked to say the least. The registration process was a total chaos. The student aides who were appointed to assist in the process were very rude and unprofessional. At one point, I became so overwhelmed with aggravation, I almost walked out. What enabled me to endure the chaos was self determination and my insatiable hunger for

knowledge. This to me was and still is an culture shock experience. The transition could have been made a bit more tolerable.

Oral-Level students are in a quandary when they write. "They don't know how to take lecture notes, they want to take down every word," a Reader-Writer observes. Or they diligently copy what the instructor writes on the blackboard but remain fearful of proceeding further on their own.

Not only what to write but also how to spell presents grave problems. "I get home and can't read the words because of my spelling," a student confesses. She is gratified when the instructor distributes outlines or lecture notes

Notsurprisingly, students postpone completing written assignments. "They're afraid that every time they write a sentence, there will be a mistake in it. And that fear is valid," declares an English professor.

Errors abound in their writing. "I correct their papers extensively," another English professor affirms, and describes his procedure.

I rewrite sentences, I rewrite paragraphs. I make sure that any correction is fully explained. In the smaller classes that I had this semester -- I only had twelve people in one class and seventeen in another -- I could actually sit down with the student every time I returned a paper and go over the grammatical points. When I have forty or forty-two people in an English composition class, there's no way I can do that, so I spell out everything on the paper. If it's a terrible paper, I ask the student to come see me. (Do they come?) No. Sometimes I have to keep pursuing them, and some I never get to see. But I try. I tell them, 'If you don't look over the paper, this whole thing is a waste of time. If you don't understand what you did wrong, come to me.' Some come.

Often they come to me with papers for other classes and ask if we can go over them. I appreciate that they take the initiative to come to see me. I'm grateful for anything they give me. If there's the slightest thing I can praise in a paper, I will. Even if the paper is full of errors, I always try to find something positive to say about it. I think our students need a lot of encouragement.

Teachers who assign papers and give essay examinations anticipate depressing results. "I think they never really had to expose themselves to this kind of activity," a history professor speculates. Required to expound on readings in a Family course, only a few students submit papers that capture the essence of the readings. An exemplary student, urged to divulge the process by which she is able to determine accurately week after week what the authors are proposing, responds merely by stating that from her earliest days her local library was her favorite haunt and she became an omnivorous reader.

Many teachers collude with students in classes other than English to insure that students are not burdened by having to write essays or take essay examinations and they, the teachers, are not burdened by having to read them. During their early years at the college, they may have given essay tests but, dismayed at student response, they resort increasingly to the easy option of examinations consisting of multiple-choice questions provided by the publishers. Students do little writing in courses where essay writing should be compulsory, a teacher in the sciences complains. "I find it astounding that there are courses here that are supposed to be writing courses, but students don't have to write term papers. They have passed some courses in social sciences where I assume they have been writing for months, for semesters, but they can't put two English sentences together. I don't think that's tolerable."

Attempting to arouse in students a love of writing, English composition teachers must perform this feat in classes ever expanding in size. Failures are inevitable, grieves one instructor. "I have about twenty-eight students in my (non-credit) remedial writing sections, which is ridiculous. I should really have half that number to have a good chance of getting them all through. Twenty-eight is almost programming some of them for failure. And then, in my composition class, a college-credit course, I have thirty-seven. You might find out the size of a class in writing at the Ivy League colleges. Those students who are so well-prepared probably have small classes and loads of help from their professors. Our more needy students get less. It's just not fair."

Anxiety is pervasive

"The anxiety baggage that our students bring to math classes is extraordinary. They are absolutely paralyzed. They dread math classes," a mathematics teacher reports.

Students especially dread taking tests, whatever the subject or their level of competence. Each test they regard as an appraisal and a vindication of self.

> Every exam counts for something. It's proof. It's final. A shock. .
> If I do good, I'm great. If I don't, I have to start all over again. . .
> I feel that my high school and family life were poor and I was in the
> Service for five year, but I will overcome it. I just have to do good,
> get good grades, make myself get good marks.

Anxiety is greatest before the first test, when students are most uncertain about their knowledge of the subject and the instructor's demands. Among Oral-Levels, test anxiety persists throughout the semester. They fear that they may know the answers but will misinterpret the questions. Their answers are likely to be terse or verbose, irrelevant or incomprehensible, and too often wrong. Teachers who test students orally discover that they often know more than the written test reveals. "Words seem so much harder on paper," laments a young student. She can tell me all about "culture" and "ethnocentrism" but she cannot remember their meaning on a written test.[11]

Students want to be forewarned about the format of a test. "What are the test questions going to be like," they query. To alleviate their anxiety, a history professor distributes a list of identification terms and study questions. "If I do that, they will go along reasonably well," he finds, "but if I don't, they're at a loss. They don't know what to anticipate."

They study differently, students maintain, depending upon the format. "To study for an essay test, you go deeper. Otherwise, you can read only the first sentence or two in a paragraph or the underlined parts." Though an occasional student prefers essay-type tests -- "students would definitely benefit more in the long run" -- many more want a multiple-choice test, dubbed by them "a nothing test," where they need not worry about grammar, phrasing, and organizing thoughts. With an increasing proportion of teachers at the college giving multiple-choice tests, an increasing number of students, though not yet an avalanche, try to pressure teachers who give essay examinations to change the format of their tests.

Describing their consternation at taking tests, students resort to metaphor.

> Every time I take a test, my mind turns into a block of ice. Everything freezes. Maybe five minutes before the test is finished, it starts coming back. . .
> Butterflies are in my stomach. I always study for an exam, but I go blank.

During the test, they sometimes reach a state of panic.

> I get very upset and nervous though I'm prepared. I flunked a test in Anatomy and Physiology. After the test, the teacher asked me the questions and I answered every one. . .
> I know certain things, and I can prove to you I know them, but what if I can't? There's a conflict in me. . .

I panic, not because I don't know what is going to be on the test, but I forget, I confuse everything. In your soc class, I didn't always remember it on tests, under pressure, but I remember it now. I retain a lot of information that I use to this day. (Her final grade in sociology was D.)

Distress mounts for those students who translate test questions into their native tongue before responding. "In sociology I get nervous and go blank," laments a Puerto Rican woman in her late thirties. "Sometimes I study. I put down what I understand." How long did she study before the most recent test, I ask. "I read the notes two times from beginning to end," she responds. The "notes" were four single-spaced, legal-size pages, distributed in class. "I didn't read the text," she continues. "Sometimes I have to translate it into Spanish to understand. It's more simple in the notes than in the text." (Early in my teaching at the college I distributed my lecture notes, but abandoned the practice when I discovered that some students were using the notes as a substitute for rather than a supplement to the text.) She recognizes the inadequacy of her preparation for the test and explains apologetically, "I come from school, run to my baby (four years old), pick up my older child (age fourteen) and my mother. I have to be running all the time. I say to my children, 'Give me a chance to study.'"

Anticipating failure, some students "give up and hand in a blank paper," a history teacher observes. "I write on their exam, 'Please see me,' but they don't come. They're afraid to be confronted." "They are accustomed to failure and will accommodate to that," explains an Education professor, "unlike what one might have expected from students of past generations, who knew that they could make up a grade the next semester if they did not show up for a final. Our students have so many other things going on in their lives that making up a final doesn't represent the same order of priority that it would represent to a student who doesn't have anything else to do but go to school."

Paradoxically, though they are accustomed to failure, they expect a grade higher than they are likely to receive. "Some of that is denial, and some is hope," a psychology professor interprets. They dream of an inevitable progression from attending class to receiving high grades to achieving occupational success. "The fact that they attend, they expect an A or a B, and expect that the degree is going to mean something. You get late papers, you get people who don't do assignments, who are not coming to class, who spend more energy trying to avoid work. It's just not going to happen for them," an English professor concludes.

Oral-Level students, it is apparent, have difficulty adapting to the reading, writing, and test-taking requirements of a college-level course, especially when they are burdened by family, job, and a multiple course load. Some do make great strides through hard work and sheer persistence, especially if they attend each class session in its entirety. Some muddle through. But a goodly number fail.

Absence or lateness without just cause?

Punctuality is regarded by students at the college as a virtue. Most even accept, perhaps reluctantly, a teacher's right to regard as absent any student who appears after class has begun, and they often run to class from all over the campus in order to arrive on time. "Lateness disrupts," they recognize, even when they themselves are the disrupters. "Teacher and students turn their heads. It's hard to start concentrating again."

Teachers are aware that students' multiple responsibilities contribute to late arrival. "I tell them I don't like my classes to be interrupted," a Spanish professor declares, "but I understand that most of them come from very poor families and don't have cars, they have to depend on public transportation. Most are older students, many are women, heads of households, who have to take the children to school first, then come to school. A child may get sick at night. Many of my Hispanic students feel responsible not only for their own children, but for their mother, their father, their sister, their brother, their cousins. This creates another problem that is not what we are accustomed to see in academia."

Absences for reasons legitimate and not so legitimate vary on any single day from five percent or less to twenty-five percent or more. Generally fewer absences occur in the physical sciences and nursing than in curricula which students find less demanding.

Teachers express sympathy for students whose absences occur for good reason, but disdain for those without just cause. On the one hand, "Students have many, many things pulling at them. If the children are sick, or if the baby sitter doesn't show up, they really can't come to class. That doesn't mean that they're not committed. I can make exceptions in cases like that," asserts an English professor. Yet, "Given their intellectual difficulties and their simple, mechanical problems, they need all the class time that they can get, and they don't take it," a history professor counterposes. "I really think they need to learn discipline. Excessive absence is a part of a general sloppiness toward responsibility that too many of our students have demonstrated."

Teachers have the option of reinstating a student who has been debarred for frequent absences. Though students may cajole a teacher to reinstate them after debarment, they accept the principle of debarment for frequent absences. A teacher should not be too rigid, though, they contend. "It's a big school. How would you know a legitimate absence? If a person can cover the material, all right." Most teachers agree, and interpret the absence-debarment-reinstatement rules with flexibility.

Seekers after Knowledge

Some students have absorbed a great deal of knowledge over the years from observing or reading on their own and come to college as Seekers after Further Knowledge.

An African-American woman in her thirties grew up in the segregated South and came North at fifteen as a live-in maid on Long Island. There she opened a book for the first time outside the classroom -- to a rape scene, she thinks, from Peyton Place -- and became "hooked on books." Now, as a nursing student, she has "no time off from learning."

A thirty-year old Jamaican left school at twelve or thirteen. He could read but not do any math. Education wasn't important in his fishing village. Arriving in the States at twenty-two, he marries a nurse who "pushes him" to go to college, feeling he is "wasting his smartness." Starting out with two mathematics remedial courses, he discovers his talent in mathematics and continues through calculus and physics. His goal now is a career in engineering, but "education means more than the degree," he asserts, he "will always go to school." He enrolls in the sociology class not in order to satisfy curriculum requirements but because he is "curious" about a course in sociology reputed to be "tough."

Embodying a love of learning, Seekers after Knowledge scoff at Requirement-Meeters who view knowledge only as a means to a very practical end: to pass, acquire the credentials, and find a good job.

> A lot of students want to get answers for tests, they don't get involved in discussion. They're here to pass, not to retain what they're learning. They just want to get out to get jobs. . .
> Chemistry and biology they take because they must. It's mandatory. And art the same. . .
> I find art history stimulating, but students detract from it. They're not interested in art. There are more students interested in learning sociology and psychology for the sake of learning.

Knowledge-Seekers are wary of teachers who limit class discussion to what has been assigned. "Most classes are very humdrum. The teachers are prepared, but the class becomes a syllabus. There's not the communication. The main goal seems to be to get through the syllabus."

They speak of their scorn for students who accept uncritically the ideas or concepts advanced by a teacher, who merely write assiduously in their notebooks in order to give back what has been presented and be rewarded for the exchange. "Many are willing to do what they have to do, like robots. It's like another high school in this place. In history or psychology or sociology, a lot of people sit down and listen and write. Listening and writing and not questioning. What is a degree going to mean for such people?"

One Knowledge-Seeker describes her own process of organizing what the teacher is saying, a process acquired in the primary grades of an academically rigorous private school.

> I put it in my mind a certain way. I talk to myself. I organize it in a pattern. I never write the words the teacher says. You have to change it to your specifications. It is important to think and draw conclusions, not to memorize the words. You start teaching children at a young age how to organize. The young child is a sponge and takes it all in. The Dalton School taught me that at a young age. Mostly we were taught to talk in class, ask questions. We were taught how to read newspapers.

Another Knowledge-Seeker deprecates classmates who fail to participate actively in class discussion. "In an English class I'm the only one talking. I took seven years out after high school, worked and travelled, and I try to put what I learned into perspective. Others have done little reading on the outside. They go home, hang out, go to work." He is unfair to students who regard English as an alien language or feel uncomfortable speaking in a college classroom or who, even after hours of study, are not sure they comprehend what they have read. For many others, though, he is on the mark.

A Jamaican student berates those students who need not rush to work or to family and do not rush either to utilize college facilities available as learning aids. "Students here are lazy. They are not prepared to work hard. I see lots of students hanging out. The facilities are here and they don't use them. The tutorial labs are excellent for biology and chemistry. We don't have them in Jamaica."

Classmates provide little intellectual stimulation, some Knowledge-Seekers complain; they offer no yardstick to evaluate one's own competence.

(Says a nineteen-year-old already professionally involved in painting and sculpture):
Most students are no challenge to me. The better I see a person's work in art, the better I want to be.

(Declares an aggrieved nurse who aspires to medical school):
The courses are good but I get depressed here. I don't feel the challenge. I get bored. I find myself with younger students who are cutting up. I like to have my peer group do well so I know how I'm doing in terms of them.

(And a young man in Engineering Technology who returns to school in his late twenties after almost a fifteen year hiatus acknowledges):
I get most stimulation from the faculty. My math professor comes to math class early. We talk about international politics. I respect a person with political opinions.

Some Knowledge-Seekers do find intellectual congeniality among peers in the more advanced classes. "As classes go higher, the number of good students increases. In Chemistry 1, there were one or two. In Chemistry 22, eight or nine. In Chemistry 32, it seems the whole class is good," notes a Guyanan Pre-Pharmacy major with a grade point average of 3.86.

Teachers are grateful for the presence of Knowledge-Seekers who challenge their account with "good, sharp questions." "They make me think. There are not many, but it helps the whole class if there are a couple of such students in a course," acknowledges a history instructor. An English professor concurs.

I like to be challenged, especially in literature. There is always the tendency to accept what the teacher says. Students have to know that there is no one approach -- sure, there are wrong answers -- but there's never any one way of looking at a novel or story or poem. I think that ideally, especially in my discipline, they could teach me because they're approaching material and they're not jaded, they have no preconceived notions about what they're going to look at, and so you get some startling insights. You could be looking at a story one way, and suddenly this woman will come up and say, 'Well, I don't think the husband is the victim, I think the wife is the victim here.' And suddenly there's a new story there. I read it twenty times, I never saw it. So this is what I mean. The student who will come out and say what he or she feels. Not be afraid.

I recall one Knowledge-Seeker in sociology whom I recognized from the first day of class as a student of uncommon ability. A black Vietnam War veteran attending class in 1990, he was considerably older than most students. He seemed to be an avid reader but not an accomplished writer. He participated actively in classroom discussion, his talk turning often to racism and the plight of African Americans, and he asked probing questions that challenged my account. He never missed a session but never came to talk to me after class or during my office hours. At semester's end he dropped out of school. I hope his absence was temporary or that he transferred to another school though I conjecture that he felt too old and too despairing to pursue academics. A tragic casualty.

As a challenge to students prepared for college-level work, the college established a Liberal Arts Academy, open to full-time liberal arts students not required to take reading or writing remedials. From its inception, Academy members attended classes together in special sections restricted in size. They enjoyed intensive contact with teachers and with one another in a program designed to provide an enriched educational experience in and out of class, their academic development presumably not compromised by underprepared peers. An English teacher deplores the inability of the college to pursue the Liberal Arts Academy program as it was originally conceived and practiced. Superior students suffer, he feels, being in a class with students who are academically less well prepared, especially when the class is large.

> At the beginning, we had Academy classes of ten or fifteen students. They were wonderful. Now, the budget realities being what they are, we undermine our own programs because one of the special things about this program is working individually with a small group. It doesn't work out with a large class. It almost makes no sense to have the program. It's unfortunate.
>
> I had an Academy group as part of an English composition class last semester. It was a large class and we didn't do anything special. I was planning additional readings, but I couldn't ask everybody to do that much work and I wouldn't give special assignments for the Academy people alone. I tried, when I gave term paper assignments, to suggest more challenging topics, but some Academy members didn't choose these topics. When we have a program of that nature, I'd like to see it preserved.

I taught two Academy classes. The students were younger than the average at the college. Their pace was fine. They were good Readers and Writers but often lacked the intellectual excitement roused by some of the older Seekers after Knowledge who may have required remediation to bring them officially up to "college level." The Academy students are not necessarily "the best" here, concedes the Academy adviser, though some have done "spectacularly well" (after leaving the college). "Some of them are babies, the lolly-pop kids. Once they grow up, they're going to be marvelous."

Innovative government-funded programs at the college give Seekers after Knowledge considering a career in the sciences hands-on research experience in off-campus laboratories after they have studied with faculty on campus in preparation. One student, concentrating in the Nuclear Medicine technology curriculum, reminisces in the sociology classroom about her exhilarating summer job working with a geneticist at a local hospital and medical school.

Knowledge-Seekers concerned with intellectual matters beyond their area of specialization appear less likely in the 1980s to major in liberal arts curricula and more likely to come from such career options as pre-engineering, pre-pharmacy, nursing, accounting, and business administration. Concentration in liberal arts and science staples such as history, English literature, or biology, common among students at Bronx Community College in the early 1970s, is rare at the end of the 1980s. I recall one Knowledge-Seeker, a retired cab driver of sixty-four, who returned to school in the mid-1970s as a liberal arts major "just to learn." His two children, starting out in an elite New York City public school, had completed medical school. Now his turn came. He exults in some intellectually gratifying experiences at the college.

> Every semester, one and another course are linked together. In English, we are reading *Crime and Punishment*. In history, we are studying the Enlightenment and discussing the Italian criminologist who devoted himself to matching the punishment to fit the crime. It is amazing how different disciplines have an effect on each other -- and fascinating. There's a wide spectrum here. Some courses are very challenging.

Many of the courses that inspired this Knowledge-Seeker in the academic era of the mid-1970s are no longer taught here during the vocational ascendancy of the 1980s.

The high status that Seekers after Knowledge are accorded in the classroom by their peers at the college they fail to receive in the community colleges researched by others. Richardson finds that Requirement-Meeters, the modal type of student, regard as "odd" those students who are eager to learn more than the minimum necessary to pass a course. London, too, notes the pressure exerted by peers against any student who enjoys reading and learning from books. And Neumann and Riesman, in their study of community college elite who transfer to selective independent colleges for their junior and senior years, document the animosity that academic achievement arouses among many students at the community college.[12] Such negative responses to Knowledge-Seekers are unlikely to surface at Bronx

Community College. Students here, both native and foreign-born, laud academic learning, though they themselves may lack the background, the time, or the discipline to acquire such learning.

Knowledge-Seekers as the Conscience of the Community

Editors of the student newspaper, the *Communicator*, published monthly, exemplify Knowledge-Seekers who are critical observers and fearless writers. Their articles published during the school year 1989-1990 touch the pulse of the college and document its concerns.

In the issue dated October 4, 1989, we are told, in bold print on the first page, that the "Library Confronts Book Shortage As Acquisitions Budget Erodes." Book selections in the humanities were excellent in the 1970s, the article notes, but humanities purchases have contracted as new and popular career programs -- paralegal, computer science, and allied health -- drain the $75,000 book allotment, a meager sum for a college with 6,000 students. "It is time for reform," suggests an editorial in the same issue and recommends ways of getting more library books into students' hands.

The newspaper focuses in its October 31, 1989 issue on the chaos in student government, its president facing charges of fraud. Stop the "shouting matches" over the allegedly fraudulent action, an editorial admonishes the student government, and remember that you represent the students, each of whom paid a $50 semester activity fee. All share the blame, the editorial continues. The Student Government president should have been confronted early, enabling her to resign without public humiliation. In a following issue, the president provides her version of the incident.

Done temporarily with prodding the student government, the paper begins to prod the administration. Only 54 percent of the courses listed in the 1988/90 College catalogue are offered in the Fall 1989 Registration Guide. The humanities are hit the hardest, the history department offering only 17 percent of its course listings. The editors seek an explanation from the Dean of Academic Affairs, who responds that twenty students must register for a course "in order for it to run." Although the demand for humanities courses is slipping, the catalogue continues to list all courses, he notes, since those not offered can be taken by students as independent study. Moreover, the catalogue serves "to showcase the diversity of the teaching staff," each of whom does not want the course in his/her area of expertise omitted. And, finally, concludes the dean, "Once we go through all of the time and trouble" to list a course, "we can't just remove a course on a whim." [13]

The dean's explanation for the disparity between course listings and offerings does not satisfy the editor, who prefaces editorial comment with the heading, "Misleading Students," and discourses at length, noting that only one percent of the students are taking independent study courses, most students not aware of this option. Furthermore, "Most of the courses offered are prerequisites and introductory level. The more advanced level courses are simply not offered or are available on a very limited basis."

"The college administration is perplexed about our high drop-out rate," the editor continues. "The suspension rate (at the college) drops dramatically, but the drop-out rate remains an area of concern. The dean believes improved faculty/student interaction will improve the situation." "It is possible," the editor suggests, "that students are actually transferring to other schools because of the limited availability of advanced level courses." "Revise the catalog," she recommends. (October 31, 1989).

"We Gotta Fight 'Da Power!'" is the title of a cartoon appearing in the March 14, 1990 issue showing students bombarding the administration building with "Gripes and More Gripes" -- "Budget Cuts," "Classes Cancelled," "Sections Closed" -- and somebody leaning out of a window of the administration building, muttering, "Uh, sir . . it's that bothersome 'student body' again!" Directly above the cartoon, the cartoonist comments editorially, "We need a unified 'student-rights' mentality if we are to strike down the ogre of benign neglect that seems to constitute the attitude of the powers that be."

The editor-in-chief interviews the president of the college and a transcript of the interview appears in the April 24, 1990 issue. What does he regard as the major accomplishments of his presidency, she wants to know. "The development of grant and community outreach programs, like drop-out prevention and employment training," he responds, and documents the tremendous increase in grant programs under his tenure.

"How do grant programs help the students on this campus?" the editor queries. "We have been faced with budget cuts practically every year. Our classes are over-crowded. Advanced courses are often cancelled. Support and counseling resources are becoming more and more scarce." The president responds that he has "been able to stabilize enrollment" and then refers to the renovation projects which have given the campus a new look.

Does he think he is "in tune to student needs?" "How accessible" is he to students?

"Now, of course, a student can't just walk into my office without an appointment and expect to see me," he concedes "No business runs like that." His assistant sees students, tries to resolve their problems, and reports everything to him. Moreover, he walks around the campus, attended two basketball games during the season, eats in the cafeteria, and can sometimes be found in the gym.

"Many students don't know who you are," the editor persists. "They have never seen you. How often are you on the campus? What exactly is your role as president?"

The president describes his perception of the function of a community college president. "Many of our students think of me as a high school principal. They should know that my major responsibility is that of chief of operations for this college. I should spend most of my time away from the campus gathering resources. That is, getting grants and funding for new projects. I make speeches for many organizations . . . "

"How do these activities benefit the campus and our students?" the editor repeats.

"My appearances help enrollment in that the campus becomes known to people and the community. The way to build an institution is to let people know about it." His biggest disappointment as president, he indicates, is that only eighteen to twenty percent of the students graduate, a rate typical for most community colleges.

The editor is relentless. "Many students are demoralized," she protests. "They often feel the college doesn't care about them. Do you think that could be affecting the graduation rate?"

At this point, the president shifts the blame. "This campus has a non-traditional student body, but we have a very supportive climate," he notes."We have the PASS Center (Personal and Academic Support Services) and the Office of Student Development. The problem is that students don't always utilize these services." [14]

Asked what he envisions for the future, the President concludes the interview by stating, "For one thing, I would like the curriculum to be reformed to include history courses that reflect the cultures on this campus. I'd like to develop more programs in the technologies and allied health professions." [15]

The same issue, April 24, 1990, announces new furor on campus with a page-one headline, "Bronx Community College Inc. Denies Funds; Forensic Society Folds." Bronx Community College Inc. is comprised of elected student representatives and appointed members of the faculty and administration who allocate funds collected from the student activities fee for extra-curricular and co-curricular activities of the college. It refuses the Forensic Society's request for $3,300 to cover the expenses of a four-day stay for eight students and their advisor at

Harvard, where Bronx Community College would have been the only two-year college among over 150 colleges participating in the National Model United Nations. "To have denied our students and this college such an opportunity is a travesty," declares the Chairperson of the Communication Department, which oversees the Forensic Society. Its faculty adviser resigns his post with the parting note that "The obstacles imposed by Bronx Community College Inc. and the lack of institutional support made it impossible to continue. Students were prepared and had done considerable research. It would have been a particularly valuable experience in broadening horizons."

A student editorial delivers its own rebuke: "I'm sure that we would all like to see the college administration lend more support to our Forensic Society which has done an outstanding job of establishing Bronx Community College as an academic force to be reckoned with among the intellectual elite, in matters of wit, reason, logic and wile. After all, that is the main reason we're all here . . . right?"

The May 16, 1990 issue ends the school year in up-beat fashion with the headline on the first page, "Former Bronx Community College Student Is Awarded Coveted Pulitzer Prize for Fiction." The Pulitzer prize winner earned sixty-six credits at the College between 1969 and 1973 and "the confidence to transfer to City College where he went on to earn his B.A. and M.A. He recalls being not unlike other students who entered Bronx Community College with little cultural sophistication. He remembers the college as a supportive place where he delighted in the information he was taking in. It was here, he said, that he discovered the fun of language. One day in an English class he realized as he never had before the fascination of alliteration. He remembers writing the phrase 'frolicking freely.' It brought him a sharper awareness of the possibilities of language and the excitement of seeing music and language as parallel modes of expression."

In an earlier issue, students are admonished to resist "A Damaging Mindset," as evidenced by the sentiment, "I don't care what happens in that class or what grade I get. Just as long as I pass!!!" Those students who come to class but hear and say nothing have already failed, warns the editor. "If we are afraid of making waves, we will never make a difference in this world. We will be destined and doomed to the robotic and assembly-line existence of 'just doing enough to pass.'" (February 13, 1990).

The editors of the campus newspaper do make waves. Seekers after Knowledge generally do.

The gulf is vast between the Oral-Level students who seek to fulfill minimal requirements and the Knowledge-Seekers who are ready academically to take advantage of the best that Bronx Community

College has to offer. Whether a teacher can inspire both groups within one class remains problematic.

Notes

1. Walter J. Ong, *Orality and Literacy: The Technologizing of the Word* (London and New York: Methuen, 1982), 11.

2. Ibid., 56.

3. David E. Lavin, Richard D. Alba, and Richard A. Silberstein, *Right versus Privilege: The Open-Admissions Experiment at the City University of New York* (New York: The Free Press, 1981), 282.

Theodore Gross speculates that "The kind of deep creativity that is manifested in a private language -- the blues of *Huckleberry Finn* or some of the poetry of Langston Hughes -- is all the more powerful precisely because its vernacular is in a tension with standard public language. The two languages must be simultaneously held in the mind of the reader as well as of the writer, at whatever counterpoint can be productively sustained." *Academic Turmoil: The Reality and Promise of Open Education* (Garden City, New York: Anchor Press/ Doubleday, 1980), 21.

4. Basil Bernstein, *Class, Codes, and Control: Theoretical Studies towards a Sociology of Language.* vol. 1. (London: Routledge and Kegan Paul, 1st ed. 1971, 2nd rev. ed. 1974).

A "restricted" speech style does not indicate "restricted" thought, though a student's poor school performance may result from the teacher's judgment that the "restricted" speech bespeaks little ability. Equating the restricted code with "linguistic deprivation" or labeling the child "nonverbal," the teacher diverts attention from the school to the child and the family. Joseph A. Scimecca, *Education and Society* (New York: Holt, Rinehart, and Winston, 1980), 100.

Riessman introduces findings reported by the Institute for Developmental Studies under Morton Deutsch (Department of Psychiatry, New York Medical College) that culturally deprived children appear to understand more language than they speak. They express themselves well in spontaneous and unstructured situations. Frank Riessman, *The Culturally Deprived Child* (New York: Harper and Row, 1962), 76-77. Many open admissions students can be similarly characterized.

5. Walt Wolfram, "Sociolinguistic Premises and the Nature of Nonstandard Dialects," *Language, Communication, and Rhetoric in Black America,* ed. Arthur L. Smith, (New York: Harper & Row, 1972), 28-40.

6. Bell hooks recounts her experience in this regard: " . . .(Every time I try to get clever and throw some vernacular black speech into my essays, they are perceived as errors and 'corrected.'). Until recently I felt that was alright, I'd been happy to keep that speech for private places in my life. Now, I recognize how disempowering it is for people from underprivileged backgrounds to consciously censor our speech so as to 'fit better' in settings where we are perceived as not belonging." *YEARNING: race, gender, and cultural politics* (Boston: South End Press, 1990) ,90.

7. In 1981, Los Angeles City College ranked first among colleges in the nation in the number of non-English-speaking students, with 61 percent of its freshman class coming from homes where English was not the primary language. Arthur M. Cohen and Florence B. Brawer, *The Collegiate Function of Community Colleges* (San Francisco: Jossey-Bass, 1987), 134.

8. Bernstein's "restricted" and "elaborated" linguistic codes could be relabeled "oral-based" and "text-based" codes. See Walter J. Ong, in *Orality and Literacy,* 6.

9. Richard C.Richardson, Jr., Elizabeth C. Fisk, Morris A. Okun, *Literacy in the Open-Access College* (San Francisco: Jossey-Bass, 1983), 90-99.

10. Fifty-five percent of freshmen remedial students at Bronx Community College in Spring 1987 passed courses in reading and mathematics and 35 percent passed courses in writing.

11. Before the nineteenth century, higher examinations were oral, not written. Greek and Roman children, when tested, recited poetry or made speeches. In the great medieval universities, graduating Masters and Doctors defended their theses by debating against rivals and critics. Gilbert Highet, *The Art of Teaching* (New York: Albert A. Knopf, 1969), 133.

12. Richard C.Richardson,Jr., Elizabeth C. Fisk, Morris A. Okun, *Literacy in the Open-Access College,* 95.
Howard B. London, *The Culture of a Community College* (New York: Praeger, 1978), 100-104.
William Neumann and David Riesman, "The Community College Elite," *New Directions for Community Colleges: Questioning the Community College Role* No. 32, ed. G.B Vaughan, (San Francisco: Jossey-Bass, 1980), 58.

13. When courses previously offered continue to be listed in the catalog, a footnote indicates that they are not offered on a regular basis.

14. The students' failure to utilize sufficiently the services available has been noted by foreign students at Bronx Community College and observed at community colleges elsewhere.
While administrators favor computer-assisted instruction over labor-intensive tutoring, minority students are resistant to the automated, self-paced, automated drop-in laboratories and prefer tutorial assistance. Richard C.Richardson, Jr. and Louis W. Bender, *Fostering Minority Access and Achievement in Higher Education: The Role of Urban Community Colleges and Universities* (San Francisco: Jossey-Bass, 1987), 48-49.

15. The student editor wants college offerings in the 1980s to duplicate "the broad range of academic programs" given at the inception of the college in 1959.   The 1990-92 College catalog places emphasis elsewhere: "In addition to serving the needs of individuals within the region, the College assumes a responsibility to help meet the local requirements for trained manpower through cooperative effort with industry, business, professions, and government."   It "has intensified its outreach to New York City's economic, educational, and cultural institutions through partnerships with business and industry and collaborative programs with the Board of Education."

Chapter 7

Cooled Out or Spoon-Fed In?

Through lowering the educational aspirations of academically poor students, community colleges have served a hidden, cooling-out function, wrote Burton Clark in 1960. All applicants are admitted to the community college, but the number of applicants exceeds the opportunities available. Through "preliminary sorting and screening," students are eased out of a transfer liberal arts curriculum into a less valued terminal vocational curriculum or else are encouraged to drop out of college altogether.[1] Cooling out from curricula or college helps to prevent four-year colleges from becoming inundated by applicants who respond to open admissions.

The student population at Bronx Community College rises precipitously with the inception of open admissions in 1970. Its fall, six years later, after the city's fiscal crisis and the imposition of tuition, is also precipitous. Enrollment rates sag for the next decade and the college embarks on an endless attempt to gain and retain students in order to insure its survival. Rather than cooling students out, it spoon-feeds them in.

Spoon-fed in to Gain and Retain Students

Admitting and retaining nontraditional students, it is assumed, requires expanding terminal vocational curricula, where students can see the direct connection between attending school and getting jobs.

Vocational programs expand during the 1980s to include paralegal, human services, nuclear medicine technology, and x-ray and audiovisual technology, while the humanities continue to shrink. Though at the inception of open admissions in 1970 almost two-thirds of the students were enrolled in curricula on the transfer track, by the end of the 1980s two-thirds turn to vocational programs leading to a terminal degree. Expanding the terminal track is seen as a way of gaining and retaining students at a time of declining enrollment and fiscal constraints though its unintended consequence is the lowering of students' aspirations.

To aid recruitment and retention, the administration actively encourages relaxing grading standards.The policy is implemented by "supportive-type" teachers who are guided by the principle that high grades "allay fear" and bolster persistence.

> I don't want anybody to fail (affirms a sociology professor). So many of these students have had bad high school experiences and are coming back after years away from school. I rarely fail anybody but this has more to do with my policies than with their level. My tendency has always been to give second chances and a lot of incompletes. I'm the supportive-type teacher. I feel personally and professionally that failure is ridiculous. That's a category that we shouldn't even have in a transitional school like this. By giving extra help and extra time, almost all students can make it. If they don't make it, it's because they don't work. . .
>
> I rarely fail anybody (says an art history professor.) I'm very helpful and easy. I tell them to speak to me if they have problems. I gear my teaching to allay fear. I say they can get A's and B's if they follow my directions.

Suspending students for poor grades after a single semester the administration considers detrimental not only to the students but also to the fiscal interests of the college. Consequently, the probationary period before suspension is extended. With suspensions occurring only once a year, they decline dramatically, and the weaker students pay fees for the entire year, a teacher observes. Another suggests sardonically, "You can do anything you want with statistics, just change the rules. If you want to cut down on suspensions, give students two semesters on probation before suspension. Next time, give them three semesters. It's an administrative game. The administration has to show success rates and therefore they have to change the rules."

Course failure or withdrawal rates vary between disciplines and even within a discipline from a low of five to ten percent of class enrollees to a high of fifty percent or more. The rate in college-level courses is likely to be highest in the "hard" sciences, nursing, and accounting. Students who are cooled out of a program do not necessarily withdraw from college. Nursing students may transfer to human services, where it is more difficult to fail. Engineering students may turn to engineering technology, nuclear medicine technology, or to business. Accounting students find majors elsewhere, perhaps in data processing.

Students determined to graduate from the college could presumably find teachers with sufficiently relaxed grading standards to spoon-feed them through to graduation. It is notable, then, that the proportion of matriculants who graduate is depressingly small, nineteen percent within four years of matriculation in the 1970s, 14 to 16 percent in the 1980s. Many students disappear from campus one or two semesters after arrival, seeming to give up on higher education. Some of them reappear either here or elsewhere several years or even several decades later.

Dropping out of college is not unique to open admissions or to community colleges. From the 1920s through the 1950s, American colleges lost, on the average, one-half their students in the four years after matriculation. Half the total withdrawals occurred before the sophomore year.[2] Academic failure is not the primary reason for dropping out.[3] In four-year colleges, the ratio of nonacademic to academic reasons for withdrawal is two to one; in two-year colleges, it is four to one.[4] The life burdens that students at Bronx Community College bear along with their studies are reason enough to anticipate countless failures and withdrawals.

Cooled Out of the Nursing Program

The nursing department has long served as the "lighting rod of student discontent" at Bronx Community College. Though several other departments have withdrawal and failure rates far exceeding the average at the college, the number of precarious points at which a prospective nurse may stumble appears more numerous and the outrage expressed, more vehement.

Students are not counselled by nursing faculty when they register for pre-nursing. "Many of them don't see us until they've already made their decision and have started the pre-nursing sequence," notes a nursing professor. "The counselors they see initially may not realize the consequences of the selection of this curriculum. But where we can be, we're candid with them. We don't say, 'You do not belong here.' I don't know legally if we can do that."

Pre-nursing students are required to achieve a 2.5 (C+) grade-point average in five courses (biology and pharmacology, English, communication, and psychology) used as a screening device to enter the nursing program and a similar grade-point average in biology and pharmacology alone. Though it was anticipated that these courses would be taken in a single semester, students often spend two to three years completing their remedial work and nursing pre-requisites. It is bandied about among pre-nursing students that "They try to keep you out," "They try to discourage you." Woeful tales are told about student averages in the screening courses a minute fraction less than the 2.5 grade point average requirement. A student laments:

> This is my fourth semester here and I'm still in pre-nursing. I need a B in English to get into nursing; I have a 2.37 average in the other courses. I'm taking English alone this summer. I don't know if I'm going to get a B.
>
> I had Mr. Z. for two courses in remedial English when I first came. He sat down and explained run-ons and fragments. He said that I should stay with him after class and he would help me out. He wouldn't let me fail. 'When I get through with you,' he said, 'You'll know all the rules of grammar.'
>
> (Her remedial English courses with Mr. Z. give no forewarning of trouble. Nevertheless, trouble ensues when she enrolls in the college-credit English Composition course.)
>
> I think there was conflict between me and the professor. In the tutorial lab the tutors said, 'Your papers are A,' but he gave me a D. Then I got a private tutor, but nothing worked. I talked to him. 'Well, Miss H.,' he said, 'Let's see how your next paper is.' I couldn't wait. He told me to stay, but I didn't want to take no chances.
>
> (She withdraws from the course. Unlike a failure, a withdrawal does not affect her grade-point average. She confesses resignedly that every semester she feels like quitting but she stays. Eventually she is admitted to the nursing program.)

Many of the one thousand pre-nursing students at the college in the early 1990s spend considerable time here without entering the nursing program, whose numbers, set by the Board of Trustees of the City University, cannot exceed three hundred. It is a debilitating experience, one student protests, "to know that after I have completed my pre-nursing courses with a grade point of average of 3.3, I have to wait until my number is called out of a waiting list." "Even if pre-nursing students don't make nursing and want to terminate, they can go into human services," a dean suggests.

Admitted to the nursing program, students encounter new stresses on the way to graduation. A young man who fails the final examination in Fundamentals of Nursing by a fraction of a point, despite being tutored by his sister, a graduate nurse, bares his grievance.

> I had a B or B+ average in pre-nursing and was in my first semester of nursing. I needed 71.6 in my final exam in Fundamentals of Nursing to get a C in the course. A D+ is failing. I studied four weeks for the test. My sister, a graduate nurse, studied with me. I got 71. I couldn't understand how I failed. They fail people either to get rid of them or to have them repeat the course, my sister told me. They want people to have A's. They don't want to pass people with C's. They want the highest grades in the community college system. I was totally devastated and didn't take the finals for my other three nursing classes. (He remains out of school for two years. Eventually he receives a letter from the nursing department indicating, "We'd like you to come in and discuss. . . He ignores the letter and when he returns to school, changes his major to human services.)

"The nursing department teaches toward the licensing test and not toward the majority of students," an instructor from another department protests. "This is wonderful if you are an A or B+ student. It does not give you any assistance if you are one of those people struggling to make this a life career." Tension rises inevitably between the tender-hearted teacher, concerned primarily about the student's personal gratification, and tough-minded nursing faculty, concerned principally that their students pass the licensing examination and become competent nurses. The faculty concur that they "teach toward the licensing test." They have experienced state board pressure to do so.

Feeling "unjustly treated," students "go to the president, they'll go to whoever they feel can help them out." Responding to student onslaughts, the nursing faculty give a single defense of its standards: "We're dealing with people's lives."

> You have to have high standards because you're dealing with people's lives. There is tension because it's a difficult program, but we're not asking them for something not attainable.

> There is frustration, we know that, and we tell the students that it's understandable if they are frustrated. Many of us have been through that ourselves. It's a profession that has a great deal of demands

because we are dealing with people's lives. And so we make no bones about that. We don't apologize for it.

The demand for nurses in the 1980s and their increasingly competitive salaries draws men into nursing, some with a baccalaureate or a masters degree in other fields. Women students generally respond in traditional fashion to the men in a field long seen as the province of women. "Sometimes they are very protective of the men, and do a lot to help them out," observes a member of the nursing faculty. "Women are not as assertive or self-confident as men in class and in the clinical situation. Men speak up more forcefully, even though some women are brighter and doing better." The all-female nursing faculty express some ambivalence at the influx of men into nursing. "Just because he has an advanced degree, it doesn't mean that that person can be a nurse," one instructor asserts, "maybe because he doesn't have the respect for nursing that he should. Some feel, 'I can walk through this.'"

In the early 1990s, the demand for nurses becomes polarized. Those nurses with higher degrees, capable of working in multidisciplinary teams and collaborating with physicians on diagnoses and treatment, are in demand, while those with lesser credentials are being squeezed out, many of their duties taken over by attendants.

Nursing graduates from the community college comprise a substantial proportion of the graduates from terminal vocational curricula who want to transfer to a senior college en route to a baccalaureate. The nursing department is attempting to articulate its program with senior colleges so that its credits will be accepted upon transfer. The reluctance of senior colleges to accept all of the community college credits is a recurring problem throughout the college.

Cooled Out at the Point of Transfer

Recognizing by the late 1980s that the two-year associate degree often has limited worth in the labor market, most graduates of Bronx Community College from both the terminal and the transfer track enter a four-year college to pursue a baccalaureate. Presumably their academic aspirations increase too as they feel more at home in the college classroom.[5] However, the terminal curricula are not designed to prepare students for transfer to a senior college. "The standards in these programs and the courses required are not the same as in the transfer programs," a mathematics professor cautions.

Students enter Bronx Community College and may say, 'I don't think I can cope with college, I'll register for one of these terminal programs.' They find out they can cope, some of them very well, and after a number of years they graduate. They then transfer to a four-year college. And these (terminal) students are at a marked disadvantage compared to students who went through a transfer program. I don't like to see students going for a degree here that really does not equip them well. The terminal track math course, Introduction to Mathematical Thought, is not designed as a transfer course to a four-year college. On the other hand, I think our calculus sequence (on the transfer track) can certainly stand up to anything they do at the senior colleges. By and large, the standards are a little higher in the transfer program throughout. I don't know whether I would be loved but I would rather see those terminal programs phased out and the higher transfer standards applied across the board.

Students on the terminal track accumulate specialization credits which the senior colleges are reluctant to accept. At the time of transfer some students "have accumulated enough credits in their major field to satisfy the baccalaureate requirements," writes Gene Maeroff in *The New York Times*, "but the corresponding department at the senior college is loath to certify as one of its majors a student who took almost all his courses elsewhere."[6] Students transfer from the community college with the least loss of credit when their courses replicate those taken during the freshman and sophomore years at the senior college.

Aggrieved teachers at the community college complain that senior colleges within the City University accept considerably fewer credits at transfer from their students than do colleges elsewhere. "The students in my curricula were losing many credits at City College in their major even if the same textbook was used," asserts an irate chairperson in the sciences. "We fought that articulation battle over a five-year period but lost. The four-year colleges circumvented it." "I think we have to do a better job of articulation so that our students don't end up losing twenty-five credits when they transfer with sixty-eight credits," declares one of the deans. "That happens all the time, especially in our very own senior colleges."

The seemingly obstructionist tactics of the senior colleges in limiting the number of credits they accept at transfer from Bronx Community College are regarded in many instances as an attempt to perpetuate a pecking order. "Our four-year colleges were never very happy getting students from the two-year college," observes a chemistry professor who has taught at both levels. "I know that from personal observation. They felt the community college students were inferior and the faculty were inferior." Nevertheless, the refusal to accept credits from Bronx Community College is not always inappropriate, observes an administrator. "Some senior colleges within the City University refuse to accept the fact that our students have passed the Writing Assessment Test given throughout the university as evidence that they can cope with English. They make them take another year of English composition. Some refusals are a kind of snobbery but some are valid, because I have seen students with degrees from Bronx Community College who either cannot write or have difficulty in speech."

The non-acceptance of community college credits may be valid, too, teachers concede, if the curriculum has become obsolete. "Sometimes, for political reasons, we allow a certain curriculum to stay on and on when it's a decade behind in terms of the job market and in terms of what the senior colleges expect us to produce," a member of the administration asserts. "We don't want some individuals to lose their jobs. We cannot revise the curriculum because what are they going to teach? That happens in this college. There are some entrenched interest groups around here. You cannot budge them. We send a graduate out and the business organizations ask, 'Where have you been? We don't do this any more.' We don't have the equipment."

To resolve the conflict over the cooling out occurring at transfer, Bronx Community College may be willing to grant "reasonable" concessions, a chairperson in the sciences suggests. "Senior college faculty are saying, 'Teach the first-year courses, the basic courses, and we'll train the students in their major.' I could accept that. The community college is not subject to the same kind of accreditation situations as the senior colleges. It could be worked out so that the bulk of the credits in the major area can be done in the junior and senior years, but it has to be reasonable. It's been political and hard to deal with."

Students themselves sometimes resolve the conflict over losing credits at transfer to a senior college through transferring early, often with the encouragement of faculty. A professor concedes advising good students to transfer the first year. "Students who are not so very good better stay and get a degree and do something with it." "Better students are transferring out earlier," another teacher agrees. "Poor students drive out good ones. Poor ones are making it through the system and graduate."

Not all teachers nor all students favor early transfer to a senior college. Recognizing that an associate degree may represent a "safety net" for the student, many teachers advise students to "graduate here first. If you have to repeat something over there, repeat it, but at least you'll have the associate degree." The losses in credits incurred are discounted.

Outstanding students often receive special attention at Bronx Community College, a professor notes. "We nurture those students, those of us who are willing to give extra time and special care to the advanced student, as much extra time as we give to the student who doesn't have the skills." Some excellent students do savor the "nurturing" they receive at at the college and stay on until graduation.

Students aspiring to a baccalaureate who start out at a community college are more likely to drop out before receiving that degree than are a controlled group of students who start out at a four-year college, according to extensively-quoted research findings.[7] However, dropout-prone students, well able to fulfill the academic requirements of a four-year institution, are more likely to begin their college venture in a community college, a possibility that Astin raises in a 1975 study.[8] Having multiple responsibilities, they want a degree in hand quickly or they are attracted by the slightly lower tuition of the community college or its proximity to their home or to work. Dropping out is not always a function of the lack of academic progress but of the overwhelming problems that confront the students. In the words of a student who transferred from a four-year city college to Bronx Community College: "There's no difference academically between students at the two colleges, but people here seem to have more problems. Everybody has two kids, and they are dragging their kids back and forth from the Day Care Center." He minimizes the academic difference and exaggerates the proportion of students "dragging their kids," but he has caught the flavor of Bronx Community College.

"There have been no accurate studies indicating how students who come out of the community college perform in the four-year schools," claims one professor. "I think it is such a hot potato that nobody has been willing to do it." He is not ready to accept either Astin's negative prognosis or Cohen and Brawer's more positive conclusion that most community college transferees do quite well after an initial shock and their records at graduation are little different from those who began at the four-year college.[9] It would seem,nevertheless, that disproportionate specialization in terminal curricula at the community college gives many students with academic ability and persistence much less than they bargain for.

We have seen, then, that when admissions and retentions lag, Bronx Community College does not look to the liberal arts and the sciences as drawing cards. Instead, the terminal track is credited with attracting nontraditional students, thus insuring the viability of the college. Spoon-feeding measures devised to retain the matriculants include not only (1) introducing flexibility in grading; and (2)extending the probationary period before suspension but also (3)reducing the substantive material covered in a course; and (4) giving "objective" tests that demand no writing or organizing skills. Some departments and some instructors do not accept such a liberalizing agenda but cool out many of their students through maintaining rigorous standards. Senior colleges later employ their own cooling-out procedure at the point of transfer through limiting the community college credits they accept. Far from "saving" time on their way to a baccalaureate, students who start out on the terminal track may find their journey interminable.

A Suggestion For Change:
The Chancellor's Preparatory Initiative

Ann Reynolds, the newly appointed Chancellor of the City University of New York, announces in 1990 that freshmen who enter any college within the City University will be expected to have completed in high school a rigorous college-preparatory curriculum. A student who lacks this background must make up the deficiency before graduating from college.[10] Requiring the prospective college student to take the college-preparatory curriculum in high school would obviate the need for an extensive remedial program at college.

All faculty members at Bronx Community College approve in theory the Chancellor's Preparatory Initiative. They regard it "a marvelous concept, to shift the burden of remediation back to the high schools. College students need not be learning what they should have learned before: how to write a sentence, how to do arithmetic, how to use a dictionary, how to take notes. We should be able to assume, in days of limited money, that students come to us prepared to perform at a college level." They can then acquire here "the reality of what they think they're now acquiring" and senior colleges will be more willing to accept community college credits at the time of transfer.

Nevertheless, there is an undercurrent of fear that the high schools will not be able to provide a rigorous academic curriculum for prospective students at Bronx Community College. Requisite funding does not accompany the Chancellor's Initiative. In the words of one fence- sitter: "Considering the demography and reality and what New York is, and the population trends and the nature of the union, and the teachers in the high school trying to keep discipline and not getting the subject matter across, I'm not sanguine about a marvelous outcome in the next couple of years."

Moreover, instituting such academic requirements for admission to college, it is feared, can mark the demise of open admissions. Two teachers who voice their fears:

I am concerned that the higher standards are going to keep certain people out. If the schools do not take the time to really prepare these students in the South Bronx and in Bed Sty, if they don't seriously deal with educating these kids, it's going to be that silent door they're going to close to keep out people like myself, an African-American, because we didn't get a proper elementary and secondary education. . .

We must be sure that we don't close the door on those who have unusual life experiences. We know that people have children at very early ages and drop out of high school. A mother may want to return at thirty after her child she had at sixteen is older. We have always been a university that has dealt with and serviced those who have had unusual backgrounds.

Other teachers, though, welcome the new admissions requirements as a screening device for students who have been using the community college as a revolving door.

Somehow we have to stop the spiral of decline. Admissions may decline but a lot of those left out will be persons who do not want to do the hard work. Maybe there are alternatives that we as a society ought to provide, some other option for those students. This may not be the choice for them. . .

We have a lot of students who come in, they're here for a semester, two semesters, and then they disappear. We're giving them something, maybe an increase in basic skills, but how costly it is. And there's an awful lot of money being spent on remediation. I would like to find out what is the cost of a degree here. . .

The Chancellor's Initiative probably will affect open admissions, but it will not eliminate minority groups. High standards are important for any ethnic group.

At the least, the Preparatory Initiative, if successful, would begin to alter the community perception of Bronx Community College as an institution of remedial studies. Yet the Initiative cannot be accomplished by fiat alone.[11]

Notes

1. Burton R. Clark, "The Cooling Out Function in Higher Education," *American Journal of Sociology* 65 (May 1960): 569-576.

2. John Summerskill, "Dropouts from College," *The American College: A Psychological and Social Interpretation of the Higher Learning,* ed. Nevitt Sanford (New York: John Wiley and Sons, 1962): 630-631.

A low attrition rate and a high graduation rate are customary measures of the success of a college.

3. David E. Lavin, Richard D. Alba, Richard A. Silberstein, "Open Admissions and Equal Access: A Study of Ethnic Groups in the City University of New York," *Harvard Educational Review* 49:1 (February 1979): 80.

4. Michael A. Olivas, With the Assistance of Nan Alimba, *The Dilemma of Access: Minorities in Two Year Colleges* (Washington, D.C.: Howard University Press, 1979), 46.

5. In a survey of students in twenty-seven community colleges, Baird found that students who succeeded academically in the community college after poor earlier academic experiences or poor background were often likely to aspire higher over time. L.L. Baird, "Cooling Out and Warming Up in the Junior College," *Measurement and Evaluation in Guidance* 4.3 (1971):160-171.

6. Gene I. Maeroff, "Better Ideas Are Sought For Two Year Colleges," *The New York Times,* 23 August 1983, C1, C10.

7. In his 1975 study, Astin attributed the relatively high dropout rate among community college students who aspired to a baccalaureate to their high dropout-proneness, insufficient student financial aid and on-campus job opportunities, absence of student housing, and difficulties in the process of transfer. Alexander W. Astin, *Preventing Students from Dropping Out* (San Francisco: Jossey Bass, 1975) , 160-161.

His indictment of community colleges is more severe a decade later. "The negative effects of attending a community college are observed even after the effects of the students' entering characteristics and the lack of residence and work are taken into account," he asserts, and refers for documentation to his earlier studies. Community colleges, he adds, "are places where the involvement of both faculty members and students appears to be minimal. All students are commuters, and most are part-timers. Thus, they presumably manifest less involvement simply because of their part-time status. Similarly, a large proportion of faculty members are employed part-time." Alexander W. Astin, *Achieving Educational Excellence: A Critical Assessment of Priorities and Practices in Higher Education* (San Francisco: Jossey-Bass, 1985) , 146.

8. Alexander W. Astin, *Preventing Students from Dropping Out,* 160.

9. Arthur M. Cohen and Florence B. Brawer, *The Collegiate Function of Community Colleges* (San Francisco, Jossey-Bass, 1987), 100-102.

10. Ann Reynolds' picture appears on page one of *The New York Times,* January 23, 1991, with the caption, "*CUNY Plans Tougher Standards That All Must Meet to Graduate.*"

11. In 1995, five years after the announcement of the Chancellor's Preparatory Initiative, the Board of Trustees of the City University of New York introduces plans to restrict senior college admission to students considered able to complete all courses in remediation and English as a Second Language within two semesters. The rejected students will have the option of attending night school or a community college

Charisse Jones, "CUNY Adopts Stricter Policy on Admissions," *The New York Times,* 27 June 1995, 1, B2; Joseph Berger, "Not the Same CUNY," *The New York Times,* 27 June 1995, B2.

If the resolutions are implemented, an extra burden of long-term remediation may be shifted to the community college.

Chapter 8

The Teachers: Student Evaluation and Teacher Rejoinder

Autonomous teachers -- this seems an oxymoron. Teachers at Bronx Community College must satisfy at least minimally their colleagues and administrators within the institution. They are limited by fiscal restraints on the courses they teach and publishing restraints on textbooks available. More than in four-year colleges, they face students with inadequate academic preparation.

Despite such constraints, given a more or less hands-off policy from administrators with regard to what happens within the classroom, teachers possess a degree of freedom, whether by design or neglect, that might well be the envy of those in other professions. They may speculate or orate with relative abandon on subject matter pertinent or irrelevant since their audience is a captive one and the lecture or dialogue is rarely recorded for future scrutiny. They may assign homework and give tests that require as much time for the teachers' evaluation as for the students' preparation or, alternatively, they may minimize their own work through extensive utilization of workbooks and computerized tests provided by publishers.

The aging of college teachers in the 1980s has been a national phenomenon and can be well documented at Bronx Community College, where the faculty is ripe in age, tenure, and rank. Perhaps over-ripe. Few teachers were hired in the lean decades of the 1970s and 1980s and few left voluntarily, though a sizeable number were retrenched during the city's fiscal debacle in 1976. The median age of the 251 full-time faculty in 1987 is fifty-two years. Almost all (94 percent) are tenured and a majority (58 percent) are associate or full professors. Missing from the institution is the excitement that comes from the continual infusion of new blood.

The full-time faculty at Bronx Community College is predominantly white (79 percent in 1987) and male (61 percent). The nonwhite proportion among faculty, though considerably lower than among students, is higher than in most American colleges.[1] Black representation in the campus establishment includes the President of the College, the Dean of Students, the Coordinator of the Humanities Division, and the Chairs of Music and Art, Chemistry, and Communication.

Community colleges have generally been reluctant to hire faculty with doctorates who, it is assumed, are immersed in research in their field of specialization at the expense of teaching. Only one-fourth of community college faculty in 1983 hold the doctorate.[2] Bronx Community College is an anomaly in this regard. A doctorate has been essential in recent years for promotion to the rank of associate or full professor or for tenure in the sciences and the humanities. In 1990 almost one-half of the full-time faculty have doctorates -- considerably more than half in social sciences, history, biology, English, mathematics, and Special Education Services. Given parity in salary with four-year college faculty within the City University, community college faculty are required to approach parity in academic degrees.

In contrast with the minimal emphasis on faculty research in most community colleges, Bronx Community College requires that an aspiring professor in the sciences and humanities show evidence of scholarly publications. Most professors, though, are "locals" and not "cosmopolitan" scholar-researchers.Their research focuses on such subjects as improving teaching methods, initiating courses and programs, and curbing attrition. "Locals" are more likely than "cosmopolitans" to be accessible to students.[3] The general atmosphere at the college bespeaks not a scholarly but a student-centered orientation among the faculty, despite the doctorate required for promotion to associate or full professor.[4] Students who transfer to a four-year city college find academic requirements there somewhat more rigorous but they miss the relaxed atmosphere and the student-teacher camaraderie of Bronx Community College.

Instructors teach twelve to fifteen hours a week. A class without the requisite number of registrants may be cancelled as late as a day before the first session, an administrative decision frustrating to students with limited time allotted to attending classes and to teachers who have worked at preparing the course or achieving a favorable time schedule. More advanced courses are more likely to be dropped -- Shakespeare rather than Fundamentals of Written Composition or Sociology of Women rather than Introductory Sociology.

Teaching at the college is a rare learning experience. The teacher is not granted the indulgence of forgetting that the literacy of some students is so limited that they may never have used or even remember reading such words as "imperiled" or"impoverished." They may never have heard of Mohandas Gandhi or Lyndon Johnson.

Though the outcome for the students of attending class is determined primarily by their intellectual capacity, motivation, and work, a good student-teacher relationship is needed to spur the intellectual trek.[5] Beginning so far behind, community college students are likely to depend more on the teacher than are students in a four-year college. Their satisfaction with the community college is more closely determined by the relationship with faculty than by any other involvement or any other student or institutional characteristic.[6] The good teacher, as described by students, is sensitive to their areas of ignorance and their consequent trepidation and is willing to personalize teaching to a degree that the instructor in a traditional four-year college may not have envisioned.

Great teachers have presumably always personalized teaching. In a 1929 study by Robert L. Kelly of responses among administrators, faculty, students, and alumni in 187 church-affiliated colleges, teachers were rated as "great" primarily if they showed interest in the students -- exhibiting "sympathy," "helpfulness," "sincerity," and "enthusiasm." "Knowledge and mastery of the subject matter" ranked third, but "breadth" and "industry" were eleventh and twelfth in importance for a teacher. The "greatness" of a college professor appeared to be related primarily to human qualities and only secondarily to intellectual distinction.[7]

A study in the 1970s by Robert Wilson and his associates reaffirms the Kelly findings. Those teachers perceived by students and faculty as most effective with undergraduates are committed to undergraduate teaching and generally prefer teaching to engaging in research. They are more likely than their colleagues to work harder at making their course presentations interesting and to talk with students about contemporary issues of importance to young adults. They meet frequently with students outside the classroom, discussing careers, educational plans, course-related ideas, campus issues, and problems of personal concern. Effective teachers, though, are not more (or less) likely than their colleagues to organize their course materials, to discuss varied points of view, or to reflect on the origin of ideas introduced in class.[8]

The students at Bronx Community College might well have written the scripts of such studies. Their evaluation of the good teacher is reminiscent of Kelly's characterization in 1929 and Wilson's, in 1975. The closer the classroom resembles the highly personal, participatory oral world with which many are familiar, the less their anxiety and the more freely do they participate in class discussion. Asked to describe the qualities they find in the good teacher, they speak of those qualities and activities that they consider fundamental to a talking relationship.

Engaging in Dialogue

Buber's "dialogic relation" encompasses what many students at Bronx Community College envisage as a learning situation at its best. Participants in a dialogue explore a given topic, trusting one another sufficiently to expose their reasoning to critical review. Though mutuality can never be complete between teacher and student,[9] teachers win the students' trust if they utilize those accouterments of learning which students deem appropriate. They engage in dialogue. Their talk is comprehensible and proceeds at an appropriate pace. They show vitality and exercise compassion, not belittling students or demeaning them in front of their peers. They recognize the students' knowledge deficits and challenge students to extend their grasp of concept and detail.

Both teachers and students are sensitive to failures of classroom dialogue and view themselves as victims of the others' deficiencies.

Students complain that many teachers "talk and talk and don't ask questions or involve the student. How would they know whether students understand? Teachers need feedback."

Teachers, they say, appear to regard questions from students as unnecessary interruptions of their own mellifluous pronouncements. Dialogue remains viable in the classroom only so long as teachers respond to questions "without too much sarcasm, no matter how trivial the questions seem to be," perhaps repeating what they have already said in a new way, not demeaning students by such rejoinders as, "That is a stupid question" or "Are you dumb? It doesn't go like that" or "I don't have the time to answer that, we'll get to it later."

Teachers curb student talk unfairly, students claim, when they regard their own rendering of a topic as the only correct version. "In some English courses, teachers seem to think an author has one thing in mind. A poem can have a thousand meanings. You can't say, 'It's a balloon,'" a student protests. Another laments his history professor's disparagement of his historical perspective, gained at Work-Study sessions of an All-African People's Revolutionary Party in California. "With math teachers there are no arguments. An Afrocenter or Eurocenter perspective on history: there's the tension."

Students concede that teachers should appropriately cut off talk when "the students argue out of ego and not out of knowledge." Teachers may respectfully disagree with irrelevant or uninformed talk and kindly but decisively correct student misstatements without causing embarrassment. "Even if you're wrong, good teachers give you credit for thinking about it. You know someone heard and is showing concern for what you said." "Students are demeaned when teachers let the student say anything and are often too quick to agree with him."

Teachers should recognize that the student's failure to participate in classroom dialogue may arise from fear of exposing educational deficiencies and language difficulties. The same students who are mute in the classroom have been heard expounding at great length on the topic under class discussion in the non-threatening milieu with classmates after the session. "Many students talk after class about the classwork. They agree or disagree with what has been said, they have different thoughts. They're insecure when they talk in class, they fear they're stupid and will be laughed at. It has a lot to do with their background, their family, what they talk about at home."

Teachers see as the major impediment to good classroom dialogue the students' failure to complete the assigned homework. Consequently, they have little of relevance to say. Not only do students misinterpret the text; too often they do not read the text. "Most of our students come into a class when they have been assigned the next topic without having prepared anything," a physics teacher complains."They walk in and sit back: 'Feed me. I'm here.'"

Student passivity in the classroom is a recurrent complaint among faculty. A biology professor recalls:

> I used to try giving misinformation, carrying that through a whole example. No one would correct me. This would amaze me. I would tell them, 'I deliberately made a mistake, and not one of you objected. Is it because you don't understand what I'm talking about? Or is it because you think I should be the one to give you all this information, while you sit there soaking it all up like a sponge?'

Whatever the reason -- whether students neglect to do the assigned reading, or read too hastily, or fear exposing their academic or language difficulties, or regard the teacher as the sole dispenser of knowledge -- too often they are not likely to ask questions or participate actively in classroom discussion.

Pondering the reasons for the students' passivity, an English professor reflects on their discomfort in the student role. Either they fail to recognize their responsibility to participate or they believe they cannot say anything of significance unless they memorize and parrot the text. "Somehow they've gotten wrong messages along the way. They have to understand that there's some effort, some responsibility involved on their part. They're tremendously passive. Maybe they believe that they have nothing of value to say. That's what I try to break them out of. It's very sad, it's very disturbing to me. Outside of class I think they are mature, adult people. In class, they tend not to ask questions simply because they don't feel comfortable in the environment. Maybe they think they're going to look foolish asking a question that's elementary. If you don't try and work with them, they tend to sit there passively."

Passivity may be a learned response to danger experienced in their community, a mathematics teacher suggests. Their life experience may foster passivity as well as aggression. "Often they expect you to teach them without realizing that it's a dynamic interchange of ideas. They can easily become passive, possibly because of the communities that many of them come from, where it may pay to be passive. You live in a world where there's real violence and you shouldn't stick your head out of the window at night when you hear a noise. A bullet could come. So they can easily become passive in order to survive. Some do become aggressive. Young adolescents tend to become aggressive because they fear that if they look too passive, they're an easy mark for violence or aggression. It's a terrible cycle."

Their weariness from multiple responsibilities may be misconstrued as passivity, notes a professor of education. "Some of them are just too tired. They're raising families, they're working and dealing with Welfare, and they're taking courses. Especially at night, watch them walking towards their classes. I know they're coming from work, at 5:30. They drag themselves, they're so tired, but they persist. I think our students have been beaten down so long, they have almost given up hope. "

Though students generally appear passive in the classroom, they respond with alacrity when a topic is introduced that relates directly to their own experience. A student who remains silent in earlier sessions of a sociology class mesmerizes the class when she describes her experiences conducting structured interviews with homeless persons who congregate around the city's railroad and bus stations. "How different they were from the stereotypes," she notes, "and how different from each other." Another student in the same class speaks up for the first time after the teacher alludes to the sensitive manner in which her young son enters the classroom, whispers to her, and then kisses her on the cheek. She talks spontaneously and relevantly about the relationship between parents and children within her own West Indian family. Such spontaneity is easier to elicit in a course in sociology, where students are considerably freer to speak about their experiences, than in mathematics or physics.

To counter student passivity, teachers must provide considerable structure, a mathematics professor proposes. "We have to provide the questions, the structure. In a sense, those are habits that are built over a long time and if they haven't done that before, they don't have the patterns to do it. We must be patient." Other teachers, though, resent the burden placed on them to provide structure. "We must teach them to formulate their own questions," a professor of education protests. "Many students are reluctant to do that. It requires time and diligence and they live in a context where everybody is in a hurry. There's this instant everything."

A fruitful interchange may evolve between the teacher and a few students. "Some students still do read, some are good readers," a history professor acknowledges. "Unfortunately, you get to the point where you, the teacher, depend on these students so much in your classes to carry the burden, and that's not fair to anyone else. Sometimes I even plead with my students: 'Now don't allow Mr. Smith to carry the full burden.'"

The teacher may unwittingly appeal to the articulate few to keep dialogue alive. "In desperation, you are trying to get a conversation going," an English professor recounts."Nothing is happening. You find yourself turning to those who will have the answer, and before you know it, it's a pattern, and those are the only people you're addressing. That's tough. I'm always aware of that. I try not to fall into that trap, but I know I do. It's almost as if you want a friendly face, some response, some recognition that you've asked the question. I think that it's very easy to ignore those who may need you the most." The active participant is, then, "pampered and catered to unknowingly," concedes a Communication professor. "The instructor is pleased that there is somebody to talk to, somebody who understands. That doesn't help the good student rise above where he or she is and have peer challenge and interaction."

To encourage underprepared students, the teacher may resort to spoon-feeding, reviewing material that needs no further review or asking questions that have long since been answered, frustrating better students in the process, since the dialogue is not proceeding at their pace. "Many teachers are very talented and even inspirational, but the students are not giving feedback," a transfer student from a large university observes. "A lot of students are spoon-fed." The teacher may view such spoon-feeding as the only way to "nurse along" a significant proportion of the class.

Classroom dialogue involving a substantial number of participants, though regarded as important by both teacher and student, appears generally to be sporadic.

Starting Out at the Students' Level

"At the students' level" is a constant student injunction. They are reiterating Willard Waller's dicta in his classic treatise on teaching: the teacher "begins where he ought to begin, somewhere near the students' present level." If the teacher "does not try to short-circuit the educational process by force of will and executive fiat, but builds up his case point by point and step by step, he may find that students respect him for his efforts." [10]

Many students, fearful that they may find the teacher's lecture incomprehensible, echo Waller:

> The good teacher puts it in a way slow students can understand and yet not make it boring. . .
> She has a gift for taking the subject and explaining it at your level, which enables you to understand it in larger terms. . .
> She illustrates the simple to get to the complex, the old to get to the new. . .
> He must talk to the student as though the student is a person. Some quote from the book, and the students just don't understand the words. . .
> Sometimes teachers talk way above you. Other students are with their level, so it's pretty tough to be a teacher.

Good teachers, students contend, are able to discern the students' level by "putting themselves in the students' place." "If they can't understand your problem, how can they help you solve it," queries a fifty-year-old student. "Drama was very hard for me. I never saw a live play on a stage, though I read novels before. I found it very hard to know the plots and the conflicts. What was the conflict in "Everyman" was the assignment. Every man has to die and didn't want to die, I said. Vices and virtues was the conflict of that play, the teacher said. Picking the wrong conflict killed my paper. After that I was nervous with the course."

Good teachers proceed not only at the students' level but also at their pace, constantly asking themselves what is being communicated and to whom. Instances are cited where teachers do not obey this injunction: "My English teacher talked on and on, not stopping to discuss or find out where we were," one student charges. "'I know it's overwhelming,' the teacher said. 'But this is college, not junior high school.'" Accusing a biology teacher of not acceding to her pace, another student drops the course. "It was so insulting," she protests. "Not everybody learns so fast."

Many teachers, too, regard starting out at the students' level a sound educational principle.

> Good teachers are able to come down from a high scholarly level to a layman's level. They have the ability to explain something at any level. . .
> They can't get too complicated at the beginning. The work they write on the board must have a simple structure. . .
> They must present something that students can grasp onto. Many of the students coming my way -- maybe I should introduce them to Mozart or Beethoven or Stravinsky. This is the only chance. They're not going to come this way again. So I try to open up their musical experience and include things they are more familiar with and less familiar with.

Teachers must not reveal consternation at the students' lack of knowledge. "You don't blanche and throw up your hands when nobody in the class ever heard of Mussolini. You say, 'This was Mussolini in his time, and this is why he is significant, and this is why an educated person should know what he did.'"

The vocabulary must be within the students' grasp, teachers concede. "Students have difficulty with some of the lectures given by my colleagues," a history instructor notes. "The vocabulary is too rich." An English teacher corroborates. "I just observed a class taught by a graduate student in her twenties, a terrific teacher, and she's going to get better. Her vocabulary included 'prosaic,' 'dichotomy,' 'de facto,' and references to Hieronymous Bosch and Picasso. I had to say to her, 'Students don't have that vocabulary in a beginning English course.'"

Teachers must recognize that they cannot take students' knowledge or understanding for granted. "In order to get students to comprehend the simplest numerical relationships in using engineering and architectural scales, I have to replicate the arithmetic involved," says an instructor in Engineering Technology. "Even dividing 1/2 over 12, I do the simple manipulations to show them how I reach 1/24. There are students in the class who are into calculus, I can see them almost dying of boredom. But for the students who are practically just off the street, with no orientation in high school to drafting or graphics or mechanical drawing, I have to proceed slowly and show them that numbers are involved in all of this."

Nevertheless, tough-minded teachers are critical of excessive deference paid to students. "We spoon-feed students. I don't think we demand independence in learning," a professor of education contends. "I think we almost prepare them for exams. We go far in giving them details. We nurse them along. In the senior colleges they're not going to get that. There's nothing wrong with that as a start. It is ending there that bothers me. You have to start from there and wean them away as the process continues."

"We start where they are. Why in our faculty culture do we place a far greater burden on the faculty than on the students?" a political science professor asks. "Their low level is at a very low level. Sometimes there is a demand to be guaranteed immediate understanding and immediate high grades. There is not enough emphasis on their coming up to my level." He concedes that "Some concepts are difficult to grasp." Sometimes he "underestimates the difficulty."

"I don't think any teacher has an obligation to start out at the students' level," a history professor demurs. "I think that we have to understand that they don't know the subject. That doesn't mean that we have to create Dick and Jane."

"Many of my students think that I teach above where they are, and I explain to them, usually at the very first class, I will not teach at the level where they are," a physics professor states decisively. "I will teach at a level that I think challenges them. They are going to have to make some strides to reach up to the level that I will teach at. After thirty-one years of experience at this game, I think I have a pretty good idea of what that level should be for the various physics courses. I tell them clearly at the beginning that a physics course is not like any other course they may ever take again in their lives. It is not history, it is not English, it is not sociology, they are not going to get through this course by writing something -- whether it is right or wrong, it makes no difference so long as they write well. That's not the way it works here. I think that I'm difficult, and my grading is difficult, and I have a lot of students that drop out of my courses."

"I think they have enough of their level in their lives," suggests an English professor. "They have to understand that there is something else out there. They have too much of one kind of reality, not enough of the other. I think that is why I always make a point of dressing for class, too. I never walk into class without a shirt and tie and jacket. I want them to see that there is such a thing as professional demeanor. I want them to see that there are people who worry about how they look and how they speak and how they behave, and I don't want to be on their level. I want to set a model for them that maybe they can aspire to."

A mathematics professor reinterprets the statement that teachers should come down to the students' level. "I think the students are really saying that they want to feel welcome in the learning environment, they want to be given a chance to learn the formal language, and they disguise it in the way they say it: 'Come down to our level.' But I don't think they want the teacher to stay at that level. They want the teacher not to embarrass them at the level that they're on, to teach the formal language, and to interface with them on their language level."

The mathematician's interpretation is probably correct. There remains, though, a difference in emphasis among teachers, the tender-hearted teacher tolerating students inching along to a higher level, the tough-minded teacher pushing for an early plunge into deep water. Later in this chapter I examine further the tough-minded and tender-hearted orientations.

Exuding Vitality

Good teachers are neither textbooks nor automatons, students reiterate, but real, live persons who convey the excitement that they feel in teaching the course. They do not impose a formal and formidable barrier between themselves and the students.

> They are interested in the subject. And lively. I don't know which way they're going to go, but I can follow. . .
> Their enthusiasm is contagious. It shows, not rattle, rattle, rattle, with no time to go back. . .
> They make the atmosphere have some beauty, not just fact, fact. Makes you want to explore the subject. . .
> They're very interested, even though they've covered the material over and over. I'm quick to perceive if the teacher is bored. .   .
> It must be in their blood.

Through the encounter with teachers who are "wholly alive and able to communicate directly to students," the subject comes alive.

Students respond well to teachers who enrich the course with illustrations or anecdotes from their work in the field. "Some one who has worked in the social service field brings examples from his own experience instead of some far-off tribe that Margaret Mead studied in 1921." "He puts something of the personal in, stepping over the boundaries just a little bit. Then students feel they know the teacher a bit. He can't step very far."

Good teachers embellish their message through cultivating the art of talking. "He shouldn't talk in a monotone or a very low voice, like to himself." "If she is too hesitant, she loses everybody's attention."

That a teacher should exude vitality, faculty agree. "If I can't convey the enthusiasm I feel, how can I expect them to get excited about what I'm asking them to read? I don't think you can be effective if you can't convey passion and love for what you are doing," an English professor reflects, and an historian concurs: "One of the greatest compliments any student can say to me is, 'My goodness, you really love your subject!' I know, then, that I haven't burned myself out."

The student though may shift the blame for any classroom mishap onto the teacher through criticizing the teacher's presentation. "If the student doesn't succeed, the onus is on the instructor. 'He talks funny.' 'You can't understand what he says.' 'He gets off the subject.' We're used to being discursive. The student has no sense of having to sift, to generate the important ideas."

Some teachers admit to having lost much of the passion they once brought to their classrooms. A professor of history comments: "We all came passionately committed to teaching the subject we were trained in. But our energies are dissipated by teaching five sections of the same course, semester after semester. I'd love to teach an elective in my field, but I can't get enough students. My energy flags and, while I am still committed to the discipline and to my students, I know that I have stopped growing. I don't keep up with the field, I don't read the literature, I don't feel challenged intellectually. "

Contributing to an erosion of the teacher's passion is the lack of positive response from administration and students. "There is the frustration of doing the same thing year after year and not getting feedback that you're doing a good job. There's no recognition from the administration. And sometimes I think many of the students don't really care. You could just as well do a poor job. Some do care. You know it by the end of the semester because they want to know the next course you are going to be teaching. A lot, though, don't care. There's not much of a challenge," an accounting instructor ruefully concedes.

Some teachers recall the early years at the college when there was a greater diversity of courses and a greater number of intellectually challenging students. "I didn't expect to be a community college teacher," a history professor reminisces. "I found I had no mobility. I came here in 1970. The students then were no worse or better than at the universities where I had taught. It was still palatable. There was an intellectual liveliness in class. It was fun to teach. Students were highly motivated. By the mid-seventies, remedial requirements had multiplied. In 1975 there were over one hundred history majors. Now there are two or three."

Other teachers allude to the pleasure they continue to derive from teaching, however underprepared their students. Of the three instructors quoted below who speak of their love of teaching, the first two have doctorates, while the third completed three years of graduate study at a major university. This fact may help to counter the notion often prevalent in community colleges that scholarly teachers have no desire to teach poorly prepared college students.

> The teaching I still love to do. I think that's really my forte. I love the students. I have good rapport. There's a lot of life. I'm more tired than I used to be. The class is still fun. I really mean that. I still get laughs. When I can't do that, I'm out of here. (sociology) . . .

> I'm a teacher. I just love teaching. Of course I would like teaching a course in abstract geometry to people who just want to know about Lobachevski in geometry. It would be marvelous. But I am not terribly unhappy teaching remedial courses. I get satisfaction out of it. . .

> Many of us found that we were teaching courses that we didn't dream would be in our future when we began teaching. Nonetheless, I've gotten to enjoy it. I enjoy teaching the introductory level in math. Often we are dealing with adults who reenter the school after many years out, we have different psychologies to deal with.

Some teachers, then, are frustrated that they fail to elicit the vitality and the passion they are capable of. Others find unexpected pleasure in engaging the new, nontraditional students.

No Role Confusion

Successful teachers demand respect and exercise control; otherwise students, abhorring a vacuum, are likely to take over. Even those students who are occasionally the culprits disapprove of disorder in the classroom.

> A teacher should be firm and in command. Some students take over and drown out the class. . .
> In Bio, when we went though the reproductive system, they would carry it completely away from the subject. They have a tendency to stray from what we're discussing. The teacher would have to demand order. . .

In Spanish, the class was crowded. Sometimes you can't hear the teacher, there are so many speaking. She doesn't say anything about it.

Good teachers maintain a clear differentiation of roles, students emphasize. A teacher who is too friendly with the students doesn't command respect. "She should be nice, but not so nice that students take advantage." "You can relate to the teacher but realize that he is the teacher and you are the student."

Teachers who are not circumspect in displaying their moods and reveal too much of their personal lives arouse the students' contempt and may lose control of the class. A teacher is accused of "snapping at everybody. He shouldn't bring his personal feelings into class. If he's mad, he takes it out on the whole class." Another is accused of failing to distinguish between his public and private persona.

There was a lot of misunderstanding in one class and the teacher hasn't regained the class. He asked the students what they wanted to know about him. They asked about his children, and he said he had three girls. 'Where do they go to school,' a student wanted to know. 'Bennington,' he responded. 'Would you send them here to the community college,' they pried. It wasn't their business and he shouldn't have hesitated. He should have said, 'No.'[11]

The distance between teacher and student, though, should not be unnecessarily stretched, students concur, teachers raising themselves inordinately high, with students far below.

The teacher in my English class was the overseer, the lord, and treated us like kids. I dropped the course. . .
A teacher who looks down on you when you make a mistake really discourages you, and you have to have great will power or that will put you back and you'll be afraid to try again, fearing embarrassment. Teachers should make a student feel that both can learn at the same time, that they are learning too, they don't know everything. They should be able to concede, 'I don't know' or even, 'I made a mistake.'

It is appropriate that students as well as teachers maintain a clear differentiation of roles. Foreign students are critical of what they see as a lack of respect for the teacher among American-born students. "It's either overt or subtle. They may change the topic of discussion. Or they feel free to say to the teacher, 'Why do you pick on me? Don't you like me?' 'Why did you give me that grade?' And a lot of teachers are afraid or don't want to get involved." In Barbados, in contrast, "Nothing disrespectful was tolerated." In Guyana, "Discipline was quite military. The teacher was likely to hit the student with a ruler for infractions. The students usually bonded together to fight the system, the best way being to get good grades." And "At home in Somalia, we respected teachers as fathers. Here, students don't respect the teacher. They don't behave politely. They interrupt with 'hey,' not, 'Can I interrupt, professor?' 'That's bullshit,' they say to the teacher."

"In foreign countries, teachers are respected and put on pedestals. No one dares to talk back to them," a teacher born in Puerto Rico confirms, whereas, "We have a lot of students here who come into the classroom with the attitude, 'Well, if you are so good, teach me.'" The freedom permitted here to be disrespectful to the teacher appears to be contagious. "Though West Indian students erect pedestals for their teachers at home, and impugn American students for their disrespect of the teacher, yet many quickly take on the coloration of the American student in the American classroom."

Disrespect from American students is hardly universal, a history professor interjects. "I can only speak for myself. I know that even when students don't know how to pronounce my name, they always say, 'professor.' Somebody even uses the simple word, 'teacher.' And one can tell after a few sessions how the initial hostility and even arrogance of some give way to respect."

The teacher at Bronx Community College, though not accorded a pedestal, is not subject to the incivility toward teachers observed by Howard London in a New England community college, whose students came from the white working class. "Social class struggle in miniature goes on in the classroom," London reports. Students there show little deference to teachers, especially to teachers in the liberal arts curriculum or middle-class teachers of vocational courses.[12] Students here are not engaged in a social class struggle with teachers in any curriculum. There may be boisterousness, and an occasional verbal attack and lack of restraint which has to be contained, but there seems a pervading respect for the teacher, despite the students' critical comments.

Respect is seen by the foreign student as a two-way street. American teachers do not always demand respect. A Jamaican student vividly describes the first encounter of a professor at Bronx Community College with his new class:

In Jamaica where I am from, professors came to the classroom appropriately dressed to suit their role. You would never see a professor smoking, and often wondered if they even used the toilet. Whenever a professor entered the classroom, students would rise to greet him, as a form of respect, and there would be total silence in the room.

When I came to Bronx Community College, my professor entered the classroom, his hair was wild, his shirt, loose around his neck, no tie, and on his feet he wore what were once white sneakers but now, dark and tattered. With a cigarette in one hand, and a styrofoam cup of coffee in the other, he placed his cup on the desk and, by lifting his leg over the back of the chair, the professor took his seat. There was no form of greeting. He proceeded to give his name and to check the names of students that were present.

I was so shocked that I heard nothing he said but noticed that he lit one cigarette after the other and that the coffee cup became his ash tray.

A woman next to me pulled out a bag of potato chips and began to crunch. She was so loud, I had no alternative but to turn and look at her. My mind flashed to Jamaica, and I remembered the day I tried to sneak a candy in my mouth and was ordered by my professor to write one hundred times: 'The classroom is not my dining room and it does not behoove me to eat there.'

I thought to myself, This is truly America. A free country.

Compassionate and Caring

Students admire the "caring" quality of teachers but are ambivalent about "spoon-feeding." Many teachers express similar ambivalence. The demarcation between "caring" and "spoon-feeding" is not always clear-cut.

Caring teachers evince a personal interest in each student primarily through helping to resolve academic problems, students assert, and they point to the personal involvement of an English Composition teacher. "Because I saw him show interest in my work, I did better. He'd put a comment on my paper, sometimes with detail. Another teacher was a maniac. The whole class was failing and she didn't know who was there."

Teachers are admired who give of their time freely, inside the classroom and out. "Teachers here care about our learning and go out of their way to help," says a student who grew up under the British system in Jamaica. "I was comparing. I'm amazed at the time the professors take to help students." They are disdainful of teachers who never have time to speak to them outside the classroom and whose lights are off in their office so students won't think they're there. "Students can walk in here any time they want," one department chairperson volunteers. "They feel so comfortable here. I was just on the phone with a student who's having difficulty with the nursing department. He said, 'Maybe you can talk to somebody.'" The last time I saw this teacher he was serving coffee to evening students in the large entrance hall of a classroom building.

Students are quick to discern a teacher's sensitivity to the culture of lower-class minority students. "The teachers here at school should understand our background, our parents didn't have the time to be interested. Many teachers here, though they come from the middle class, do understand points of view of students who are lower class. They understand the cultures." Teachers unfamiliar with the cultures that students grew up in can transcend their deficiency. "My English teacher gave us black writers to read," an African-American student recalls. "She herself doesn't understand where they're coming from. I soon realized what was the problem. I wrote my disagreement and she gave me an A, said I was a good writer."

Students scoff at teachers who fail to comprehend the meaning of time in students' non-leisured lives. "Some teachers are like machines. They're so, 'We do this at a certain time.' They don't allow for things like a train was late or a baby was sick, or you had to spend the whole day at Social Service to get money for Day Care fees, and then they said, 'Come back tomorrow.' You couldn't do your homework. They think you have nothing to do but go home and study for this class."

They deride teachers who reveal their discomfort with inner-city minority students through avoiding confrontation on racial topics. "'I'm not going to mess with these people,' one teacher said. Male teachers get uptight, they're supposed to be able to control the situation." Teachers who protest too much that they do not discriminate are also revealing their discomfort. "There's the teacher who says, 'It doesn't make any difference whether you're black or white, you'll get the same grade.' Why does he remind us? A person who has constantly got to tell me."

They are disconcerted by teachers who seem to equate blackness with dullness. "Why do some teachers talk down to you as though you were a child," a student queries. Teachers who anticipate dullness among minority students may have their anticipations rewarded.[13] "In Communication, the entire class is black. It seems to be moving so slowly. When the teacher talks, it's as though he's speaking to a bunch of morons. He repeats and repeats. He anticipates a slow class and gets it."

Antagonism between minority students and white faculty has surfaced in other research. Weis attributes such antagonism to the low academic level of the students at the urban community college she studied and the differences in class and race between faculty and

students. White faculty enjoy their experience at the predominantly
black school, but their enjoyment derives from non-teaching activity
such as becoming dean or head of a department, coaching the baseball
team, or establishing good relations with colleagues and
administrators. Only black teachers among the faculty she interviewed
indicate that the students they taught contributed to making their
experience at the college enjoyable. Generally only teachers who have
lived in the ghetto or had other previous contact with ghettoized
minorities can feel comfortable with those "other" than themselves,
Weis concludes.[14] In their study at the City University of New York,
Lavin and associates also indicate that some faculty see minority
students as strangers, distinguished by physical appearance, dress,
manner, and language. Though many faculty members are sympathetic
to open admissions, "in all probability the antipathy to minority
students was widespread enough to surface" in their data.[15]

Teacher-student relations at Bronx Community College appear to
have a different texture.[16] Teachers are appalled at the low academic
level of students, but most give little indication of antipathy to the
color, class, or cultural style at this predominantly third-world school.
Nevertheless, racism is alive and well at the college, at least among
faculty, a nonwhite instructor attests.

> I never talked about this with anybody at the college because it's
> damaging. A lot of good things have happened here, but there are
> people here who are clearly racist. It happens inadvertently. A
> person who said, in a room with about eight people present, some of
> the top-ranking people in the college, 'If you've seen one black,
> you've seen them all.' The black president of the college was sitting
> there and he turned and gave a very mild admonishment. That is his
> responsibility but it is also his style. I wasn't even astonished. The
> other people were silent. Nobody made another comment about it.
>   There were other instances. After certain confrontational
> departmental business was over, a person in my department said,
> 'Those blacks stick together.' That startled me but I wasn't surprised
> because, again, I had had other subtle references. That was said
> openly in front of all members of the department. No one in the
> department, white or black, stood in outrage, to say, 'What in the
> hell are you talking about? This is crazy.'

Students, though, "are likely to read many behaviors as racist when
it's absolutely not true. Charging somebody as racist is easy," the
instructor points out. He does not give credence to such charges until
he himself has investigated. Teacher activity in the classroom may be
misinterpreted by students as racist.

Most of the teachers here are good, but some have behavioral characteristics that are not just elitist but are arrogant and they might very well have nothing to do with race or ethnicity or gender. It's some personal characteristic that turns students off. A faculty member who closes the door to his classroom and locks it from the inside when the bell sounds. I know several faculty members do that. The student has to interpret that. He could say, 'Well, I was late, I deserved it.' There will be at least one student who is going to say, 'That person can't stand Latinos. He locks the door to keep me out.' And then he tells three more and it starts floating around out there and it' s alive. I don't think that's necessary behavior. You can make demands without doing those things which put the image at risk.

There are teachers who are not very good at the most important interaction that we have -- the technique of questioning students in the classroom. You can ask a question of the student without putting the student down, making students feel that they're ignorant or dumb. There's nothing racist about being a poor questioner, but students read it that way.

Are minority students more comfortable with minority faculty? Student opinion appears divided. Questioned by a white interrogator whom they know and feel comfortable with probably tempers their responses. Some students favor increasing the number of minority teachers. Students, they say, are likely to feel more at ease and more motivated with one of their own.

I don't like to mention this point. At last I have a black professor. In chemistry. I never looked forward to a professor being white or black. I've been geared all the time to seeing white professors. But with him I was aware. It's a fleeting feeling. (Black Guyanan)
Maybe they need some more minority teachers. Sometimes students respond more easily. It shouldn't matter. (Jamaican)
I think there should be more minority teachers, especially in sciences. There are none in physics, one black in engineering. Students probably would be more motivated with minority teachers. (Jamaican)
If they are professionals, if they have the ability to teach, why not? (African American)

A black female professor recognizes that she serves as a magnet for many black students who see her in maternal guise. "Coming from the same ethnic background as a majority of my students, they find me," she observes. "I was born here, my family's from the Caribbean, and I'm obviously black. I know the different languages, I know the different cultures. And then, my late husband was from Guinea. So, my students send their friends to me. There's this perception of me as being very much like them. Then there's this whole thing that if I grew up in the South Bronx and I made it, they can too. So I'm a role model, even for the guys. That transcends my gender, which for many of our male students is a problem because they come from these paternalistic, patriarchal cultures. Also I'm old enough now to be their mother and they don't want to disappoint me. When they take exams, they ask me, was I proud of them. I'm not sure I want it to be that way, but it is that way."

Some students are equivocal about increasing minority teachers on campus. If teachers have an empathic understanding of cultural differences, their ethnicity or race should not become an issue.

> I think it's just fine the way it is. The ones they have, they know what they're talking about. (Puerto Rican)
> It doesn't bother me at all that most students are black and teachers are white. (African-American)
> I'm not into too much of the minority thing. You may think they will help you better, but they don't. Black Americans, so far down, so much animosity. They are very resentful toward black West Indians. They envy West Indians. They see you taking their jobs away. (Barbudan-Antiguan)

Again, are minority students more comfortable with minority faculty? Their responses are divided between "We need more minority faculty" and "Let well enough alone." The "need for more" appears to be in the ascendancy.

The care and compassion that teachers at Bronx Community College offer students seem to derive largely from the students' dependence. "They'll initiate the contact," a teacher observes. "A student at a private college would probably try solving the problem without contacting the faculty member. Here there's a tendency to rely on the faculty."

Students are deficient not only in academic background but also in motivation for academic study. Motivating them requires personalized teaching. "Here at the community college we can't assume the lecture means much to them, that they have the same interest, the same drive to do homework," an English professor observes. "We need to motivate the students. We have conferences with them, do group work, individualize. If you taught in high school, you know what to do. You learn their names -- know their names the first week. A more personal touch. Praise them. You have to get them to trust you, win their confidence. They feel cared for here. We're a social agency and an academic institution."

Teachers refer with pride to the accolades they have received from former students. A chemistry teacher recounts one prideful experience.

Students come in and expect us to recognize them from five years ago because of what they felt was a warm cocoon here. There are enough of them who come back, they really make us feel good.
I had one yesterday, a young woman, she's still here in the college; she came back to talk with me. She was in my lecture and in somebody else's lab class . She was failing lab. I invited her to come to my office. I talked with her for a while and we went through some exercises on how to learn. I was trying to teach her how you know when you know something. A nice little exercise that we all learn. You've got to be able to describe it, you have to be able to talk to somebody about it, you've got to be able to write about it extemporaneously. We went through some exercises to prove to her that she could do it, around some objectives in the course. She was thrilled. She said, when she left, 'This has been so helpful. I think I can make the honor roll if I do this all the time.' And I said, 'Come back and tell me when you do.'
She came back yesterday to tell me she made the honor roll. I can tell you how she will affect me. I'll remember her as forty people who came back, it felt so good.

Most students who leave the college do not return to acknowledge care and compassion, the teacher cautions. Nobody is likely to hear from the students who neither graduate nor continue their studies elsewhere.

Pushing Students To Extend Their Grasp

Good teachers know their subject intimately, students indicate, and know what they want to cover each class hour: "They make the pupils feel they are really interested and dedicated when they come with good lectures and not all out of the textbook. They give information that is new and not thought of before." "They must know the material so well, be so comfortable in presenting it to you, they make it enjoyable. Sometimes not enough information is coming through, the course is not put together well enough."

Can teachers at a community college provide intellectual challenge and excitement for the best students and at the same time accommodate the underprepared? Burton Clark answers in the negative. Teachers in the Open Door college, "controlled by the multitude," cannot lead their students, he says, but must adapt to them. The mass enterprise in higher education encourages a "sovereignty of the poorly qualified" and inevitably entails lowering standards of admission and attainment.[17]

Teachers at Bronx Community College stand before a class where only a minority of the students are ready to immerse themselves in and weave their lives around the learning process. They display two dominant orientations in their relations with students: the academic orientation of the tough-minded, who maintain rigorous academic standards and cool out students failing to meet these standards, and the social-service orientation of the tender-hearted, who spoon-feed students, reducing or simplifying course content and inflating grades so that failures or withdrawals are minimal. Perhaps all teachers at the college combine the two orientations in some measure, though for each teacher one orientation predominates.

Tough-Minded Teachers:
An Academic Orientation

Tough-minded teachers adhere to what they regard as a single academic standard throughout the university and are reluctant to compromise in teaching open admissions students. "There's a liberal form of racism here," a professor of physics warns. "Teachers feel that students don't have what it takes; therefore, be charitable to them. They do have capabilities, but they have not been challenged. They are survivors. They cope. It's better if they are challenged earlier. If we tell them what it takes to succeed, some will do it." "Teachers give up too quickly on students," an English professor affirms. "I can see that in attitudes, in snide remarks. 'Oh yeah. I'm asking them to read Madame Bovary. Ha! That's a laugh.' Why not? Why not teach Flaubert? Why not, Dickens? Just because it's a bulky novel, you think they won't read it? Why lower the standards? Why lower the level?"

The teachers require that students engage in what Richardson, Fisk, and Okun define as "texting" rather than "bitting."[18] With "texting," students are expected to read critically the assigned material and write an essay or report, evaluating and applying the material in a manner appropriate to the discipline. The process is slow and arduous, not only for the students but also for the teacher, who has to prepare students for the task and review their products. "Bitting," in contrast to "texting," usually requires that students learn discrete facts such as a list of names or dates or definitions outside a larger context and then give them back, perhaps on a multiple-choice test.

Tough-minded teachers devise a variety of approaches to preserve high standards without losing students, although the failure/withdrawal rate in their classes remains considerably higher than that of their tender-hearted colleagues.

A professor of history stresses broad historical patterns, "not cluttered with minutiae."

> I would have high standards, but not necessarily trivial standards. There is a distinction between detail and profundity. Much of what passes for knowledge in a four-year college is that of detail. (He has taught at New York University, City College, and The New School). I think one can eliminate some of that and still give the broad lessons of history.
>
> The fact is that no one civilization ever developed everything completely by itself, and that we are the product of what the Europeans did, who in turn were influenced by the Muslims and by the Byzantines, who were influenced by the Romans, who were influenced by the Greeks and the Egyptians. So there's a sort of relay race in all of history. And one of the reasons we stand so high is that we stand on other people's shoulders. The third world is now standing on our shoulders. At any one time in history the so-called advanced peoples were relatively backward, whether they be the German barbarians at the time of the fall of Rome or the Japanese at the beginning of the nineteenth century; this shows that there is no innate ethnic superiority. That is a profound lesson which has nothing to do with detail. And so it is possible to give a meaningful course at any level and not clutter it with minutiae.

Another history professor prepares students exhaustively for essay examinations: "I tell them what an essay should be, the elements of the essay that a teacher would expect.I give them lists of potential questions, and I tell them that they should study to get the big picture rather than try to get bogged down with minutiae because nobody remembers all the facts."

Professors of mathematics work at routing student fears of their subject. "Everybody is capable of learning calculus," one professor remarks. "It's a matter of having the will. Many of our students believe they cannot, they believe that minorities cannot. American-born blacks have some of that belief. Our African students don't have that belief at all. They're very clear about the fact that they can do math." "Often students think that they must have a special gift in math even to succeed on a normal, average level," says another professor. "Once you get below the level of the truly endowed individual, students, I think, are pretty much the same. If they develop certain skills and certain strategies, they can attain the necessary knowledge. You can make them aware of this."

Students of calculus receive more help in and out of class than is customarily available in a college mathematics course. "We hold ourselves to a high standard in calculus, but we're willing to extend ourselves, I think, in a very special way to help students reach that standard," a mathematics professor affirms. "We enhance our high expectations with a reasonable learning environment. Our faculty has changed with the open admissions experience. We reach out more. We put into place more learning avenues. With good notes given to the students, with tutoring laboratories, and with frequent testing and retesting, we can have high standards without a high failure rate." This professor inadvertently discovers verification of his own high academic standards. Wandering around the hall in the mathematics building at Rutgers, he sees a differential equations examination and the answers on the bulletin board. "I teach differential equations here year after year, so naturally I had to look. It was my exam. They ask the same questions at Rutgers as we do at Bronx Community College." (There are three calculus tracks at the college, the most rigorous being for students entering mathematics and science-based fields.)

Students of varying ability in physics are encouraged to study together in groups, good students serving as mentors for the underprepared. "Those students who want to learn will gravitate to the better students and ask them for help," a physics professor observes. "I think having a mixture in a class is beneficial to all groups. The better students who try to explain the material sharpen their own skills and their own understanding."

Teachers striving to prepare their students to meet the standards of senior colleges or accrediting authorities find tough-mindedness a necessary attribute. "We have an obligation here, especially for engineering students. Our graduates are going to go on to the four-year college, if not to City College, then to Rensellaer Polytechnic and other fine schools. Those who do make it through here are getting an excellent preparation," notes a physics professor. An accounting professor speaks of his obligation to the students and to the college. "When we send a graduate off to work at Con Ed or Nynex, they expect a certain minimum skills level. The American Institute of Certified Public Accountants has determined what our students have to know. Our reputation becomes worthless if we don't produce good students. It would be easy to say, 'Let's just inflate the grades and pass everybody through,' but in the long run, it's detrimental. I probably have a very poor reputation as far as grades go when I have 50 percent failure or dropouts, but I try to make up for it by giving a good course." (The introductory accounting course at the college meets five hours a week, in contrast to an equivalent three-hour-a-week senior college course.)

Tough-minded professors demand more from students than they think they are capable of giving. A history student expresses her gratification.

> History was the biggest challenge for me. There is a lot of reading. You have to know your work or the teacher will embarrass you. He assigned a book on the Russians. I'm learning so much at once. Now, when I read the papers, I know what's going on.
> He gives all essay tests. You have to practice writing before his exam. I try to get a rough form for the essay -- all the important questions and supporting data. (How do you know the test questions?) I know what he spends the most time on. (A tenth-grade dropout who started out at the college with all remedials, she anticipates transferring to a university and majoring in international law.)

Students who seek the challenge of a tough-minded instructor feel their intellectual capacity denigrated when teachers water-down their courses, including only what a student needs to know in order to pass. Such teachers are initiating a self-fulfilling prophecy, one Knowledge-Seeker asserts, "demanding little and then seeing the student not as victimized but as getting away with murder." Other students agree.

> The worst quality a teacher can have is to make the work too easy. He just tells enough of what you need to get by. He should go into more detail. . .
> One teacher treats us like children. She asks simple, dumb questions, gives us simple assignments, not college level. . .
> Students should have three to five books on a subject, really looking at the subject from various angles. If we had even two books to read, it would be more of a learning experience. The more that is required of me, the more I will do. . .
> Students complain when teachers expect a lot, and some teachers get intimidated. I prefer and respect a teacher whom everybody hated. He stood his ground.

Tender-hearted teachers imperil a student's transition from the two- to the four-year college, students preferring a tough-minded teacher fear. "English and Math at Hunter seem much harder. When you transfer, you must feel at home, be used to it." "It's absolutely a disservice to students here not to be prepared for what they're going to get in a four-year college." Students are apprehensive that, like Sisyphus, they will continue stumbling up the steep hill but at the critical juncture of transfer to a four-year college, they may fall, to begin again the long, laborious trek.

Tender-hearted teachers are accused not only of deflating the content of a course but also inflating the grade, indiscriminately doling out high grades that cannot be maintained after transfer to a four-year college. "A community college with open enrollment is a weeding ground, a preparatory thing for a four-year college. But if I get all these good grades for doing not quite superior work and then go to a four-year school, it would be a trauma, blow my mind. What happened to all your brilliancy, I'd ask myself."

Potential transferees to a four-year college suspect that standards are lowered and grades raised at Bronx Community College as a salve for the minority student population. Hunter and Lehman are perceived as more rigorous academically than Bronx Community College because they have more students who are white and middle class. "There's a slacker policy here in workload and grades. Hunter College is more acceptable because there are middle-class students there, not only minorities. And at Lehman, the teacher expects you to know more. They give you more paper work, their tests are harder. The teacher expects more of them because they have mainly a white population."

It may be asked why students who seek high academic standards are attending a community college. Let them matriculate at a four-year college in their freshman year, where they can more easily get the higher standards they opt for. Many of them, out of school for a number of years, are unsure of their academic competence when they matriculate.[19] They have heard that teacher-student relations at a four-year city college are likely to be more impersonal than at Bronx Community College and they do not want to forego the nurturing relation with teachers they find here. "There is a wide range of students here. I think this is an excellent school to give people a chance," one Seeker after Knowledge declares, shortly before her departure. "Some students here are even better than many at Dalton and Bronx Science (which she attended). I'd recommend this school to anyone out of school for a long time, but not to stay for a long period. I felt I had been out of school so long, I couldn't compete." (She is twenty-nine. She remains at Bronx Community College for three semesters and shortly after the interview transfers as a scholarship student to a private college nearby).

Students seeking tough-minded teachers are more likely to have attended Bronx Community College in the early 1970s, when the college was regarded by the community as an academic institution, than in the late 1980s, when remedial and terminal vocational curricula predominate. Nevertheless, every class in the two decades has proponents of high academic standards.

I have assumed high standards throughout the senior colleges. Academic standards were not high in the City University during the 1960s, the decade prior to open admissions, though perhaps in retrospect they seemed so, observes the psychology professor, Kenneth Clark, who taught at City College for almost thirty years prior to open admissions. The past has been romanticized, he asserts, the process of higher learning has always been a gamble. Very few students at any time, even among the privileged groups, were ever able to think independently and creatively. Rather, students were trained to get good grades.[20] Thomas Sowell notes that double academic standards exist on practically every campus, although not necessarily in a majority of courses.[21] The assumption that high standards are always maintained at most four-year colleges, then, may be illusory.

Tender-Hearted Teachers:
A Social Service Orientation

Many students enter Bronx Community College with multiple handicaps. They have been immersed from early years in a predominantly oral and not a reading and writing culture and they have had insufficient exposure to the English of the classroom. A year or two of remedial courses may not prepare them adequately for college-level work. "Our students come to us so ill-prepared that they could not survive in a four-year college," a mathematics professor affirms. "The teachers in a four-year college are not willing to put up with the terrible study habits and, in a sense, we hold their hands and try to turn them into sufficiently well-performing students. Our function is vital and singular."

Given students' inadequate preparation, all teachers at the college must of necessity "level down" in varying degrees, perhaps through redoubling efforts at defining concepts and providing illustrations, through repetition, and through distributing outlines or study questions. Nevertheless, teachers veer in the direction either of the tough-minded, who attempt to uphold rigorous standards in course content and grading, or the tender-hearted, who are more lenient on both counts.

Tender-hearted teachers agree with students who say, "This is remedial, open admissions, a good place for people with a minority education to build themselves up to a four-year college. The senior system I imagine to be much harder, rougher than this. You go through the hurdles here, train for that." Teachers are likely to reduce the scope of the course and simplify reading and writing assignments. Tests in most subjects are multiple-choice and grades are likely to be high.

"We do tend to water down," concedes a foreign language professor. "Back in the late 1970s and in the 1980s I saw a lot of departments going into their syllabi and saying, 'Well, we're having trouble completing this. Let's move it on to the next course.' I don't know what's happening in the senior colleges. They might have been doing the same thing." "I think in fact there are two standards within the City University," declares a sociology professor. "The community at large expects there to be two standards. Community college students might be devalued by ten points or so. My expectations are lower and so I participate in this two-tier system in content and grading. The hope is that as students go from introductory to more advanced classes at the community college they are building their skills so that they can do better at the senior-college level. I have a higher standard in my more advanced classes. I require writing throughout -- papers and research -- but I still feel that if I were in a different setting I would probably expect more. There's no doubt about that. I say openly in my first class that my good students will find this class relatively easy, that if I have to make a choice, I'm going to choose the struggling learners."

Tension between Tough-Mindedness and Tender-Heartedness

Tension is on occasion palpable between the tough-minded and the tender-hearted among the faculty. A physics professor complains:

> We are a training ground and we should not be passing students through who are going to fail later on. This is a place for them to try and see how far they can go with their lives. Many of them are late bloomers, as we know. But we're spoon-feeding them and lulling them into a false sense of security that they're 'A' students because they show up and sit in class. I have students who want to know, 'How can I fail? I've been here every hour. I go to other courses every time and I pass.'
>
> I think that we are misrepresenting ourselves if we don't have some reasonable set of standards. I don't have a lot of failures because students withdraw before they have a chance to fail. I

would say that in a typical class of engineering physics, I could start out with 25 students and finish with 50 percent. For liberal arts courses (in physics), we tend to lose a little bit less. Engineering physics courses are more difficult, taught at a higher level.

I think those that succeed are well able to go on. We've always had excellent reviews by the four-year colleges of our engineering students. However, we can start with 100 engineering science students and two years later graduate only 10 or 15. After six or seven or eight years, maybe 25 will get out. Not much more than that. Some are here a long time because they're working full time, so the percentages are very, very small. Those that do get through can handle it. And the others were given an opportunity. It didn't work out for them in engineering. They may have switched into another field, into accounting, and succeeded there. And that's what the community college should be: a place for opportunity.

Has the college over-extended itself, this physics professor ponders, "letting students come back over and over, keep taking academic suspension, and coming back again. Maybe we've overdone that, and that's become very costly." He concludes by embracing the notion that, "In principle, I think we are doing what we are supposed to do, we are supposed to provide an opportunity."

All tough-minded teachers do not have the fortitude of the physics professor. Despite their attempts to adhere to tough-mindedness, faculty generally concede that assignments are not as rigorous as they might be for an academically well-prepared class. "What would challenge that truly superior student would cause the teacher to lose eighty or ninety percent of the remaining class members. I think that anybody who denies that is lying," declares a professor in Communication, and a political scientist assents. "In content, in substance, I do not give as much as I might give in a senior college. It's slow going. There are copious explanations. Community college instructors realize they will have to make allowances. A maturation process is going on here. If we challenge them as much as we can within their maturation parameters, they will go on and hopefully, eventually transfer."

Lower educational standards become inevitable in music with the elimination of admission requirements for music majors. A professor of music expresses her consternation: "When I started teaching here twenty-one years ago we had to audition on an instrument each student who became a music major. We had an interview and placement exams. Gradually over the years, the auditions stopped. To keep the department functioning, we've had to accept anybody who comes in off the street and says he or she wants to be a music major. A person with no music background can now be a music major. They don't have to play an instrument, they don't have to know how to read music. That is a gross compromise in educational standards, even to get students into a classroom. If you don't have students, you don't have a job. I highly disapprove of that."

The poorly qualified, if not sovereign, at the least are highly influential. Though teachers are troubled by the relaxation of academic standards, they find themselves in an insoluble bind. "I think it's a very real issue," concludes a Communication professor. "We can't deny it. I don't know how to answer it. I don't know that we are really trying to answer it, and I don't think that politically we can answer it."

Tough-minded teachers from departments of physics, biology, accounting, and history pour out their sense of disillusion.

> I do believe there was a long period in which faculty felt they were making some gains. They thought they were raising the levels of the students' aspirations and getting them to work a little bit harder. I think that many faculty are beginning to feel they failed. (physics)

> It is frustrating teaching the basics over and over again, semester after semester, and not seeing much evidence of excellence. (accounting)

> There are failures and withdrawals and repeats. That is wearing. (biology)

> I had a kind of commitment to dealing with kids who were very much like me. The kind of background, in terms of lower class, working class. And I always felt that the kids would be the kind of student that I was, that they would be really interested in education. That's probably one of the greatest disappointments I had in my years here. (history)

> Most troubling is that I cannot convey the intellectual beauty of the science to more of the students. There are so many of them that are just not prepared mentally or psychologically for this encounter and go away with far less than I would like them to go away with,, and that's a tremendous frustration. (physics)

There is some gratification in discovering students, who, initially apprehensive, gain understanding and pleasure in learning.

If I'm teaching a concept in class that I know is difficult, and the students have no awareness of what's going on, even though they're supposed to have read about it, usually it would be a particular topic in accounting, then when I see by the nodding heads or a smile, some feedback, that I've broken through, that's most encouraging. I know that I've accomplished something.

I have a lot of students who come to history very apprehensive, with anger at the requirements, at being forced to read, and who somehow move from not understanding to showing an ability to amass facts and put them into some kind of sensible order, and to showing by their questioning and writing that they are enjoying learning -- not just history, but enjoying learning. That's most satisfying. I'm gratified when I see students, although there aren't enough of them, turn not into scholars but into people interested in learning and give every prospect that they will be knowledgeable, thinking citizens. What's most troubling is that so many of them don't.

Most poignantly underlined in the teachers' criticism of the students who sit before them is their frustration at the institutions of our society who, from the students' early years, have allowed such academic underdevelopment to come to pass.

Tension inheres not only between tough-mindedness and tender-heartedness but also between advocates of the terminal vocational and the transfer track. "The lack of progress among students here may be due to the preponderance of terminal degree programs," a physics professor conjectures. "I think we have seen a whole shifting of emphasis (since the early 1970s). Emphasis is very, very important in a college. The college can do a lot of things of a peripheral nature so long as the academic faculty feel they are the central core, that the academic program has to come first, and then we'll worry about the peripherals. The emphasis is in the wrong place."

The good teacher at the community college, it is apparent, must transcend what is usually considered to be good college teaching. He or she must have a touch of the scholar who imparts knowledge, the counselor who engages the student in talk, the actor who presents theater, and the parent who cares. A pervasive disillusionment combined with varying degrees of gratification appears to be the lot of teachers who struggle against the odds to maintain high academic standards.

Notes

1. In the early 1980s blacks comprised only 4 percent of higher education faculties in this country, and Hispanics less than 2 percent. R. Wilson. and S.E. Melendez, *Second Annual Status Report: Minorities in Higher Education* (Washington, D.C.: American Council on Education, 1983), 10.

At John F. Kennedy High School in the Bronx, a school Sara Lawrence Lightfoot selected as a "good" high school, its principal boasts that the minority representation among faculty is 12 percent, though 77 percent of the students are Hispanic, black, or Asian. *The Good High School: Portraits of Character and Culture* (New York: Basic Books, 1983), 72, 86.

2. Arthur M. Cohen and Florence B. Brawer, *The Collegiate Function of Community Colleges (*San Francisco: Jossey-Bass, 1987) , 66-67.

3. Gouldner characterizes *"cosmopolitans"* as low on loyalty to the employing organization, high on commitment to specialized role skills, and likely to orient themselves to an outer reference group. *"Locals,"* he says, are high on loyalty to the employing organization, low on commitment to specialized role skills, and likely to orient themselves to an inner reference group. Alvin W. Gouldner, "Cosmopolitans and Locals: Toward an Analysis of Latent Social Roles, I and II," *Administrative Science Quarterly* 2 (1957): 290.

4. A festering frustration at Bronx Community College is the predicament of faculty in the liberal arts and sciences with fine records in teaching and service to the college community who do not rise above the assistant professor level, despite departmental and college-wide faculty approval, because they lack a doctorate. See chapter nine, "The Doctorate Dilemma." 172-174.

5. Theodore Newcomb, "Student Peer-Group Influence," in *The American College: A Psychological and Social Interpretation of the Higher Learning,* ed. Nevitt Sanford (New York: John Wiley and Sons, 1962):485.

6. The "community college elite" whom Neumann and Riesman interviewed at the selective institutions to which they transferred indicate that, though friends contributed to their success at the community college, faculty interest and support were even more important.. William Neumann and David Riesman, "The Community College Elite," in *New Directions for Community Colleges: Questioning the Community College Role* 32, ed. George B. Vaughan (San Francisco: Jossey-Bass, 1980) 59.

7. Robert L. Kelly, "Great Teachers -- And Methods of Developing Them," in *Association of American Colleges Bulletin* XV1 (March 1929): 49-67, 215-216.

8. Robert C. Wilson, Jerry G. Gaff, Evelyn R. Dienst, Lynn Wood and James L. Bavry, *College Professors and Their Impact on Students* (New York: Wiley-Interscience, 1975), 104-107, 192.

"Students almost universally link their most significant educational experiences to teachers with whom they have had some personal relation in and out of the classroom," Katz and Sanford concur. Joseph Katz and Nevitt Sanford, "The Curriculum in the Perspective of the Theory of Personality Development," in Nevitt Sanford, ed., *The American College: A Psychological and Social Interpretation of the Higher Learning* (New York: John Wiley and Sons, 1962), 427

9. Martin Buber, *Between Man and Man* (New York: MacMillan Co., 1965; London: Routledge and Kegan Paul, 1947).

Maurice S. Friedman, *Martin Buber: The Life of Dialogue* (Chicago: The University of Chicago Press, 1955; New York: Harper Torchbooks, 1960).

10. *Willard W. Waller, On The Family, Education, and War: Selected Writings,* eds. William J. Goode, Frank Furstenberg, Jr., and Larry R. Mitchell, (Chicago: The University of Chicago Press, 1970) , 242.

11. This student appears to be saying, "The school is good enough for us, but I wouldn't expect the professor to send his children here."   The negative appraisal anticipated from the teacher at Bronx Community College contrasts with the positive assessment   from teachers at Miami-Dade Community College in Florida, where faculty seem proud to let it be known that their children and their nieces and nephews have been students at the college.   L. Steven Zwerling, "The Miami-Dade Story: Is It Really Number One?" *Change* January/February 1988: 19.

12. Howard B. London, *The Culture of A Community College* (New York: Praeger, 1978) 75-81.

13. Ray Rist, "Social Class and Teacher Expectations: The Self-fulfilling Prophecy in Ghetto Education,"   *Harvard Educational Review,* 40 (August 1970): 411-451.

14. Lois Weis, *Between Two Worlds: Black Students in an Urban Community College* (Boston: Routledge and Kegan Paul, 1985), 90-93, 97, 85.

15. David E. Lavin, Richard D. Alba, and Richard A. Silberstein, *Right versus.Privilege: The Open-Admissions Experiment at the City University of New York* (New York: The Free Press, 1981), 283.

16. Students who feel generally positive about the faculty and are willing to change aspects of their own culture appear to be   considerably more numerous at Bronx Community College than at Weis' Urban College. Lois Weis, *Between Two Worlds,* 115 ff.

17. Burton R. Clark,*The Open Door College: A Case Study* (New York: *McGraw-Hill Book Company, 1960), 154-155.*

18. Richard C. Richardson, Jr., Elizabeth C. Fisk, Morris A. Okun, *Literacy in the Open-Access College* (San Francisco: Jossey-Bass, 1983), 65-72.

19. Community college students who transfer to elite colleges also recall their lack of self-confidence when they entered the community college. Neumann and Riesman, "The Community College Elite," *New Directions for Community Colleges: Questioning the Community College Role ,* ed. George B. Vaughan, (San Francisco: Jossey-Bass, 1980), 53-71.

20.   Council for Basic Education, *Open Admissions: The Pros and Cons* (Washington, D.C., 1972), 26, 27, 46.

21.   Thomas Sowell, *Education: Assumptions Versus History: Collected Papers* (Stanford: Hoover Institute Press, 1986), 136-137.

Chapter 9

Further Faculty Frustrations

Low Repute in the Local Community

Bronx Community College is well regarded among education professionals. The number of research grants from government, industry, and research foundations awarded the college exceeds that of most community colleges and many four-year institutions. The number of faculty having doctorates is disproportionately high compared with other community colleges.

Yet the college stands in low repute in the local community. Its parents are loath to select Bronx Community College as the college for their children."There is a self-selection process here," a Communication professor observes. "We are not seeing that kid from the New York City public schools whose mother says, 'Let me see your homework. Why did you not have homework?' When teachers say, 'We have students who come from Asia or Africa or the Caribbean and they pay great attention to homework and the homegrown kids don't, what they're not dealing with are all those parents in Harlem and the Bronx and Bed Sty and East Harlem who say to a kid, 'End up at Bronx Community College and I will kill you.' Where parents are concerned about homework and the attitudes toward learning, the children don't end up here because their parents have the sophistication to have made sure that they go elsewhere."

Local high school teachers and guidance counselors try to ensure that their good students do not attend Bronx Community College. They attribute what they consider its low academic quality to an open admissions policy which allows students to drop out of high school, yet pass an equivalency examination and enter college. "I had not realized how seriously open admissions has undermined the position of the teachers in the high schools," remarks a mathematics instructor. "They can no longer say to students that if you do not do X, Y, and Z, you cannot go to college." High schools "steer their better students away from us," a dean complains, "even students who can profit tremendously from starting out in a community college, gaining confidence before moving on to a four-year school."

The academic reputation of Bronx Community College lags in the community even in comparison with other community colleges. "We have a reputation as a school of remediation," notes the Communication professor closely attuned to community sentiment. "I have heard the grandiose things about what returning students say, but we must face the issue of what people say on street corners, and what parents say to their children, and what relatives say, and what high school teachers say."

She cites the chilling reaction to the college displayed by a physician and a cleaning woman she encounters at a local hospital: "I was meeting a friend who is a physician at Harlem Hospital. Hanging around,I was asked, 'Where do you work?' When one of the physicians heard that I work at Bronx Community College, he gasped, 'Oh my God,' and went into a three-minute tirade. A woman who was cleaning chimed in that she would not allow her daughter to attend this college. We see it and we hear it and faculty talk about it because faculty know it. And nobody wants to deal with it."

The telephone call the professor receives from a local high school teacher is equally devastating. "I acquired this little darling in September as a result of domestic difficulties in his family," she continues. "I called all the schools I could think of to enroll him, and they were all quite filled. The only other place for him was the local public high school. In the middle of his first semester he was required to have a series of surgical operations. While he was in the hospital, he kept carrying on about missing his regents exams and going to miss his SATs. People assumed I was doing this, that I was harassing the kid. 'Get well,' I said. 'And if you miss all of the deadlines, for the first year you'll go to a community college and during that year you'll do all of those things. Then you'll transfer in your sophomore year.' I thought I had done God's good work. I got a phone call from the kid's teacher. She's in a rage. She'd been to the hospital to see him and he told her. . . We got into this long battle on the telephone. First, I had not said which community college. I said that it seemed to me a sensible kind of thing, that her rage and hysteria were only going to upset the the kid, and, furthermore, all the things she was saying were just not true. The woman concluded that I was deranged.   She was beside herself that this child was going to come here. There's a message in that."

The community views Bronx Community College as not only a remedial but also a terminal vocational college. Consequently, students opting for a liberal arts transfer curriculum have little reason to want to matriculate unless they are guided by non-academic considerations. "Our entering students perceive that the intellectual atmosphere is not at a high level," the Communication professor continues. "They prefer not to be here. They believe the poor press clippings and they believe their friends. They don't understand how well-educated the professors are. "

The negative community reaction to Bronx Community College may have been energized not only by its emphasis on remediation and terminal vocational programs but also by the unkind words of students who withdrew or failed here. "We need to do something about that. When they come through the door, there's got to be a way of starting the nurturing from the very beginning," suggests a chemistry professor.

Despite local community perceptions, most students at Bronx Community College do not say that they are attending the college because they are "dunces" whereas, if they were smart, they would be at a four-year college and on their "way to becoming something." [1] They are more likely to perceive themselves as "successes," having advanced academically beyond the reach of family and old friends. Limited in their choice of college, they appear grateful that some door to higher education is open to them.

We are looking at a diverse student body. Among students matriculating at the college in Fall 1987, one-third are recent high school graduates, another third are graduates who have been out of school for a number of years, and the final third are equivalency recipients. The population of foreign students is large and continues to grow. Students most sensitive to the low rank of the community college within the community are likely to be recent high school graduates.

The School as a Cultural Wasteland

Students at Bronx Community College lack a rich extracurricular life. At the end of the 1980s the college loses its forensic society and drama workshop. Only two outside speakers appear on campus during the 1989-1990 school year -- Jessie Jackson and Leonard Jeffries.[2] They come at the behest of the Black Student Caucus. "To the students who make the decisions, Jeffries is a hero," a member of the administration explains. "What we consider Culture -- the ballet, the arts -- the Black Student Caucus sees as an all white man's culture. They want to know, 'Why should Bronx Community College have that when our student body is fifty percent Hispanic and forty percent black?' The administration cannot or will not interfere. Sometimes there's a risk in the administration making decisions and easier to let things go. They don't want to invite student ire, especially since the Black Student Caucus represents a large segment of the population. Unfortunately, students at large are not given the chance to evaluate and then possibly to appreciate what other cultures offer."

The failure of the administration to intercede provokes the anger of some faculty, who charge the administration with abdicating its responsibility to provide a viable institutional culture beyond the classroom for its students. "A college by the very nature of being a college is a representative of an elitist process," declares a Communication professor. "There are standards one expects in an elitist institution, and our job is to make sure that students are aware of them, exposed to them, and then make choices. The standards of social decorum and the social graces that are expected to accompany the college experience are neither taught nor encouraged nor reinforced at this institution because it is believed the students are only the students of the street, poor and black and Latino. The week that the Kingsboro Community College was doing "The Messiah" we were showing an Eddie Murphy movie. We never replaced the art exhibit in Tech Two that was part of the building's interior design when a private university had the campus. The cement enclave had been used as a mini art gallery on each floor and there was one bench in the little gallery area where students could sit and enjoy the works. It was not there for my students to see.

"Things here would not be tolerated at Howard University and at the University of Puerto Rico. Things of tone. Students have formal experiences where they sit at a table and have napery and they have other experiences where they wiggle their hips 'til two in the morning. Both make for the totality of the undergraduate experience. We have seen only one side of that. Often in the classroom the instructor is overwhelmed with the task of getting through the syllabus. Ours is a challenging task. Much of what I am asking, I suggest, often has to happen outside the classroom."

Bronx Community College was not always a cultural desert. In the early 1970s, it had an Artistic Manager whom teachers used to joke about as "the Cultural Commissar, who sat in his office and decided which ballet company and which of the touring groups of the Metropolitan were coming," a professor recalls. "We had the Joffrey and the Alvin Ailey and the Julliard. We had theater, lectures, and films. This was an ongoing process. All that stopped at the time of the fiscal crisis in the mid-1970s. The attempt to revive it failed."

The Artistic Manager then turned his considerable talents to theater direction and provided an active theater workshop whose repertoire included Sophocles' *Antigone*, Moliere's *Tartuffe*, Masters' *Spoon River Anthology*, Duberman's *In White America*, Ntsange's *For Colored Girls Who Have Considered Suicide When The Rainbow Is Not Enough*, modern musicals, and more. "He used to work eighteen hours a day when he had a production. Nobody appreciated him. They would destroy his scenery. I think the last thing that happened was that he had scenery on stage ready for a production and somebody destroyed it. Nobody cares." His final production was Oscar Wilde's, *The Importance of Being Earnest*, in 1986. Attempts to revive the theater failed.

"The money's there for outside activities," an English professor discloses. "There's no excuse. They have a budget of $700,000 or $800,000 that can't be put to any other use by law other than for student activities. That money is wasted. We undermine our own projects."

Little effort is expended to make of this multicultural campus an educational and aesthetic resource. "We have so many different cultures here, students are really proud of who they are," the English professor continues. "I see this in class. They love to talk about their traditions, their customs. We don't even take advantage of that. Nothing is done. We have two or three people in the Office of Student Activities and we have no student activities."

Students may have to be gently pushed to attend extracurricular functions, given the "realities of their lives," it is conceded. "One time I went to a lecture here where Rosalind Yallow was the featured speaker," another English professor recalls. "You know, she's a Nobel Prize winner. Her lecture was very sparsely attended. Embarrassingly so. We were sitting with five and six spaces between us. And she was a little annoyed. She said, as I recall, that students must recognize intellectual values. They should have come. If she had been able to hear a Nobel Prize Winning speaker, she would have made it her business to go. Perhaps it could have been better publicized. But look! When she was a college student, did she have to run home and get her child out of Day Care? Did she have a part-time job to go to? It's very hard for our students. I think that people should realize that."

Students at Bronx Community College do not go home to a rich cultural life -- and the college often fails to fill the void.

Teachers versus Administrators

Tension permeates the relationship between administrators and faculty
-- a quiet rumbling, not at all surprising since ultimate decisions
relating to budgetary allocations, faculty hiring, firing, promotions, and
class offerings are made by key administrators.[3]

The tension between the president and faculty began at the
president's first convocation, when he indicated to faculty that he meant
to establish his distance. The tenor of his first address to faculty
continues to rankle. One impassioned reaction:

> At his first convocation speech, he made the announcement: 'I want
> to let you know that I do not have an open door. If you have a
> problem, you will have to go through channels to get to me.' Why
> is he telling me he's not going to have an open door? Why
> doesn't he just say, 'I welcome everybody,' and then tell his
> secretary to make appointments and kind of screen?

The mission of the college changed when the president assumed
office in the late 1970s. "There is a greater emphasis now on the career
(vocational) programs and much less on the college as a miniature if
of Harvard at least of City College. The latter disappeared," notes the
former Acting President. "The change was partly due to the new
president's approach and partly due to the demographic changes in the
borough. Fewer young people were graduating from the high schools
and the quality of the graduates was going down. The president felt that
this was the way we had to go to survive institutionally. If we had
tried to remain a miniature City College, the college would have
continued to shrink."

Admission and retention of students becomes the prime goal of the
new president's administration. To ensure student retention, new career
programs are introduced in the 1980s, notably, paralegal, human
services, nuclear medicine, and x-ray and audiovisual technology. The
college is also increasingly involved in continuing education and
community services.

Liberal Arts faculty view with dismay and resignation the
predominance of vocational studies. "We're a totally anti-intellectual
institution," maintains a sociology professor. "I don't think it's true of
all community colleges. We used to have a strong intellectual push.
Now most of the liberal arts people are just happy to have a job as
appendages to more vocational-oriented departments. Where once they

tended to dominate the landscape at Bronx Community College, now they're very quiet." [4]

Academic faculty serve as administrators for new vocational programs. "I find more and more duties being heaped on my shoulders, and less and less time to carry them out," grieves the chairperson of the physics department. "I have under me nuclear physics, engineering science, astronomy, nuclear medicine, x-ray technology, automotive mechanics, and aviation technology -- seven different areas that I'm involved in, where paper work has to be taken care of. It's just impossible. I can spend four to six hours a week just in meetings. And to have to teach nine hours on top of that!"

Long-standing vocational curricula suffer from the urge to expand vocational programs. "The college gets a block grant," the chair of a long-established vocational department illustrates. "Everything allotted comes out of one pie. The amount is based on enrollment. Whatever a new curriculum gets comes out of your hide and my hide, and it better be a damn good thing for the students and the college!"

Prodded to do so, the president agrees to talk to faculty about his educational philosophy. One professor, eagerly anticipating the talk, is devastated. "He came down and read a nine-year old paper. He's unwilling to come into a room and just talk to us, tell us how he feels about education." The president emphasizes in his talk the critical importance of teachers' commitment, as measured by their zeal in admitting and retaining students. A student body of 8,000, he notes, is bound to have a greater number of successes than a student body half that number.

It is appropriate that the president be concerned with headcount, since the school's budget is determined by enrollment. Nevertheless, he and other administrators introduce a demeaning note when they question faculty commitment, arising perhaps out of their frustration that they themselves cannot directly affect retention. "The president's approach to the faculty is that they are responsible for the success or failure of the students, and that if they don't do what they are supposed to be doing, students will not succeed, that there is a direct correlation between faculty performance and student success," observes the professor who has served as Acting president. "Faculty feel that their role is only part of the picture, that student motivation, student preparation, and institutional support are also important, and this is not in his mental frame."

Other administrators join the fray in quietly derogating faculty. The Dean of Academic Affairs speaks in his newsletter to the faculty of the Retention Handbook that he produced "with checklists of items that faculty should be doing. While we are blessed with a very experienced staff, everyone can benefit by taking a little time to review what we are doing and not doing." He recalls the remark of a retired professor that this was the first time in forty years that he took time out to think about his teaching and to talk about his teaching in and out of his department.[5] "Faculty and students don't get together as much any more," another administrator complains, and recommends that faculty increase their office hours.

The teachers respond in kind. In a survey of teacher attitudes in Spring 1989, most respondents indicate satisfaction with colleague relationships and with teaching. An overwhelming proportion, however, find the academic preparation of students and faculty participation in college decision-making "below average" or "poor," and one-half the respondents also regard academic standards, intellectual climate, and college-wide leadership "below average" or "poor." [6]

Teachers deplore the president's inattention to day-to-day activities on campus. "He is a national leader in so many organizations, on so many boards, he's on a skateboard all the time," asserts a professor of long-standing. "This is a community college. We need a president who can lead, but we also need a president who can lead on the campus."

Though teachers recognize the commitment of the Dean of Academic Affairs to the college, they question the propriety or effectiveness of the Dean assuming the on-campus duties of the president. "The Dean is everywhere. He's the hatchet man. The brunt of everything is on him. He doesn't have an enviable job." "He is extraordinarily dedicated to this college and works incredibly long hours, and really looks to see how many ways he can make things better at the college for students. Nobody can do that for a long time." "He runs the college. Nobody will deny that he is a very hard worker. He badgers everyone, even though he doesn't have jurisdiction. More and more it just causes conflict."

The Dean of Students appears to be caught in another crossfire. To whom does he owe allegiance: the administration or the student? "The Dean of Students in most colleges seems to have more to do with the students than here," a teacher speculates. "His position is so unclear to me. When we had the hearings on the student strike (against higher tuition), the Dean as prosecutor was absolutely bizarre. I thought that they put him in an untenable position. As a student advocate, he should at least have been allowed to stay out of it and not be put in a position where he had to try to make the students seem guilty. It was very strange."[7]

Despite inattention to everyday campus affairs, the president is accused of establishing "an imperial presidency," eroding faculty power, "pushing through changes in the governing structure which are counter-productive." Faculty committees are formed at the administration's request to consider long-term policy, they "make recommendations, the administration expresses thanks, and doesn't even look at the report."

Administrators are insufficiently concerned with the quality of teaching, some teachers conclude. "That's secondary to financial considerations. Look at the incentives for early retirement! The administration wants to get out the high salaries of the experienced teachers that have years under their belt and bring in the low salaries." "They see the faculty as production machines. If we have to raise the class size to produce more, I don't see any difference between that and the Toyota auto factory." [8]

Complaints against the president and his administration continue to escalate. He interferes with departmental elections. "We were told that we couldn't have the person we elected as chairperson. Reasons were given.They didn't satisfy most of us. It's not democratic." His administration spends too much money frivolously and too little for the library. "We know that they get new carpeting regularly; we see that happening. And then we're told that there isn't money for this journal or that journal in the library." He could "challenge university policy" and recommend a waiver or equivalency for a teacher who lacks a Ph.D. but he appears unwilling.

Faculty remain passive in the face of the president's assault, asserts a professor whose tenure antedated open admissions. "The faculty have not taken advantage of their power as a faculty to take a stand on issues in the college senate and come out publicly, even if it entails motions of censure. We've been reluctant to flex what muscles we do have, to take advantage of what publicity we could get. When I was a younger member here, back in the sixties, I was a rebel. I'd write white papers and circulate them all the time and push against what we thought was wrong. We have a lot of people now who either have given up or decided that it's not worth the effort. Maybe they feel it's too uncomfortable to fight, or maybe they feel they don't have the students' support to do the kind of fighting they would like to do. If the faculty are recalcitrant, the president can't force things on them. They've got academic freedom and tenure. Nobody is thwarted from coming up with an idea that he or she is willing to fight for. If the president vetoes a faculty committee decision, both reports must go downtown (to the Board of Higher Education)."

A minority among the faculty look upon the president favorably, preferring his "laissez faire style to a hands-on, dictatorial style," crediting him with "keeping the college on the map, in the limelight," "giving us a positive public image," seeing him as articulate and aware of university problems. "His manner may be a little acerbic at times, and people may be turned off by that. But he's presiding over contraction, like Mayor Abraham Beame, who gets blamed for the contraction of New York City, while Lindsey was a mayor in a period of largesse. People are disappointed for many reasons and focus their malaise at the top."

The president is a political animal with a constituency that encompasses not merely the college but also the central administration, the borough, the city, and beyond. A highly visible participant in city-wide affairs, he has frequent media exposure. He has to satisfy many masters, one of whom is the accrediting agency, the Middle States Association of Colleges and Schools, which scrutinizes school statistics on retention and attrition. The Association deferred renewing the accreditation of one of the senior colleges within the university despite its admirable faculty and academic program because of high minority student attrition and too few minority faculty and administrators.[9] Such fiats are not lost on college administrators.

My interview with the president never takes place. He suggests alternative dates for our meeting but shortly before the scheduled time postpones the interview. Several weeks later, he announces that he is resigning, effective the end of the following school year.

The Doctorate Dilemma.

The dilemma of the doctorate has persisted at Bronx Community College for more than two decades.

Most of the current full-time faculty came to the college during the 1960s or early 1970s, with teaching experience at the primary, secondary, or college level. Among those who began teaching as graduate students, many eventually received their doctorate. Some did not.

Before 1976, a doctorate was not needed for advancement. The rules changed that year when the City University required that community college faculty have parity in degrees with faculty in the senior college in order to maintain parity in salary. Consequently, some highly committed and intellectually astute teachers at the college have been frozen at the assistant professor level for more than twenty years. All have the masters degree -- sometimes two -- and some have completed three years of course work on the doctorate, but lack the qualifying credential needed for promotion. Waivers have been rather freely granted in vocational fields, with an "industrial equivalent to a Ph.D," but not in most liberal arts and sciences. An accounting professor has an "equivalency" based on his Masters and CPA. A professor of Engineering Technology substitutes his Professional Engineering license for the Ph.D. A nursing instructor receives an "equivalency," as does an instructor of music.

The issue of the missing doctorate and consequent immobility among teachers in the humanities and sciences arouses considerable resentment. A chairperson in the sciences, who holds the doctorate, speaks for many, though not all, of the faculty, in regarding the situation "deplorable that we have faculty members who have been in the same rank for twenty-six years. I don't care if they have a Ph.D. or not. For anybody who serves for twenty-six years at a level that has been complimented by faculty and students alike, there should be some way to give academic recognition. That whole thing has demoralized the faculty tremendously." Resentment focuses on the president, who is reputed to have neglected to submit certain departmental recommendations for the promotion of faculty members in the liberal arts and sciences to the Central University Office but grants waivers or equivalencies to others.

Faculty regard the doctorate as important primarily in enhancing a teacher's status rather than promoting good teaching. The degree confers recognition in academic circles. "Four-year colleagues and graduate school colleagues are forced to deal on a somewhat more equal footing with people who have comparable educational backgrounds," declares one teacher, and another, "With a Ph.D. beside your name, it's easier to publish in professional journals."

Students "accept the mystique that goes with the doctorate," speculates a Communication professor. "A Ph.D. is important perceptually for the student who feels that he or she has a 'real' professor. Students will often comment that I possess the degree. If they belong to ethnic groups that are viewed in this country as traditionally minority, it is important for them to feel that their instructors hold these 'real' titles, since to be minority in America means that you have to be better and brighter in order to be equal."

The learning entailed in earning a doctorate may serve the teacher well in the community college classroom, several holders of the doctorate suggest. "There is material which may never be taught at the community college level that sharpens the mind of the instructors and allows them to explain often elementary concepts in a much better, well-informed manner," observes a physics professor. And a political scientist adds that "Going through the Ph.D. process provides a certain academic orientation. It gives an immunity to educational leveling that occurs at community colleges. It makes one part of a broader community."

The teaching load and departmental responsibilities at the college leave little time during the school year for the research usually associated with having a doctorate. The community college professor with an international reputation as a scholar is not likely to assume rigorous departmental duties, an English professor observes. "I respect and admire the true scholar in our department very, very much, but my perception of him is that he's totally detached from the realities of the day-to-day running of the department. He's very rarely here; he's not a participating member of the department. I respect that because I know he's putting his time to very good use. He's doing excellent work. But I don't think we could run a department with thirty people like him."

Through the years faculty frustration over the dilemma of the doctorate continues to mount.

The Problem of the Adjunct

In 1976, during the city's fiscal crisis, the college was closed for two weeks, many faculty members were retrenched, and teachers stood in unemployment lines. Since then, the college has endured perennial budget cuts. Talk about non-reappointment, incentives for early retirement, and replacement of retirees with non-permanent adjuncts dramatizes the fiscal woes.

The failure to hire new full-time faculty is decried. "The fact that our department has not hired a new faculty member for twenty years is unthinkable," laments the chairperson of the chemistry department. "It means we are obsolete. We no longer have people who have experience at using some technologies invented in the last twenty years. I subscribe to eight of the prominent journals in the field, I read them, and I am obsolete because I don't get to go into the laboratory. When you don't bring on new people and thrive on them, and learn from them, and build with them, you lose your ability as a professional chemist."

Adjuncts teach fifty percent of the courses in an average department. Faculty decry the infusion into teaching ranks of an inordinate number of adjunct part-timers who contribute to the university's efforts to run the system as cheaply as possible.

> Many of them teach here and run to another campus to teach another course to scrape together a little bit of a living and run off to graduate school to learn. They cannot have the same devotion that a full-time teacher would have to the university. (mathematics)
>
> They may be fine teachers, with expertise from the business and scientific world, yet they are not required to have office hours, confer with the students, or take part in registration or advisement, and they need not come to departmental meetings. (biology)
>
> Depending on adjuncts deprives the school of new blood, new leadership, new ideas, and a commitment to the college. (sociology)

The Dean of Academic Affairs deplores the situation where "in entire departments, there has not been a new appointment for sixteen or seventeen years. There is no opportunity for a renewal of the faculty. When we had the last early retirement incentive, we lost twenty-seven teaching faculty, and the university immediately reduced our budget by 2.2 million dollars and said, 'Don't hire anybody.' I go to the Freeze committee and say, 'Our Communication Department lost five people. Give me two.' They say, 'We'll give you one.' What kind of gamesmanship is that? We lost twelve of the nursing faculty. 'Give us five.' They say, 'We'll give you three.' What kind of nonsense? The bill on early retirement incentives stipulates one-on-one replacements for the faculty lost. We hope over a period of time we will do that, though not necessarily in the same department. We got a radiology program, so we appointed three radiologists. Appointments will be selective, where they are really needed." Or where accreditation regulations mandate certain teacher-student ratios. The need will rarely be in the humanities.

A physics professor pithily elucidates the recurring dilemma: "Without adjuncts, we'd be in dire straits financially, so you have to balance the financial exigencies and the needs of the students."

Underserviced and Overcrowded

All departments -- most notably, the sciences -- lack basic supplies and equipment. Chemistry classes lack "the sophisticated instruments required in the laboratory today." In biology "there are not enough microscopes or other kinds of equipment to serve this level of student." And the physics department has been unable to purchase new equipment "without cheating" for at least five years. The cheating involves utilizing the breakage funds contributed by students. "I have to pray that an old piece of equipment dies so that I can get a state-of-the-art piece of equipment," the physics chairperson confesses."We submit proposals year after year on what we need so that we can at least be competitive with other schools, but there's just no money."

Contributing to faculty despair is "something simple like the telephones," recounts the chemistry chairperson. "Four of my faculty members on the floor below who occupy four different offices with the same telephone number don't pick up their phones any more. If they do, they usually have to walk down the hall to summon someone or give a message. I don't believe it's worth the money to do that to people who are on the front lines. I think the phone has become such an important part of what we do. Students can get me on the phone when they can't come to class, or I can get them. Right now, when I want to call members of my faculty, I have to walk downstairs to contact them because they're not going to pick up the phone. I understand why the college is doing it. The dean has a budgetary imperative that he has to live by, and they've cut everything, from released time to paper, phones, and the works."

Simple maintenance is postponed, a history professor muses. "Most of the teaching is done in this run-down building. It's dirty because they don't have the people to clean it. I remember a classroom which, once the door was closed, didn't open from the outside. Students trying to get in would giggle and pound on the door. I'm happy to say the door is now open. Things like this seem small but they're not, really. There's no soap. There are no towels For a long time they had an electric dryer that wasn't functioning. Now I'm happy to see that it's functioning."

Faculty complain of the "unconscionable class size." In the art studio, "There are more people than we have easels. An upper limit of twenty-eight is too much." In the biology lab, " Our maximum class size has increased from twenty-four to twenty-eight and we have as many as thirty-two. Class size reaches a point where you cannot give individual attention and that is critical in biology."

Especially arduous are classes where students write and teachers review compositions "I don't know how in the world the English department can survive," states the chair of the chemistry department. "I know the teachers must be great but I can't believe they can read and evaluate all that writing in the amount of time they are given. I believe they can be three times as effective if they have half the number of students. We could get rid of the institutional malaise here by dealing with issues like that."

A funded experimental writing program limiting the number of students per class produces exciting results. "Teaching in the Title III Immersion program was probably one of the best teaching experiences I ever had in my twenty-six years here," an English professor reports. "Twelve students in one class and eighteen in the next! The work we did was phenomenal. I met the students in conference twenty times. They wrote eighteen compositions in twenty days and I corrected and reviewed all of their compositions. The students were grateful. It was wonderful, and I attribute it to the class size."

As class size continues to expand and supplies and equipment become depleted, many of the teachers express resignation and despair. They feel helpless against the tidal wave of budget deficits.

Some teachers carry their frustration into the classroom and wait eagerly for early retirement. Others seem indefinitely to feel the spark derived from subject and students. There is, however, a consensus that, "In the classroom, while teachers are doing their job, they are not necessarily enhancing the job. The commitment, the passion, has been defused. It is not an intellectually stimulating or academic campus, but it's not for lack of personnel that could make it so." A professor of history reflects on what has come to pass :

> There is a gap between what teachers should be doing and what they actually do, myself included. You just can't help it. You can compartmentalize a bit, but at times things seep over. The anger and frustration that we feel at this endless situation of budget cuts and lack of positive feedback from the administration and from students results in an inevitable decline in our own commitment, I believe. I think it's true of everyone. I'm aware of it and try to fight it, but I think it's there.
>
> I'm angrier with students who don't work than I was before. I'm more pessimistic about the future than I was before. I feel that there's less hope for a generation of students than I felt before. I think that our students reflect a generation which is not going to be as successful as preceding ones because they lack both discipline and fundamentals.

The vision of what teachers at Bronx Community College might achieve was forged in the 1960s, the chair of the English department recalls. "Most of us really care for the students. We came from an historic period. The sixties was very powerful for us. The civil rights movement. We're here to complete Dr. King's dream. We have no high expectations but we go on."

Very troubling to faculty is society's failure to provide the conditions to make the dream come true -- the students given a raw deal in their earlier education, the burdensome teacher workload, the lack of basic supplies and equipment, and the overcrowded classes. "We're part of a wonderful experiment that we can't fulfill because society doesn't provide the resources." That is the anguish.

Notes

1. A student's comment in Howard B. London, *The Culture of a Community College* (New York: Praeger, 1978), 20.

2. Leonard Jeffries, the Chairman of the Black Studies Department at City College, is a charismatic leader well-known for his invective against whites and more specifically against Jews.

Jeffries represents "the deep currents of anti-intellectualism, and the appetite for consolatory myths, that ran through large parts of the black community," concludes Traub in his intriguing chapter on "Dr. J's Theater of Racial Outrage." James Traub, *City On A Hill: Testing the American Dream at City College* (Reading, MA: Addison-Wesley Publishing Company, 1994) , 229-271.

3. Bronx Community College feels bound by budgetary demands to require a twenty-student minimum enrollment in each class. As a consequence, many courses listed in the catalogue are offered sporadically, at best, especially in the humanities.

4. The frustration and isolation experienced by professors in the humanities who teach underprepared students and provide service courses for vocational curricula while distancing themselves from the research orientation and professional organizations important to them in the earlier days of their career are poignantly described by McGrath and Spear, two community college professors. Dennis McGrath and Martin B. Spear, "A Professoriate is in Trouble," *Change* ((January/February 1988): 26, 53.

5. Newsletter #22, 1983, Dean of Academic Affairs. Missing in the adminiustrator's comments is the high regard for teachers found in abundance in the six "good" high schools studied by Sara Lawrence Lightfoot, who "was struck by the centrality and dominance of teachers and by the careful attention given to their needs. . . The high regard for teachers and their work expressed in the six high schools . . marked them as different from a great many schools where teachers are typically cast in low positions in the school's hierarchy, and not treated with respectful regard." Sara Lawrence Lightfoot, *The Good High School: Portraits of Character and Culture* (New York: Basic Books, 1983) 333, 334.

6. Conflict between administration and faculty is apparently muted at Miami-Dade Community College, due at least in part to the administration's open show of respect for faculty. The president "undoubtedly sets the tone at Miami-Dade with his unwavering commitment and strong emphasis on the basic philosophy that equal access must be accompanied by a demand for high standards." John E. Roueche and George A. Baker, III, *Access and Excellence: The Open Door College* (Washington, D.C.: The Community College Press, 1987), 120, 126.

All was not perfect at Miami-Dade. Faculty felt that excellence in teaching was not sufficiently rewarded. Ibid.,107. And students expressed some concern about the quality of the required core courses, which seemed to stress rote learning rather than analytic thought, presumably in preparation for the exit test which students were required to pass before graduation.   L. Steven Zwerling, "The Miami-Dade Story: Is It Really Number One?"   *Change,* 20.1 (Jan./Feb. 1988):10-23.

7. In defense of the deans, a faculty member indicates that "The college is under-deaned, if you compare this college with other colleges within the university.   There are not as many administrators.   By and large, I think they're all overworked.   Nobody's complaining when faculty go home at one, and administrators work until five."

8.   College faculty   generally express favorable attitudes toward academic life yet remain frustrated and dispirited.   Howard Bowen and Jack Schuster refer to the powerful demographic, economic, and political forces that contribute to the waning of faculty influence during the period from 1970 to 1985.   *American Professors: A Natural Resource Imperiled* (New York: Oxford University Press, 1986).

9.   *The New York Times,* 5 April, 1990, B1, 6.

Chapter 10

Conclusion

The birth of open admissions in the late 1960s and early 1970s is recalled with nostalgia and anguish by the teachers at Bronx Community College twenty years later. "We were growing too fast. But with hindsight we could say those were the glory days of the college. Most people had a positive feeling that we were on the right track." [1] What then went wrong?

As the years under open admissions become a decade and then two, teachers feel buffeted on all sides. They confront students in oversized classes, burdened by family and job, who seek the rewards of a college education without the necessary immersion in college-level study. They confront administrators within the college who chide them for much of student failure, and administrators beyond who do not provide the resources to facilitate their efforts. High school teachers dissuade their good students from matriculating at the college, and senior college teachers express reluctance at accepting their credits. Part-time adjuncts increasingly replace full-time faculty, many of them rewarded for early retirement, while the extracurricular responsibilities of the remaining faculty continue to expand.

Teachers recall the promising years in the early 1970s when admission to undergraduate colleges of the City University is declared open and free to all high school graduates, and students ranging widely in age and academic preparedness enter the classroom in escalating numbers. Often informed in earlier years that they were "not college material," they come with trepidation but with the belief that through attending college they can achieve the mobility they crave. Women predominate. A substantial number in the 1970s leave men behind who feel threatened by their return to school and a substantial number in the 1980s are single mothers who bear the burdens of family alone. Students come increasingly from developing countries of the Caribbean, Africa, and Asia. African-American men of the inner city are conspicuous by their underrepresentation.

Remediation courses giving no college credit are introduced to provide some measure of equity for underprepared students. Those entering with minor deficiencies in reading, writing, or mathematics, remedied in a single semester or two of remedials, usually advance without difficulty to college-level courses. It becomes apparent, though, that twelve years devoted to acquiring the substance and discipline of learning in primary and secondary grades cannot be condensed into a year or two of remediation for students who never read a book in any language outside of class and cannot write a coherent paragraph. Remedials soon overwhelm the curricula. Sixty percent of the English sections in 1987 and eighty-five percent of the mathematics sections are remedial.

In an attempt to reduce remedials throughout the City University, its Chancellor recommends, in 1990, that all prospective matriculants be required to complete a college-preparatory curriculum in high school. "When she talks about two years of high school lab science, she must know that some high schools don't even have laboratories," a dean comments, indicating disbelief that the city high schools will be given the resources to accomplish the Chancellor's goal. The fear is pervasive among faculty. There is the apprehension, too, that the Chancellor's proposal, when implemented, will emasculate open admissions.

Open admissions is out of the bottle and will not be put back. The hopes and aspirations of thousands of students cannot be stifled. The palliative offered is a community college transformed from an academic transfer to a terminal vocational institution. The transformation manifests the reality that the playing field cannot easily be leveled; hence it is essential that underprepared students progress quickly toward a terminal vocational degree and a job. Whereas in the early 1970s students at Bronx Community College were more likely to enroll in curricula on the transfer track in preparation for study at a senior college, in the later 1970s and the 1980s they turn most frequently to terminal vocational programs. "I would like to see more emphasis on the liberal arts but I can understand the needs of the students for some sort of immediate ability to go into the job market," acknowledges a proponent of the change.

The city colleges of New York have from their inception prepared students for jobs, but vocational studies were subordinate to a rich academic curriculum. Now, with the change of emphasis at Bronx Community College from the academic to the vocational, the liberal arts have become marginalized. Students are rarely told that, whatever their specialization, greater exploration in the liberal arts and the sciences would enable them to move more easily from one field to another in a rapidly changing world. One ex-student describes his inadvertent stumble into liberal arts from a terminal vocational curriculum.

> Bronx Community College is billed as a two-year associate program. Get your associate degree, you'll get a raise on the job or move into another position. Going into higher education is never really pushed.
>
> Students come here and something opens up for them that they didn't expect. When I came, I was an electrician. I liked to read. That didn't mean I wanted to teach English. Electrical Technology made more sense to me. Most of the courses I needed weren't available for me as an evening student so I filled in with others. Before I turned around, I had enough credits for liberal arts. And my love of English classes! Early on, they asked me to tutor in the writing lab, so I got to meet really great people.
>
> I'm very prejudiced in my feelings about this institution. I just feel so indebted to it. It was like a corridor for me to move from one life into another life that has been much more fulfilling. (Starting out as a tutor, he now teaches English composition as an adjunct while pursuing graduate studies.)

Students discover that early vocational specialization may not lead to the jobs they seek. Either the waiting lists for admission into coveted terminal vocational programs are prohibitively long, or the demand for workers is shrinking, or their own academic background lags behind that of other job applicants with higher degrees. Admitted to the college under standards of equity, they may be confronted by job standards that are severely meritocratic.

There is little assurance, too, of college graduation. Less than twenty percent of matriculants graduate from the community college. Students who do graduate, whether from the the terminal or the transfer track, are likely to apply to a senior college to pursue a baccalaureate. Terminal track graduates belatedly discover that the senior college is reluctant to accept all their vocational credits and that their limited pursuit of the liberal arts and sciences has not prepared them well for transfer.

The seemingly insoluble quandary that often arises when community college studies become largely remedial and terminal vocational must be addressed. We start by recognizing, reluctantly, that although all who want to enter college should be admitted, open admissions cannot preclude some early selectivity after admission. Those students who display little interest in or aptitude for the academic and are likely to read little in books, assigned or unassigned, but have some aptitude for a trade must be confronted early with the options available. Some cooling out must occur early, not in the interests of the institution but in the interests of the student. A strongly recommended alternative to college might be a trade school which offers rigorous vocational or on-the-job training, "not beguiled by college degrees," a political science professor suggests.[2] The community college, often lacking the equipment and the experience with the newest technologies in a variety of areas, may not provide such instruction. Students exposed to the best in vocational training at schools designed optimally for that training may begin to comprehend the relationship between work and academics and become motivated to return to the academic classroom to master the subjects that they spurned earlier.[3]

All students in the community college who perform adequately at the college level should pursue a course of study in preparation for transfer to a senior college. They may take introductory courses in any area of specialization, but all curricula must meet standards for community college graduation high enough to ensure admission to the junior year of a four-year college without loss of credits. Requirements would entail (1) Eliminating all watered-down courses now being offered throughout the liberal arts and the sciences; (2) Meeting senior college standards in reading and writing; and (3) Including study in the liberal arts and sciences approximately equivalent to that of the first two years of the four-year college. Students with insufficient exposure to an academic curriculum in high school should be informed early how long their stay here is likely to be. The entrance to the community college must remain open to all who wish to come and learn, but the exit at graduation must be circumscribed.

Students may start out at the community college poorly prepared for college-level study but, with persistence and assistance, master their subjects and continue to graduation and beyond. The remarks of a history professor bear repeating.

We are capable of taking people who might not be interested in learning and opening up a new world to them, and there are enough of those that I think it makes it worth while. We're in danger of losing that function because of the college emphasis on jobs, jobs,

jobs. The danger to the long-term existence of the community college will be if it becomes nothing more than a glorified trade school because I think that broad learning is not emphasized as much as I feel it's supposed to be and in fact once was.

The student body also includes those well able to meet college-level requirements with little remediation, who were diverted from formal study and now return to the fold. Some discover unexpected academic opportunities here under the tutelage of professors as mentors. A young woman, urged by her English professor to give vent to her grumblings through writing for the school newspaper, becomes its gifted editor-in-chief. Two years after transfer, she receives the journalism award at her senior college graduation. Another, at the recommendation of her adviser, applies to an elite liberal arts college and receives a full scholarship for her junior and senior years. Graduating with honors, she enrolls at the Sorbonne. A student in engineering is awarded a scholarship to Rensellaer Polytechnic Institute and a student in mathematics, a scholarship to New York University. Some students turn to careers in science through hands-on experience in medical research laboratories off campus. Such students are a small minority, but they offer gratification to their teachers and serve as inspiration to their peers.

If all students were required to take whatever courses were necessary to facilitate transfer to a senior college without loss of credits, tender-hearted teachers might see fit to become increasingly tough-minded, prodding students to extend their reach. Though sympathetic to the students' burdens, they would recognize that to reduce course requirements and inflate grades deceives and derogates students.[4]

Students stumbling up the steep hill will not all get to the top but may transmit to others the richness they themselves derive from their college experience.[5] A parent's love of reading even now increasingly penetrates the home. A twenty-seven-year-old Puerto Rican father of five vows:

Nothing would make me stop. I have shown my wife what my going to school has brought to the home and to the relationship that has been very creative. I have the kids reading and I told her she should reinforce this by her reading. After a while she says, 'Get me a book.' Already I'm a success, just to be here, learning the things I'm learning. I went to college and none of my brothers did. My life is an accomplishment. I can give this to my children and they can take it a step further.

And knowledge of calculus radiates from a student in the classroom to a community of cousins. A mathematics professor's vignette:

> I had a Cambodian student five years ago in a calculus course that I taught until 10:15 at night. I wanted to go home at 10:15. He would always wait, and he was one of the best students in the class. He would say, 'Professor, I didn't quite understand this.' Finally I asked him, 'Han,' I think was his name, 'You are an A student. Why do you have to have a perfect score? No one is perfect.' And he said, 'Professor, I live with fifteen of my cousins. The fifteen work; they send me to school. When I come home from school, I must teach the other fifteen what I learned in the classroom.'
>
> It was a mind-boggling experience to realize that I was his teacher and he was their teacher. This is what the community college is all about. We are bringing knowledge to a community, not just to an individual, and that community is a very complex thing. And I think that was decided in this particular nation of ours, that we did not want a stratified society locked into certain levels.
>
> To come from a family that has labored with poverty and with welfare, to take an individual like that and have him succeed in only a two- year college is a wonderful thing and removes negative and dangerous tensions in our society. The second and third member of the family may then swim right through here and go on. When we look at change, we have to be patient. We are looking at twenty-five years in the City University versus thousands of years. I understand it's an expensive proposition, but I don't see any alternative other than to allow hope. We are a place for hope, and success for some.

The emphasis on academics that the college espoused in its early days must not be allowed to lapse.

Notes

1. A quotation from the former Acting President.
2. The recommendation resembles the three (or four) tier system of the University's 1968 Master Plan, scheduled to have begun in 1975, which specified that students unable to meet the requirements for the senior college or the community college would be eligible for vocational

apprenticeship or college transition programs in Education Skills Centers. This plan was scuttled in favor of a policy of open admissions, beginning in 1970, accepting all applicants in a four-year senior college or a two-year community college.

3. Hedrick Smith, *Rethinking America: A New Game Plan from The American Innovators: Schools, Business, People, Work* (New York: Random House, 1995) 134-141.

4. Important in a black student's success is an outstanding teacher who intervenes at a crucial point in the student's development. Thomas Sowell, *Black Education: Myths and Tragedies* (New York: David McKay Company, 1972) 231.

The Coleman data too (1966) indicate that teacher quality is a major determinant of scholastic achievement among black students. Samuel Bowles, "Toward Equality of Educational Opportunity?" *Harvard Educational Review* (Winter 1968):94.

5. Theodore L. Gross, *Academic Turmoil: The Reality and Promise of Open Education.* New York: Anchor Press/Doubleday, 1980.

Appendix

Interview Schedule
for Students

1. When you decided to attend college, what was your first, second, and third choice?

2. Why was Bronx Community College one of your first three choices?

3. Do you plan to get an associate degree? to go on to a four-year college? To get a baccalaureate?

4. Do you know now what job or career you aspire to? What is your area of concentration? Have you changed your area of concentration during the course of your college career?

5. Were you reared to take much interest in going to college? If not, what sparked your interest?

6. Do you feel that life-long satisfaction comes from marriage and family or from career? Which is primary? Which secondary?

7. If your goal were to become a doctor, would you be satisfied being a medical technician?

8. Suppose you end up doing unskilled or semi-skilled work for which a college education is not required. If you knew this now, would it still be worthwhile to continue your education?

9. Rank your reasons for wanting to attend college.

10. What do you regard as the most desirable characteristics in a man and a woman who are close to you?

11. What was the last grade that you completed before attending college? What was your curriculum in high school (academic, commercial, vocational, or general)? What was your grade level there? Did you graduate or take an equivalency examination?

12. What is your grade level here? How long have you been in college? How many college credits (and non-college credits) have you earned?

13. Do you feel that you have done as well here as you are capable of ? If not, what do you feel are the reasons for not doing better?

14. How many hours do you study, on the average, each week (for how many courses) When and where do you study?

15. Do you prefer a multiple-choice or essay test? Why?

16. What feelings do you have when you take a test? If anxious, do you feel that your anxiety is realistic; that is, is it due to your being unprepared?
Do you feel that your pre-college preparation was so poor that it is difficult to make up now for your deficiencies in learning?

17. Should our grading standards be the same as those of a four-year college? Do you think they are the same?

18. What are the qualities in a teacher which you think help a student to learn?

19. Do you think an instructor should let absenteeism affect a student's grade? Would you consider that you have had excessive absences for varied reasons? What have been the reasons?

20. Do you think your classes have been challenging here? If some are not, for what reason(s)?

21 Are you now working? What kind of work and how many hours a week do you work? What are your wages?

22. Do you have children? What are their ages? Whom do they stay with when you are at school?

23. How many people live with you? Whom do you spend most of your free time with? Do they agree with you about the importance of education?

24. What would you consider a serious enough financial problem to make you quit school? For what other reasons might you quit?

25. What grade level average would make you want to drop out of school?

26. What other reasons would make you want to drop out of school?

27. Are you apprehensive about getting a good job after you leave here?

28. If you were different from what you are-- in age, sex, race, class -- would it be easier of more difficult to achieve what you want?

29. To what would you attribute any possible failure? (discrimination by race, class, sex, age, educational discrimination; fear of failure, lack of ability, lack of hard work, poor choice of program).

30. Do you think the black man is a threat to the white man? the black woman, to the white woman? Vice versa? In what way?

31. Do you think an instructor should present issues in a classroom setting which would arouse controversial discussion around change in the social structure, or should the instructor try to avoid such controversy in the classroom ?

32. Do you have any close friends on campus whom you meet outside the classroom? Do you belong to any clubs or organizations on campus? off campus?

33. age.   34. sex.   35. ethnic group   36. marital status 37. veteran status.

Interview Schedule
for Teachers

1. (Educational history)   Subject, degree, year. Do you think holding the doctorate is important for community college teachers?

2. Have you taught elsewhere? How long? How long here? Why here?

3. Do students appear to work hard at learning (as indicated by homework, exams, absences, and class discussions)? What does homework involve?

What is the format of your examinations? Do you assign essays and give essay examinations?

Do you regard absences as excessive?

Do most students participate actively in class discussions?

Students speak of wanting teachers to start out "at the students' level." Is this level difficult to determine? Can you illustrate how low you must go?

Do students fear failure? Whom are they likely to blame if they do poorly?

4. Have you noted differences in performance among students by age, gender, ethnic group, or curriculum?

5. Do you think there should be a single standard in course content and grading for equivalent courses throughout the university or should there be a lower standard in community colleges?

6. Do high standards produce a high failure rate? suspensions? dropouts?

Suspensions declined from 19.2% in Spring 1980 to 10.6% in Spring 1989. Why? Did grades become increasingly inflated? Should grades be based on "the value added" rather than on some absolute standard?

7. What type of student inspires you?

8. "There needs to be in all teachers a passion for the subject matter and a commitment to the students," says Patricia Graham, Harvard School of Education. Are the teachers here outstanding in the former compared with teachers in four-year colleges? In the latter? Do you think teacher-student relationships are different here than in four-year colleges within the university? In what way?

9. What do you think of the Chancellor's College Preparatory Initiative, designed to improve academic standards of students?

10. Is there a dominant peer culture at the college? (e.g., high culture and counter culture? rebels? preponderance of outsiders?) Do you think the students are a rather passive lot in the classroom? Outside the classroom?

11. When was the last full-time faculty member appointed to your department? Adjuncts now perform most of remedial teaching and more than 40% of all undergraduate instruction at the university. Is this good for your department? for the students?

12. In Fall 1987, 17% of the students at the college were in AA-enrolled curricula, 14% in AS, and 62.5% in AAS. Do you think this is a good division for a community college? Are there divided loyalties among faculty at the college?

13. The articulation policy adopted by the university states that senior colleges shall grant to incoming transfer students at least nine credits, but not necessarily more, in the students' major. Do you think the failure to receive credit for all courses taken at the community college seriously reduces the number of transfers?

14. Bowen and Schuster base the findings in their book, *American professors: A Natural Resource Imperiled*, on more than 500 interviews at 38 institutions, including community colleges, four-year colleges, and universities. They conclude that since 1970, the condition of the nation's faculties has deteriorated, their influence has declined, their morale has dropped precipitously, their sense of security has suffered, and the work milieu has degenerated. Is this an accurate description of the situation for faculty at this college?
Is teacher morale affected by increase in class size?
Faculty at the college appear satisfied with departmental leadership but much less so with college-wide leadership. Why?
Is there faculty participation in decision making? In which decisions?

15. Forty-three percent of respondents to a Faculty Survey considered the Intellectual Climate at our college Below Average. Do you?
Have our teachers suffered much from burnout? Do they recover?

What are the reasons for the large numbers of early retirees?

16. What gives you the greatest gratification here? What is most troubling?

17. Why should there be community colleges? Do they duplicate the function served either by trade schools or by the first two years of a four-year college?

Works Cited

Anderson, Elijah. *StreetWise: Race, Class, and Change in an Urban Community*. Chicago: University of Chicago Press, 1990.

Arbeiter, Solomon. "Black Enrollments: The Case of the Missing Students," *Change* 19.3 (May/June 1987): 14-19.

Aries, Pillippepe. *Centuries of Childhood: A Social History of Family Life*. Translated by Robert Baldick. New York: Alfred A. Knopf, 1962.

Astin, Alexander W. *Preventing Students from Dropping Out*. San Francisco: Jossey-Bass, 1975.

----------. *Achieving Educational Excellence: A Critical Assessment of Higher Education*. San Francisco: Jossey-Bass, 1985.

Baird, L.L. "Cooling Out and Warming Up in the Junior College." *Measurement and Evaluation in Guidance* 4.3 (1971): 160-71.

Berger, Joseph. "Not the Same CUNY." *New York Times*, 27 June 1995, B2.

Bernstein, Basil. *Class, Codes, and Control : Theoretical Studies towards a Sociology of Language*. Vol. 1. 2nd rev. ed. London: Routledge & Kegan Paul, 1974.

Blake, Elias Jr.."Equality for Blacks: Another Lost Decade or New Surge Forward?" *Change* (May/June 1987): 10-13.

Bond, Horace Mann. *Black American Scholars: A Study of Their Beginnings*. Detroit: Balamp Publishing, 1972.

Bowen, Howard R.. and Schuster, Jack H. *American Professors: A National Resource Imperiled*. New York: Oxford University Press, 1986.

Bowles, Samuel. "Toward Equality of Educational Opportunity?" *Harvard Educational Review* (Winter 1968).

Boyer, Ernest L. *College: The Undergraduate Experience in America*. New York: Harper and Row, 1987.

Brint, Steven, and Jerome Karabel. *The Diverted Dream: Community Colleges and the Promise of Educational Opportunity in America, 1900-1985*. New York: Oxford University Press, 1989.

Buber, Martin. *Between Man and Man*. New York: MacMillan, 1965; London: Routledge and Kegan Paul, 1947.

Carnegie Commission on Higher Education. *New Students and New Places: Policies for the Future Growth and Development of American Higher Education.* New York: McGraw-Hill, 1971.

Clark, Burton R. "The Cooling Out Function in Higher Education." *American Journal of Sociology* 65 (May 1960): 569-76.

----------. *The Open Door College:A Case Study.* New York: McGraw-Hill, 1960.

Clark, Kenneth B. *Dark Ghetto: Dilemmas of Social Power.* New York: Harper & Row, 1965; Middletown, CN: Wesleyan University Press, 1989.

----------. "No, No. Race, Not Class, Is Still At the Wheel." *New York Times,* 22 March 1978, A-25.

Cohen, Arthur M. "What Next for the Community Colleges? An ERIC Review." *Community College Review* 17.2 (1979) : 55.

Cohen, Arthur M. and Florence B. Brawer, *The Collegiate Function of Community Colleges.* San Francisco: Jossey-Bass, 1987.

Cole, Johnnetta B. "The Black Bourgeoisie." In *Black and White on American Race Relations.* Edited by Peter I. Rose, Stanley Rothman, and William J. Wilson. New York: Oxford University Press, 1973.

----------. *Conversations: Straight Talk with America's Sister President.* New York: Doubleday, 1993.

Council for Basic Education. *Open Admissions: The Pros and Cons.* Washington, D.C., 1972.

Cross, K. Patricia. *Beyond the Open Door.* San Francisco: Jossey-Bass, 1971.

Cross, K. Patricia and Jones, J. Quentin. "Problems of Access." In *Explorations in Non-Traditional Study.* Edited by Samuel B. Gould and K. Patricia Cross. San Francisco: Jossey- Bass (1972): 39-63.

Cruse, Harold. *Plural But Equal: A Critical Study of Blacks and Minorities and America's Plural Society.* New York: William Morrow, 1987.

Cummings, Judith. "Breakup of Black Family Imperils Gains of Decades." *New York Times,* 20 November 1983, 1, 56.

Davis, Angela Y. *Angela Davis: An Autobiography.* New York: Random House, 1974.

----------. *Women, Race & Class.* New York: Vintage Books, 1983.

Du Bois, W.E.B. *The Souls of Black Folk..* Introduction by Arnold Rampersad. New York: Alfred A. Knopf, 1993. First published, 1903.

Eells, Walter Crosby. "A Suggested Basis for a New Standard." *Junior College Journal* 3.1 (1932):1-2.

Epstein, Cynthia Fuchs. "Positive Effects of the Multiple Negative: Explaining the Success of Black Professional Women." *American Journal of Sociology* 78 (1973): 913-918.

Fitzpatrick, Joseph P. *Puerto Rican Americans: The Meaning of Migration to the Mainland.* Englewood Cliffs: Prentice-Hall. 1971.

Franklin, John Hope and Alfred A. Moss,Jr. *From Slavery to Freedom: A History of Negro Americans* 6th ed. New York: Alfred A. Knopf, 1988. First published, 1947.

Friedman, Maurice S. *Martin Buber: The Life of Dialogue.* Chicago: The University of Chicago Press, 1955; New York: Harper Torchbooks, 1960.

Friedman, Murray. "The Jews." *Through Different Eyes: Black and White Perspectives on American Race Relations.* Edited by Peter I Rose, Stanley Rothman, and William J. Wilson. New York: Oxford University Press (1973): 148-165.

Furstenberg, Frank F., Jr. "Good Dads-Bad Dads: Two Faces of Fatherhood." *The Changing American Family and Public Policy.* Edited by Andrew J. Cherlin. Washington, D.C.: The Urban Institute Press (1988): 193-218.

Giddings, Paula. *When and Where I Enter: The Impact of Black Women on Race and Sex in America.* New York: William Morrow, 1984.

Glenn, N.G. "Negro Prestige Criteria: A Case Study in the Bases of Prestige." *American Journal of Sociology* 68 (1963): 645-657.

Goldfarb, Robert. "Black Men Are Last." *New York Times,* 14 March 1980, A27.

Gorelick, Sherry. *City College and the Jewish Poor: Education in New York, 1880-1924.* New Brunswick, New Jersey: Rutgers University Press, 1981.

Gouldner, Alvin W. "Cosmopolitans and Locals: Toward an Analysis of Latent Social Roles, I and II. " *Administrative Science Quarterly* 2 (1957): 281-306, 444-480.

Greer, Colin. *The Great School Legend.* New York: Basic Books, 1972.

Gross, Theodore L. *Academic Turmoil: The Reality and Promise of Open Education.* New York: Anchor Press/Doubleday, 1980.

Hacker, Andrew. *Two Nations: Black and White, Separate, Hostile, Unequal.* New York: Ballantine Books, 1992.

Henriques, Fernando. *Family and Colour in Jamaica.* 2nd ed. London: MacGibbon and Kee, 1968.

Higginbotham, Elizabeth, "Black Professional Women: Job Ceilings and Employment Sectors," *Women of Color in U.S. Society.* Edited by Maxine Baca Zinn and Bonnie Thornton Dill. Philadelphia: Temple University Press (1993): 113-131.

Highet, Gilbert. *The Art of Teaching.* New York: Albert A. Knopf, 1969.

Hofstadter, Richard. *Anti-Intellectualism in American Life.* New York: Random House/Vintage, 1962.

hooks, bell. *Ain't I A Woman: Black Women and Feminism.* Boston: South End Press, 1981.

------------. *YEARNING: race, gender, and cultural politics.* Boston: South End Press, 1990.

Houle, Cyril O. "Commentary: The Motives of New Adult Learners." In *New Colleges for New Students.* Edited by Laurence Hall and Associates: San Francisco: Jossey-Bass (1974): 59-65.

Jones, Charisse. "CUNY Adopts Stricter Policy on Admissions." *New York Times,* 27 June 1995: 1, B2.

Jones, Jacqueline. *Labor of Love, Labor of Sorrow: Black Women, Work, and the Family from Slavery to the Present.* New York: Basic Books, 1985.

Katz, Joseph and Nevitt Sanford. "The Curriculum in the Perspective of the Theory of Personality Development." In *The American College: A Psychological and Social Interpretation of the Higher Learning.* Edited by Nevitt Sanford. New York: John Wiley and Sons, 1962.

Kelly, Robert L. "Great Teachers -- And Methods of Developing Them." *Association of American Colleges Bulletin* XV. 1 (March 1929): 49-67, 215-216.

Kessner, Thomas, and Caroli, Betty B. *Today's Immigrants, Their Stories: A New Look at the Newest Americans.* New York: Oxford University Press, 1981. 105-122.

Kincaid, Jamaica. *A Small Place.* New York: Farrar, Straus, Giroux, 1988.

Lavin, David E., Richard D. Alba, and Richard A. Silberstein, *Right versus Privilege: The Open-Admissions Experiment at the City University of New York.* New York: The Free Press, 1981.

----------. "Open Admissions and Equal Access: A Study of Ethnic Groups in the City University of New York." *Harvard Educational Review* 49.1 (1979): 53-92.

Lightfoot, Sara Lawrence. *The Good High School: Portraits of Character and Culture.* New York: Basic Books, 1983.

London, Howard B. *The Culture of A Community College.* New York: Praeger, 1978.

Maeroff, Gene I. "Better Ideas Are Sought For Two Year Colleges." *New York Times,* 23 Aug 1983, C10.

McGrath, Dennis and Martin B. Spear. "A Professoriate is in Trouble." *Change* (January/February 1988): 26, 53.

Milner, Murray Jr. *The Illusion of Equality: The Effect of Education on Opportunity,Inequality and Social Conflict.* San Francisco: Jossey-Bass, 1972.

Nettleford, Rex M. *Mirror, Mirror: Identity, Race and Protest in Jamaica.* London: William Collins and Sangster, 1970.

Neumann, William and David Riesman. "The Community College Elite." *New Directions for Community Colleges: Questioning the Community College Role,* No. 32. Edited by George B. Vaughan. San Francesco: Jossey-Bass(1980): 53-71.

Newcomb, Theodore. "Student Peer-Group Influence." *The American College: A Psychological and Social Interpretation of the Higher Learning.* Edited by Nevitt Sanford. New York:John Wiley and Sons (1962): 469-488.

Ogbu, John U. "Minority Status and Literacy in Comparative Perspective." *Literacy in America, Daedalus.* (Spring 1990): 141-168.

Olivas,Michael A. With the Assistance of Nan Alimba, *The Dilemma of Access: Minorities in Two Year Colleges.* Washington, D.C.: Howard University Press, 1979.

Ong, Walter J. *Orality and Literacy: The Technologizing of the Word.* London and New York: Methuen, 1982.

Padilla, Elena. *Up from Puerto Rico.* New York: Columbia University Press, 1958.

Pinkney, Alphonso, *The Myth of Black Progress.* New York and London: Cambridge University Press, 1984.

Richardson, Richard C., Jr., and Louis W. Bender.: *Fostering Minority Access and Achievement in Higher Education: The Role of Urban Community Colleges and Universities.* San Francisco:Jossey-Bass, 1987.

Richardson, Richard C.Jr., Elizabeth C.Fisk, and Morris Okun. *Literacy in the Open-Access College.* San Francisco: Jossey- Bass, 1983.

Riesman, David and Christopher Jencks. "The Viability of the American College." In *The American College: A Psychological and Social Interpretation of the Higher Learning.* Edited by Nevitt Sanford. New York: John Wiley (1962): 74-192.

Riessman, Frank. *The Culturally Deprived Child.* New York: Harper and Row, 1962.

Rist, Ray. "Social Class and Teacher Expectations: The Self-Fulfilling Prophecy in Ghetto Education." *Harvard Educational Review* 40 (August 1970): 411-451.

Rose, Willie Lee. *Slavery and Freedom.* Edited by William W. F Freehung. New York: Oxford University Press (1982): 23-28.

Rossman, Jack E., Helen S. Astin, Alexander W.Astin, and Elaine El-Khawas. *Open Admissions at City University of New York: An Analysis of the First Year.* Englewood Cliffs: Prentice-Hall, 1975.

Roueche, John E. and George A. Baker III. *Access and Excellence: The Open-Door College.* Washington, D.C.: The Community College Press, 1987.

Rudy, Solomon Willis. *The College of the City of New York: A History 1847- 1947.* New York: The City College Press, 1949; Arno Press, 1977.

Sanford, Nevitt. *Where Colleges Fail.* San Francisco: Jossey-Bass, 1967.

Scimecca, Joseph A. *Education and Society.* New York: Holt, Rinehart, and Winston, 1980.

Smith, Hedrick. *Rethinking America: A New Game Plan from The American Innovators: Schools, Business, People,Work.* New York: Random House, 1995.

Sowell, Thomas. *Black Education: Myths and Tragedies.* New York: David McKay Company, 1972.

----------. *Education: Assumptions versus History.* Stanford: Hoover Institute Press, 1986.

----------. *Ethnic America: A History.* New York: Basic Books, 1981.

Stack, Carole B. *All Our Kin.* New York: Harper and Row, 1974.

Summerskill, John. "Dropouts from College." *The American College: A Psychological and Social Interpretation of the Higher Learning.* Edited by Nevitt Sanford. New York: John Wiley and Sons (1962): 627-657.

Thomas, Laurence. "Next Life, I'll Be White." *New York Times* 13 August 1990, A 15.

Traub, James. *City On A Hill: Testing the American Dream at City College.* Reading, MA: Addison-Wesley Publishing Company, 1994,

U.S. Bureau of the Census. *Current Population Reports*, Series P-20, No. 443, Table A-7, on high school graduation status, college enrollment and attainment by sex, race, and Hispanic origin, 1967-1988.

U.S. Department of Education. National Center for Education Statistics. *The Condition of Education,* 1990, Vol. 2, *Postsecondary Education.,* Indicator 2:2, 2:3, pages 20-21.

U.S. Department of Education. National Center for Education Statistics. *Digest of Education Statistics*, 1992, Table 168, on freshmen college enrollment, sex, attendance status, and type and control of institution, 1955-1990.

Wallace, Michele. *Black Macho and the Myth of the Super-Woman.* New York: The Dial Press, 1978.

Waller, Willard W.*On The Family, Education, and War:Selected Writings.* Edited by William J. Goode, Frank Furstenberg, Jr., and Larry R. Mitchell. Chicago: The University of Chicago Press, 1970.

Weber, Max. *From Max Weber: Essays in Sociology.* Edited by H.H. Gerth and C.Wright Mills. New York: Oxford University Press, 1946.

Wechsler, Harold S. *The Qualified Student: A History of Selective College Admissions in America.* New York: John Wiley, 1977.

Weis,Lois. *Between Two Worlds: Black Students in an Urban Community College.* Boston: Routledge and Kegan Paul, 1985.

West, Cornel. *Race Matters.* Boston: Beacon Press, 1993.

Wilson, Robert C., J.G. Gaff, E.R. Dienst, L. Wood, and J.L. Bavry, *College Professors and Their Impact on Students.* New York: Wiley-Interscience, 1975.

Wilson, R. and S.E. Melendez. *Second Annual Status Report: Minorities in Higher Education.* Washington, D.C.: American Council on Education, 1983.

Wilson, William Julius. *The Declining Significance of Race: Blacks and Changing American Institutions.* 2nd ed. Chicago: The University of Chicago Press, 1978.

----------. *The Truly Disadvantaged: The Inner City, the Underclass, and Public Policy.* Chicago: The University of Chicago Press, 1987.

Wolfram, Walt. "Sociolinguistic Premises and the Nature of Nonstandard Dialect." *Language, Communication and Rhetoric in Black America.* Edited by Arthur L. Smith. New York: Harper and Row, 1972. 28-40.

Zwerling, L. Steven. "The Miami-Dade Story: Is It Really Number One?" *Change* (Jan./Feb. 1988): 10- 23.

Index